Matt Miller

biblegateway.com

NASV

UNDERSTANDING
the Bible

JOHN STOTT

UNDERSTANDING
the Bible

JOHN STOTT

Baker Books
A Division of Baker Book House Co
Grand Rapids, Michigan 49516

This edition © 2001 Angus Hudson Ltd/
Tim Dowley and Peter Wyart trading as
Three's Company

First published in the USA in 2001 by Baker Books
a division of Baker Book House Company
P.O. Box 6287, Grand Rapids, MI 49516-6287

ISBN 0-8010-1229-5

Library of Congress Cataloging-in-Publication
Data is on file at the Library of Congress,
Washington, D.C.

Scripture is taken from the HOLY BIBLE, NEW
INTERNATIONAL VERSION®. NIV®
Copyright © 1973, 1978, 1984 by International
Bible Society. Used by permission of Zondervan
Publishing House. All rights reserved

Designed and created by
Three's Company,
5 Dryden Street,
London WC2E 9NW

For current information about all releases from
Baker Book House, visit our web site:
        http://www.bakerbooks.com

Printed in Singapore

Picture acknowledgments

Photographs
Tim Dowley: pp. 19, 26, 28, 30, 31, 32, 37, 45,
48, 51, 57, 63, 66, 79, 80, 81, 83, 94, 97, 98, 101,
103, 104, 105, 111, 123, 125, 156, 163
Hanan Isachar: p. 49
Jamie Simson: pp. 15, 141, 151
Peter Wyart: pp. 1, 25, 36, 40, 64, 65, 85, 88, 91,
93, 107, 113, 127, 129, 131, 137, 139, 145, 155,
159
Sa'ar Ya'acov: p. 38

Illustrations
James Macdonald: pp. 73, 119
Alan Parry: pp. 58, 149

Chart
Tony Cantale: p. 36

Contents

Preface to the Second Edition

The publisher's decision to produce a second edition of *Understanding the Bible* has given me the opportunity to reread it and make a number of additions. Over ten years have elapsed since the first edition. During this decade the international situation has changed considerably. The worldwide student revolt at the end of the sixties has been replaced by apathy among the majority and anarchy among a comparatively small, but very vocal and radical, minority. The areas of theological controversy have shifted, as symbolized by *Honest to God* (1963) which denied personality to God and *The Myth of God Incarnate* (1977) which denied deity to Jesus. New challenges as well as new problems face Christians in these times.

I have tried to ensure that this new edition reflects this changing mood. Some fresh material has been added on religion and science, creation, evolution and the flood. I have elaborated the section which considers the interpretation of Genesis 2 and 3, and how we can distinguish between the literal and the figurative in Scripture. I have rewritten the introduction to the chapter on "The Authority of the Bible." Echoes of the inerrancy debate are heard in several passages. My position is to endorse and explain the principle stated in the Lausanne Covenant (1974) that Scripture is "without error in all that it affirms." I have enlarged the reference to cultural transposition and have also commented on the so-called "new hermeneutic," emphasizing the need to go beyond the elucidation of each biblical text to its application, beyond its original meaning to its contemporary message. Further, practically all the biblical quotations are now taken from the New International Version.

My hope and prayer are that, in his grace, God may help readers of this second edition to love the Bible more and understand it better.

John Stott
April 1984

Acknowledgments

For about 20 years I have lectured on the authority and interpretation of the Bible to our students at the London Institute for Contemporary Christianity. I am grateful to them for their penetrating questions, which have helped to clarify some of the material in this book. I am even more grateful to my two most recent Study Assistants, namely John Yates (1996-1999) and Corey Widmer (1999-2001). Both of them have read the whole book through the eyes of the younger generation and have suggested some improvements, which I have mostly – and gratefully – adopted.

JRWS
Christmas 2000

Preface

Every author owes it to the reading public to explain himself. Why has he thought fit to swell the torrent of books – especially religious books – which pours from the world's printing presses every day? Can he justify his rash enterprise? Let me at least tell you frankly the kind of people I have had in mind while writing. They fall into two categories.

First, the new Christian. With the spread of secularism in our day, an increasing number of people are being added to Christ and his church who have no religious background whatever. Here, for example, is a young man from a non-Christian family. The Christian instruction he received at school was minimal, and possibly misleading. In any case the fashion was to pay no attention to it. He did not go to Sunday School as a child, and he has seldom, if ever, been to church. But now he has found Christ, or rather been found by him. He is told he must read the Bible daily if he is to grow into spiritual maturity. The Bible is a closed book to him, however – an unexplored, uncharted territory. Who wrote it, he asks, and when, where and why? What is its message? What is the foundation for its claim to be a "holy" or special book, the book of God? And how is it to be read and interpreted? These are proper questions to ask, and some answer must be given to them before the new Christian can derive maximum benefit from his Bible reading.

Then, secondly, there is the Christian of several years' standing. In the main, he (or she) has been a conscientious Bible reader. He has read a passage from the Bible faithfully every day. But somehow it has become a stale habit.

The years have passed, and he himself has changed and matured as a person. Yet he has not developed as a Christian in any comparable way. A sign (and cause) of this is that he still reads the Bible as he did when he was a child, or a new convert. Now he is tired of his superficiality, his immaturity, and not a little ashamed. He longs to become an adult, integrated Christian, who knows and pleases God, fulfills himself in serving others and can commend the gospel in meaningful terms to a lost, bewildered generation.

My desire is to assure such a Christian that the secrets of Christian maturity are ready to be found in Scripture by all who seek them. There is a breadth to God's Word which few of us ever encompass, a depth which we seldom plumb.

In particular, our Christianity is mean because our Christ is mean. We impoverish ourselves by our low and paltry views of him. Some speak of him today as if he were a kind of hypodermic syringe to be carried about in our pocket, so that when we are feeling depressed we can give ourselves a fix and take a trip into fantasy. But Christ cannot be used or manipulated like that. The contemporary church seems to have little understanding of the greatness of Jesus Christ as Lord of creation and Lord of the church, before whom our place is on our faces in the dust. Nor do we seem to see his victory as the New Testament portrays it, with all things under his feet, so that if we are joined to Christ, all things are under our feet as well.

It seems to me that our greatest need today is an enlarged vision of Jesus Christ. We need to see him as the One in whom alone the fullness of God dwells and in whom alone we can come to fullness of life (Col. 1:19; 2:9-10).

There is only one way to gain clear, true, fresh, lofty views of Christ, and that is through the Bible. The Bible is the prism by which the light of Jesus Christ is broken into its many and beautiful colors. The Bible is the portrait of Jesus Christ. We need to gaze upon him with such intensity of desire that (by the gracious work of the Holy Spirit) he comes alive to us, meets with us, and fills us with himself.

In order to apprehend Jesus Christ in his fullness, it is essential to understand the setting within which God offers him to us. God gave Christ to the world in a specific geographical, historical and theological context. More simply, he sent him to a particular place (Palestine), at a particular time (the climax of centuries of Jewish history) and within a particular framework of truth (progressively revealed and permanently recorded in the Bible). So the following chapters are concerned with the geography, history, theology, authority and interpretation of the Bible. Their object is to present the setting within which God once revealed and now offers Christ, so that we may the better grasp for ourselves and share with others the glorious fullness of Jesus Christ himself.

Abbreviations

AV: Authorized Version/King James Version
NEB: New English Bible
RSV: Revised Standard Version
REB: Revised English Bible
NRSV: New Revised Standard Version

1. The Purpose of the Bible

❖ *What does it mean to say that the Bible is primarily a book of salvation?*

❖ *In what ways do we see Jesus Christ in the Old Testament as well as in the New Testament?*

❖ *How does Scripture draw from us a response of faith?*

The choice of a book to read and the way in which we read it are determined largely by the author's purpose in writing it. Is it a textbook of science or history intended to inform, or a novel meant purely to entertain? Is it a piece of serious prose or poetry in which the writer reflects on life and stimulates the reader to think about it too? Does it speak in any meaningful way to the contemporary world? Or is it perhaps a controversial work in which he deliberately sets out to argue his point of view? Moreover, is the author qualified to write on the subject? Questions like these are often in our minds when we ask, "Is it worth reading?"

Most books supply prospective readers with the information they want about who wrote them and why. Either the author tells us candidly in a preface about himself and his object in writing, or the publisher does so in the "blurb" on the cover. Most readers spend time examining these before committing themselves to buy, borrow or read the book.

It is a great pity that readers of the Bible do not always ask the same questions. Many appear to pick it up and begin their reading at random. Some start at Genesis and get stuck in Leviticus. Others may doggedly persevere from a sense of duty, even setting (and achieving) a target of reading the whole Bible through section by section in five years, but without deriving much benefit from their study because they lack understanding of the book's overall purpose. Or indeed many give up Bible reading altogether, or never start it, because they cannot see how the tale of a faraway people in a faraway age could have any relevance for them today.

In any case, how can the Bible, which in fact is not a book but a library of sixty-six books, possibly be said to have a "purpose"? Was it not compiled by different authors at different times with different objectives? Yes and no. There is indeed a wide variety of human author and theme. Yet behind these, Christians believe, there lies a single divine Author with a single unifying theme.

The Bible itself declares what this theme is. It is stated several times in several places, but perhaps nowhere more succinctly than by the apostle Paul to Timothy:

From infancy you have known the holy Scriptures, which are able to make you wise for salvation through faith in Christ Jesus. All Scripture is God-breathed and is useful for teaching, rebuking, correcting and training in righteousness, so that the man of God may be thoroughly equipped for every good work. (2 Tim. 3:15-17)

Here the apostle brings together both the origin and the object of Scripture, where it comes from and what it is intended for. Its origin: "God-breathed." Its object: "useful" for human beings. Indeed, it is useful for us only *because* it is God-breathed – inspired by God. The subject of biblical inspiration I must leave to a later chapter; in this chapter I want to investigate the nature of the Bible's usefulness. For this I will take up three words which Paul used – "salvation," "Christ" and "faith."

A book of salvation

Perhaps no biblical word has suffered more from misuse and misunderstanding than the word "salvation." Some of us Christians are to blame for the caricature of it which we have presented to the world. As a result, the word "salvation" has become for many a source of embarrassment, even an object of ridicule. We need to rescue it from the narrow concept to which we have often debased it. For "salvation" is a big and noble word, as I shall soon elaborate. Salvation is freedom. Yes, and renewal too; ultimately the renewal of the whole cosmos.

Now the supreme purpose of the Bible, Paul writes to Timothy, is to instruct its readers "for salvation." This immediately indicates that Scripture has a practical purpose, and that this purpose is moral rather than intellectual. Or rather its intellectual instruction (its "wisdom," as the Greek word implies) is given with a view to the moral experience called "salvation."

In order to grasp more firmly this positive purpose of Scripture, it may be helpful to contrast it with some purposes it does not have.

First, the purpose of the Bible is not scientific. This is not to say that the teaching of Scripture and of science are in conflict with one another for, when we keep each to its proper sphere and discern what each is affirming, they are not. Indeed, if the God of truth is the author of both, they could not be. Nor is it to say that the two spheres never overlap and that nothing in the Bible has any scientific relevance, for the Bible does contain statements of fact which can be (and in many cases have been) scientifically verified. For example, a number of historical facts are recorded, such as that Nebuchadnezzar King of Babylon

besieged, took and virtually destroyed Jerusalem, and that Jesus of Nazareth was born when Augustus was Emperor of Rome. What I am asserting rather is that, though the Bible may contain some science, the *purpose* of the Bible is not scientific.

Science (or at least natural science) is a body of knowledge painstakingly acquired by observation, experiment and induction. The purpose of God through Scripture, however, has been to disclose truths which could not be discovered by this method (called by scientists the "empirical" method), but would have remained unknown and undiscovered if he had not revealed them. For instance, science may be able to tell us something about our physical origins (even this is an open question); only the Bible reveals our nature, both our unique nobility as creatures made in the Creator's image and our degradation as self-centered sinners in revolt against our Creator.

Next, the purpose of the Bible is not literary. Some years ago a book was published entitled *The Bible Designed to Be Read as Literature*. It was beautifully produced. The traditional verse-arrangement was abandoned. And the layout indicated plainly what was poetry and what was prose. All this was helpful. Further, no one can deny, whatever his or her beliefs or disbeliefs, that the Bible does contain noble literature. It deals with the great themes of human life and destiny, and handles them with simplicity, insight and imagination. So fine was its original translation in some countries, such as England and Germany, that the Bible has become part of the nation's literary heritage. Nevertheless, God did not design the Bible as great literature. It contains some glaring stylistic weaknesses. The New Testament was written largely in *koine* Greek, the everyday language of market and office, and much of it lacks literary polish, even grammatical accuracy. The purpose of the Bible is to be found in its message, not in its style.

Thirdly, the purpose of the Bible is not philosophical. Of course Scripture contains profound wisdom, in fact the wisdom of God. But some of the great themes with which

Books of the Bible

The Bible is made up of a "library" of sixty-six books, thirty-nine in the Old Testament, twenty-seven in the New. The writings of the **OLD TESTAMENT** first appeared as separate scrolls in Hebrew; we do not know how or when they were first gathered into a single volume. The thirty-nine books of the Old Testament vary in authorship and style and can be divided into four major groupings:

Law
Sometimes called the Pentateuch, or "five scrolls."

History
Tracing the story of God's people from their entry into the Promised Land to the Exile.

Poetry and Wisdom
Full of proverbs, riddles, parables, warnings, and wise sayings.

Prophecy
God's prophets explained what had happened in the past, spoke out against evil in the present, and told what God would do in the future.

The Apocrypha
The Apocrypha (not illustrated) is a collection of books and additions to the Old Testament books written between 300 BC and AD 100. It was not accepted by the Jews as part of the Old Testament Scripture, and most Protestant denominations do not accept it as part of genuine Scripture. The books are interesting and valuable historical documents that range from historical narratives to pious fiction.

The twenty-seven books of the **NEW TESTAMENT** were written in Greek and can also be divided into different types of writing:

History
The four Gospels and the book of Acts are considered history. The Gospels, however, are not simply historical records; they were written to persuade readers to believe in Jesus and form portraits of Jesus as the Messiah.

Letters
These include Paul's letters to churches in various cities, his letters to individual Christians, and letters written by other apostles.

Revelation
This book opens with letters to seven churches in Asia Minor, but continues with vivid visions about the last days.

philosophers have always wrestled are not given a thorough treatment in Scripture. Take the great problems of suffering and evil. As phenomena of human experience they figure prominently throughout the Bible. On almost every page men and women sin, and men and women suffer. And some light is thrown – supremely by the cross – on both problems. But no ultimate explanation of either is offered, nor are the ways of God justified in relation to them, in terms acceptable to human philosophy. Even in the Book of Job, which concentrates on the problem of suffering, Job in the end humbles himself before God without understanding God's providence. I think the reason is simply that the Bible is more a practical than a theoretical book. It is more concerned to tell us how to bear suffering and overcome evil than it is to philosophize about their origin and purpose.

So the Bible is primarily a book neither of science, nor of literature, nor of philosophy, but of salvation.

In saying this we must give the word "salvation" its broadest possible meaning. Salvation is far more than merely the forgiveness of sins. It includes the whole sweep of God's purpose to redeem and restore humankind, and indeed all creation. What we claim for the Bible is that it unfolds God's total plan.

It begins with the creation, so that we may know the divine likeness in which we were made, the obligations which we have repudiated and the heights from which we have fallen. We can understand neither what we are in sin nor what we may be by grace until we know what we once were by creation.

The Bible goes on to tell us how sin entered into the world, and death as a result of sin. It emphasizes the gravity of sin as a revolt against the authority of God our Creator and Lord, and the justice of his judgment upon it. There are many salutary warnings in Scripture about the perils of disobedience.

But the main thrust of the biblical message, as will be elaborated in chapter 5, is that God loves the very rebels who deserve nothing at his hand but judgment. Before time began,

Scripture says, his plan of salvation took shape. It originated in his grace, his free and unmerited mercy. He made with Abraham a covenant of grace, promising through his posterity to bless all the families of the earth. The rest of the Old Testament is devoted to an account of his gracious dealings with Abraham's posterity, the people of Israel. In spite of their obstinate rejection of his word, as it came to them through law and prophets, he never cast them off. *They* broke the covenant, not he.

The historical coming of Jesus Christ was in fulfillment of his covenant:

> Praise be to the Lord, the God of Israel,
>   because he has come and has redeemed
>   his people.
> He has raised up a horn of salvation for us
>   in the house of his servant David
> (as he said through his holy prophets of
>   long ago),
> salvation from our enemies
>   and from the hand of all who hate us –
> to show mercy to our fathers
>   and to remember his holy covenant,
>   the oath he swore to our father
>   Abraham:
> to rescue us from the hand of our enemies,
>   and to enable us to serve him without fear
> in holiness and righteousness before him
>   all our days.
> (Luke 1:68-75)

It is important to observe that the promised "salvation" from "our enemies" is understood in terms of "holiness and righteousness" and – later in the same passage – of "the forgiveness of their sins, because of the tender mercy of our God."

So the New Testament concentrates on the outworking of this salvation, on the way of "forgiveness" and of "holiness" through Jesus Christ's death, resurrection and gift of the Holy Spirit. The apostles emphasize that forgiveness is possible only through the sin-bearing death of Christ, and a new birth leading to a new life only through the Spirit of Christ. Then the Letters are full of practical ethical

"Christ at Emmaus," Rembrandt. Jesus rebuked the two disciples from Emmaus for their ignorance of Scripture.

instruction. As the New English Bible translates 2 Timothy 3:16, Scripture is profitable not only "for teaching the truth and refuting error" but "for reformation of manners and discipline in right living." It also portrays Christ's church as the society of the saved, who are called to a life of sacrificial service and witness in the world.

Finally, the New Testament authors insist that although God's people have already in one sense been saved, in another their salvation lies still in the future. We are given the promise that one day our bodies will be redeemed. "In this hope we were saved" (Rom. 8:24). And in this final redemption the whole creation will somehow be involved. If we are to be clothed with new bodies, there is also going to be a new heaven and a new earth pervaded by righteousness alone. Then and only then, with no sin either in our nature or in our society, will God's salvation be complete. The glorious liberty of God's children will be the freedom to serve. God will be everything to everybody (Rom. 8:21; 1 Cor. 15:28).

Such is the comprehensive salvation set forth in Scripture. Conceived in a past eternity, achieved at a point in time and historically worked out in human experience, it will reach its consummation in the eternity of the future. The Bible is unique in its claim to instruct us for "such a great salvation" (Heb. 2:3).

Christ in the Law

The salvation for which the Bible instructs us is available "through faith in Christ Jesus." Therefore, since Scripture concerns salvation and salvation is through Christ, Scripture is full of Christ.

Jesus himself understood the nature and function of the Bible in this way. "The Scriptures," he said, "testify about me" (John 5:39). Again, walking with two disciples after the Resurrection, from Jerusalem to Emmaus, he rebuked them for their folly and unbelief due to their ignorance of Scripture. Luke who tells the story adds:

And beginning with Moses and all the

Prophets, he explained to them what was said in all the Scriptures concerning himself. (Luke 24:27)

A little while later the risen Lord said to a wider group of his followers:

This is what I told you while I was still with you: Everything must be fulfilled that is written about me in the Law of Moses, the Prophets and the Psalms. (Luke 24:44)

Christ's assertion was, then, not only that the Scriptures bore witness to him in a general way, but that in each of the three divisions of the Old Testament Scripture – the Law, the Prophets and the Psalms (or "Writings") – there were things concerning him, and that all these things must be fulfilled.

The fundamental relation between the Old Testament and the New Testament, according to Christ, is that between promise and fulfillment. The very first word Jesus uttered in his public ministry (in the Greek text of the Gospel of Mark) indicates this. It was the word "fulfilled":

The time is fulfilled, and the kingdom of God is at hand; repent, and believe in the gospel. (Mark 1:15 RSV)

Jesus Christ was deeply convinced that the long centuries of expectation were over, and that he himself had ushered in the days of fulfillment. So he could say to his apostles:

Blessed are your eyes because they see, and your ears because they hear. For I tell you the truth, many prophets and righteous men   longed to see what you see but did not see it, and to hear what you hear but did not hear it. (Matt. 13:16-17)

In the light of this claim, we shall look first at the Old Testament in its three divisions, then at the New Testament, and try to see how our Savior Jesus Christ himself (in terms of promise and fulfillment) is Scripture's uniting theme.

By the "Law" was meant the Pentateuch, the first five books of the Old Testament. Can we really find Christ in them? Yes indeed.

To begin with, they contain some foundation prophecies of God's salvation through Christ, which underlie the rest of the Bible. God promised first that the seed of Eve would bruise the serpent's head, next that through Abraham's posterity he would bless all the families of the earth, and later that "the scepter will not depart from Judah . . . until he comes to whom it belongs," whom the people will obey (Gen. 3:15; 12:3; 49:10). Thus it was revealed – already in the first book of the Bible – that the Messiah would be human (descended from Eve) and Jewish (descended from Abraham and of the tribe of Judah), and that he would crush Satan, bless the world and rule as king forever.

Another important prophecy of Christ in the Law represents him as being himself the perfect Prophet. Moses said to the people:

The LORD your God will raise up for you a prophet like me from among your own brothers. You must listen to him. . . . "I will put my words in his mouth, and he will tell them everything I command him." (Deut. 18:15, 18)

It was not only by direct prophecies that the Law pointed forward to Christ, however, but also by more indirect pictures. In it the Messiah was foreshadowed as well as foretold. Indeed, God's dealings with Israel in choosing them, redeeming them, establishing his covenant with them, making atonement for their sins through sacrifice, and causing them to inherit the land of Canaan all set forth in limited and national terms what would one day be available to all people through Christ. Christians can say today: God has chosen us in Christ and made us a people for his own possession. Christ shed his blood to atone for our sins and ratify the new covenant. He has redeemed us not from Egyptian bondage but from the bondage of sin. He is our great high priest who offered himself on the cross, as one

Paul was probably imprisoned in this jail in Philippi, Macedonia. Paul portrays the Law as a jailer.

sacrifice for sins forever, and all priesthood and sacrifice are fulfilled in him. Further, by his resurrection we have been born again to a living hope, "into an inheritance that can never perish, spoil or fade," and is reserved in heaven for us (1 Pet. 1:3-4). These great Christian words, which portray various aspects of our salvation through Christ – election, atonement, covenant, redemption, sacrifice, inheritance – all began to be used in the Old Testament in relation to God's grace towards Israel.

There is yet a third way in which the Law bears witness to Christ. It is elaborated by the apostle Paul in his Galatian letter:

> Before this faith came, we were held prisoners by the law, locked up until faith should be revealed. So the law was put in charge to lead us to Christ that we might be justified by faith. (Gal. 3:23-24)

The law is vividly portrayed by the Greek words Paul used as a military garrison hemming us in ("held prisoners"), a jailer keeping us under lock and key ("locked up") and a tutor charged with the discipline of minors ("put in charge"). All this is because the moral law condemned the lawbreaker without in itself offering any remedy. In this way it pointed to Christ. Its very condemnation made Christ necessary. It held us in bondage in order "to lead us to Christ," who alone could set us free. We are condemned by the law, but justified through faith in Christ.

Christ in the Prophets

As we turn now from the Law to the Prophets, we need to remember that the Old Testament division known as "the Prophets" included the history books (Joshua, Judges, Samuel and Kings) as "the former prophets" because the authors were judged to have written prophetic or sacred history, as well as "the latter prophets" whom we call the major and minor prophets.

Many readers of the Bible have found the history of Israel extremely tedious and cannot imagine how all those dreary kings could have anything to do with Christ! When we remember, however, that Christ's first words about "the time is fulfilled" immediately led on to "the kingdom of God has drawn near," we have in the word "kingdom" the clue we need. Israel began as a "theocracy," a nation under the direct rule of God. Even when the people rejected the divine rule by demanding a king like the other nations and God granted their request, they knew that ultimately he continued to be their King, for they continued to be his people, and that their kings reigned as it were as his viceroys.

Nevertheless, the rule of the kings, of both the northern kingdom Israel and the southern kingdom Judah, left much to be desired. The monarchy was spoiled externally by foreign wars, and internally by injustice and oppression. Both kingdoms also had the instability of all human institutions, as king after king acceded to the throne and reigned and died. And sometimes they shrank to tiny territories, as their land was overrun by invading armies, until in the end both capitals were taken and both nations suffered a humiliating exile. It is not surprising that God used their experience of the limitations of human government to clarify their understanding of the perfections of the future Messianic kingdom and to strengthen their longing for it.

Already God had made a covenant with King David to build him a house and through his posterity to establish his throne forever (2 Sam. 7:8-17). Now the prophets began to describe what would embody the ideals of kingship which the kings of Israel and Judah, and even David himself, so imperfectly foreshadowed. In his kingdom oppression would give place to justice, and war to peace. Further, there would be no limit to either its extent or its duration. For his dominion would stretch from sea to sea, even to the ends of the earth, and would last forever. These four characteristics of the kingdom of the Messiah – peace, justice, universality and eternity – are brought together in one of Isaiah's most famous prophecies:

> For to us a child is born,
>   to us a son is given,
>   and the government will be on his
>   shoulders.
> And he will be called
>   Wonderful Counselor, Mighty God,
>   Everlasting Father, Prince of Peace.
> Of the increase of his government and
>   peace
>   there will be no end.
> He will reign on David's throne
>   and over his kingdom,
>   establishing and upholding it
>   with justice and righteousness
>   from that time on and forever.
> The zeal of the LORD Almighty
>   will accomplish this. (Isa. 9:6-7)

If the prophets foretold the glory of the Messiah, they foretold his sufferings also. The best-known such prophecy, obviously definitive for our Lord's own understanding of his ministry, is that of the suffering servant in Isaiah 53. He would be "despised and rejected by men, a man of sorrows, and familiar with suffering" (v. 3). Above all, he would bear his people's sins:

> He was pierced for our transgressions,
>   he was crushed for our iniquities;
> the punishment that brought us peace was
>   upon him, and by his wounds we are
>   healed.
> We all, like sheep, have gone astray,
>   each of us has turned to his own way;
> and the LORD has laid on him
>   the iniquity of us all. (Isa. 53:5-6)

Christ in the Writings

The third division of the Old Testament was "the Writings," sometimes called "the Psalms," because the Psalter (our book of Psalms) was the chief book of this section. Several psalms are applied to Jesus Christ in

King Jehu of Israel brings tribute to Shalmaneser III of Assyria. Israel was often overrun by invaders.

the New Testament, psalms which include references to his deity, humanity, sufferings and exaltation. Thus the words "You are my Son; today I have become your Father" were used (at least in part) by God the Father in direct address to his Son at both his baptism and his transfiguration. The allusions in Psalm 8 to man as "made . . . a little lower than the heavenly beings" and "crowned . . . with glory and honor" are applied to Christ by the author of the Letter to the Hebrews. Jesus himself quoted Psalm 22:1 from the cross: "My God, my God, why have you forsaken me?" claiming that he had personally experienced and fulfilled the terrible God-forsakenness which the psalmist expressed. He also quoted David's saying in Psalm 110:1, "The Lord says to my Lord: 'Sit at my right hand until I make your enemies a footstool for your feet,'" and asked his critics how the Messiah could be both David's Lord and David's son.

"The Writings" contain, in addition, what is often called the wisdom literature of the Old Testament. The "wise men" appear to have become a distinct group in Israel during the later period of the monarchy, alongside the prophets and the priests. They knew that the beginning of wisdom was to fear God and depart from evil. Often they extolled wisdom in glowing terms, as more precious than gold, silver and jewels, and occasionally they appeared even to personify wisdom as the agent of God's creation:

> I was there when he set the heavens in
>   place,
>   when he marked out the horizon on the
>   face of the deep,
> when he established the clouds above
>   and fixed securely the fountains of the
>   deep,
> when he gave the sea its boundary
>   so the waters would not overstep his
>   command,
> and when he marked out the foundations of
>   the earth.
>   Then I was the craftsman at his side.
> I was filled with delight day after day,
>   rejoicing always in his presence,
> rejoicing in his whole world
>   and delighting in mankind. (Prov. 8:12,
>   27-31)

Christians have no difficulty in recognizing that this wisdom of God is uniquely incorporated in Jesus Christ, the personal "Word" who was in the beginning with God and through whom all things were made (see John 1:1-3; Col. 2:3).

The Old Testament expectation of Christ – in the Law, the Prophets and the Writings – is seen to have been extremely diverse. Jesus himself summed it up in the comprehensive question: "Did not the Christ have to suffer these things and then enter his glory?" (Luke 24:26). The apostle Peter took up the phrase, conceding that the prophets did not fully understand "the time and circumstances to which the Spirit of Christ in them was pointing when he predicted the sufferings of Christ and the glories that would follow" (1 Pet. 1:11). But this double strand of prophecy was there, representing him as the priest who would offer himself as a sacrifice for sin and the king whose glorious reign would know no end.

In fact, another way of summing up the Old Testament witness to Christ is to say that it depicts him as a greater prophet than Moses, a greater priest than Aaron and a greater king than David. That is to say, he will perfectly reveal God to man, reconcile man to God and rule over man for God. In him, the Old Testament ideals of prophecy, priesthood and kingship will find their final fulfillment.

Christ in the New Testament

If the idea of discovering Christ in the Old Testament seems at first sight strange, there is no similar difficulty about finding him in the New. In the Gospels – each with its own viewpoint, as we shall see in chapter 4 – we find the story of his birth, life, death and resurrection, together with a sample of what he said and what he did.

These "memories of the apostles," as they used to be called in the early church, came rightly to be known as "Gospels," for each evangelist tells his story as "gospel" or good news of Christ and his salvation. They do not present him as a biographer might. They are essentially witnesses, directing their readers' attention to one they believed to be the God-man, born to save his people from their sins,

whose words were words of eternal life, whose works dramatized the glory of his kingdom, who died as a ransom for sinners, and who rose in triumph to be Lord of all.

You might suppose that the Acts of the Apostles, which tells the story of the early days of Christianity, is more about the church than about Christ. Yet this would misrepresent its nature. Luke, its author, has a different emphasis. In introducing his work to Theophilus (for whom he is writing) he describes his first book (the Gospel of Luke) as containing "all that Jesus began to do and to teach." The implication is that the Acts story will contain all that Jesus continued to do and teach through his apostles. So in the Acts we listen to Christ as he was still speaking to men, though now through the great sermons of the apostles Peter and Paul which Luke records. We also see the miracles which he did through them, for "many wonders and miraculous signs were done by the apostles" in the name and with the power of Jesus Christ (Acts 2:43). And we watch Christ building his own church by adding converts to it:

And the Lord added to their number daily those who were being saved. (Acts 2:47)

The Epistles extend the New Testament's witness to Christ by unfolding further the glory of his divine-human person and saving work, and by relating the life of the Christian and of the church to him. The apostles exalt Christ as the one in whom "God was pleased to have all his fullness dwell" and through whom we ourselves have "fullness in Christ" (Col. 1:19; 2:9-10). In Christ God has "blessed us . . . with every spiritual blessing," they say (Eph. 1:3), so that we can do all things through him who inwardly strengthens us (Phil. 4:13). The Christ the apostles present is an all-sufficient Christ, who is able to save to the uttermost and for all time "those who come to God through him" (Heb. 7:25).

The Bible's showing-forth of Christ reaches its climax in the Revelation of John. He is portrayed in the vivid imagery which characterizes

Remains of the theater, Laodicea, Asia Minor. The church here was one of the "lampstands" of Revelation 2–3.

this book. First he appears as a glorified man "among the lampstands." These represent the churches, which the risen Christ is seen to patrol and superintend, so that he is able to say to each, "I know your deeds" (Rev. 2–3). Then the scene changes from earth to heaven, and Jesus Christ appears as "a Lamb, looking as if it had been slain." The countless international crowd of the redeemed are even said to have "washed their robes and made them white in the blood of the Lamb," by which John means that they owe their righteousness to Christ crucified alone (Rev. 5:6; 7:14). Then towards the end of the book Christ is seen as a majestic rider on a white horse, going forth to judgment, with his name inscribed upon him "KING OF KINGS AND LORD OF LORDS" (Rev. 19:11-16). Finally we are introduced to him as the Heavenly Bridegroom for, we are told, "the wedding of the Lamb has come, and his bride has made herself ready." His bride is the glorified church which is then seen "coming down out of heaven from God, prepared as a bride beautifully dressed for her husband" (Rev.

19:7-9; 21:2). Almost the last words of the Revelation are "The Spirit and the Bride say, 'Come!' And let him who hears say, 'Come!' . . . Come, Lord Jesus" (Rev. 22:17, 20).

There is great diversity of content, style and purpose among the books of the Bible, and in some of them the witness to Christ is indirect, even oblique. But this brief survey of the Old and New Testaments should be enough to demonstrate that "the testimony of Jesus is the spirit of prophecy" (Rev. 19:10). If we want to know Christ and his salvation, it is to the Bible we must turn. For the Bible is God's own portrait of Christ. We can never know him otherwise. As Jerome put it in the fourth century AD, "Ignorance of the Scriptures is ignorance of Christ."

Just as in a children's treasure hunt, one is sometimes fortunate enough to stumble immediately upon the treasure but, more usually, has to follow laboriously from clue to clue until at last the treasure is found, so it is with Bible reading. Some verses point one direct to Christ. Others are remote clues. But a painstaking pursuit of the clues will ultimately lead every reader to that treasure whose worth is beyond price.

Through faith

The Scriptures are "able to make you wise for salvation through faith in Christ Jesus," wrote Paul (2 Tim. 3:15). Since their purpose (or the purpose of the divine author who spoke and speaks through them) is to bring us to salvation, and since salvation is in Christ, they point us to Christ, as we have seen. But their object in pointing us to Christ is not simply that we should know about him and understand him, nor even that we should admire him, but that we should put our trust in him. Scripture bears witness to Christ not in order to satisfy our curiosity but in order to draw from us a response of faith.

There is much misunderstanding about faith. It is commonly supposed to be a leap in the dark, totally incompatible with reason. This is not so. True faith is never unreasonable, because its object is always trustworthy. When we human beings trust one another, the reasonableness of our trust depends on the relative trustworthiness of the people concerned. But the Bible bears witness to Jesus Christ as absolutely trustworthy. It tells us who he is and what he has done, and the evidence it supplies for his unique person and work is extremely compelling. As we expose ourselves to the biblical witness to this Christ, and as we feel its impact – profound yet simple, varied yet unanimous – God creates faith within us. We receive the testimony. We believe.

That is what Paul meant when he wrote:

Consequently, faith comes from hearing the message, and the message is heard through the word of Christ. (Rom. 10:17)

We have seen that God's purpose in and through the Bible is severely practical. He has ordained it as his chief instrument for bringing people to "salvation," understood in its widest and fullest sense. The whole Bible is a gospel of salvation, and the gospel is "the power of God for the salvation of everyone who believes" (Rom. 1:16). So it points its many fingers unerringly to Christ, so that its readers will see him, believe in him and be saved.

The apostle John writes something very similar at the end of his Gospel. He has recorded only a selection of the signs of Jesus, he says, for Jesus performed many others. He goes on:

But these are written that you may believe that Jesus is the Christ, the Son of God, and that by believing you may have life in his name. (John 20:31)

John sees the ultimate purpose of Scripture ("what is written") just as Paul sees it. John calls it "life," Paul "salvation," but the words are virtually synonymous. Both apostles are further agreed that this life or salvation is in Christ, and that to receive it we must believe in him. Both present exactly the same sequence of steps: Scripture – Christ – faith – salvation. Scripture testifies to Christ in order to evoke faith in Christ, in order to bring life to the believer.

The conclusion is simple. Whenever we read the Bible, we must look for Christ. And we must go on looking until we see and so believe. Only as we continue to appropriate by faith the riches of Christ which are disclosed to us in Scripture shall we grow into spiritual maturity, and become men and women of God who are "thoroughly equipped for every good work" (2 Tim. 3:17).

2. The Land of the Bible

✤ *Why is it important that we know the geography
   and the history of the people in the Bible?*

✤ *Why was rain so important to the Israelites,
   and how is this importance shown in the Bible?*

✤ *What was the significance of the three festivals of the Israelites?*

God's purpose to call out from the world a people for himself began to unfold on a particular part of the world's surface and during a particular period of the world's history. It is not possible to understand its meaning, therefore, without some knowledge of its historical and geographical setting.

Yet the very mention of history and geography, especially Bible history and Bible geography, is enough to switch some people off. They shudder as they recall boring Sunday school lessons, with date-lists of dreary Israelite kings to memorize and Paul's interminable missionary journeys to plot on a map. If you feel like that, I sympathize with you. I suffered that way too. So evidently did the theological student who was required in an exam to distinguish between the prophets Elijah and Elisha. As he did not have the slightest notion which was which, it is rumored that his essay began: "Let us not haggle over the differences between these two truly great men. But let us rather give a list of the kings of Israel and Judah in their chronological order."

Some folk who have no taste for either history or geography may ask rather impatiently why God did not give us instead a simple set of dogmas to believe and rules to obey. Why did he have to reveal himself in a rather remote historical and geographical context, so that we have to struggle to understand the context before we can grasp the revelation? One reply might be: "Because God chose to do it that way" and "Stop asking impertinent questions." But the questions are perfectly proper ones.

A better answer would be that the living God is a personal God, who made us as persons in his own image and insists on treating the persons he has made as persons. So the whole process of revelation has been the self-disclosure of a Person to persons, to real persons like ourselves who actually lived in a certain place at a certain time. In saying this, I am not denying that God has revealed his truth in words. I am rather asserting that his revelation has been "personal" and "propositional" at one and the same time. That is, the truths he has revealed have not descended from heaven by parachute. They have instead been made known in and through the living experience of human beings, culminating in his own Son, the Word made flesh.

Moreover, if God had simply supplied us with a systematic catalogue of dos and don'ts for everyday belief and behavior, it would have been far too abstract to be useful. And if such a list had been expressed in the idiom of one age or generation, it would have been largely meaningless to others. But as it is, God revealed himself in personal situations, which, being human, are concrete and readily intelligible in every generation. Their record in Scripture enables us to see for ourselves.

God's dealings with the nation of Israel and with individuals are recorded, we are told, "to teach us" (Rom. 15:4; 1 Cor. 10:11). The instruction they give consists of both encouragement and warning. "The encouragement of the Scriptures" (Rom. 15:4) is tremendous. Even the great men of the biblical story, it is emphasized, were "like us" (see Jas. 5:17; Acts

14:15). Yet we watch them overcoming in their struggle with temptation and doubt; refusing to bow down to idols and willing to accept death rather than compromise their allegiance to the living God; believing the promises of God in spite of every evidence to the contrary; standing alone in an age of prevailing apostasy; loving and serving their own generation; and bravely bearing witness to the truth.

Scripture contains warning as well as encouragement, for it refuses to conceal the faults even of its great men. It tells us frankly how righteous Noah got drunk; how Abraham, the giant of faith, fell so deeply into unbelief that he was ready even to expose his wife to moral danger in order to save his own skin; how Jacob schemed and Joseph boasted; how Moses, the meekest man on earth, lost his temper; how David found favor in the sight of God, yet committed theft, murder and adultery in a single surrender to passion; how Job, "blameless and upright, a man who fears God and shuns evil" (Job 1:8), under the provocation of great adversity, cried out in bitterness and cursed the day that he was born; and how the whole nation of Israel, despite its many unique privileges, broke the covenant of God. The Bible is equally candid with its New Testament characters. They too were human beings of flesh and blood like us, who gave way sometimes to unbelief, compromise, boastfulness, indiscipline and disobedience. "Now these things occurred as examples" (1 Cor. 10:6, 11).

God wants to deal with us in our situation of time and place, as he dealt with the biblical characters in theirs. So to understand his ways with us, we must understand his ways with them. And to understand this, we must know something of both where and when it all happened. We must be able to visualise it. So our look at the land of the Bible in this chapter and at the story of the Bible in the next two becomes a fascinating, even indispensable, study. For this history and this geography constitute the arena in which God chose uniquely to speak and to act.

It used to be seriously argued by Christian geographers in the Middle Ages that Jerusalem was the centre of the earth. Their maps illustrated their belief. And in the ancient Church of the Holy Sepulchre in Jerusalem (which is built over the supposed site of the burial and resurrection of Jesus) a stone is set into the floor to mark what was thought to be the precise spot.

Of course this is sheer nonsense, geographically speaking. Theologically, however, Christians would defend it as true. To them Palestine is "the Holy Land," a region distinct from all others. It is also the center of the world's history and geography in the sense that here lay "the promised land," which God pledged to Abraham some two thousand years before Christ; here the Savior of the world both lived and died; and here the Christian mission was born, which was to outlive the Roman empire and change the course of world history.

Further, Christians believe in the providence of God. We cannot therefore imagine that the choice of Palestine as the stage for the drama of salvation was an accident. One of its obvious features is that it acts as a kind of bridge between three continents. Europe, Asia and Africa converge at the eastern seaboard of the Mediterranean, and their citizens have always mingled with each other on its trade routes by sea and land. Consequently, not only has Palestine been invaded and subjugated by armies from all three – first Egyptian, then Assyrian, Babylonian and Persian, and finally Greek and Roman – but it became an admirable springboard for spiritual counterattack, the soldiers of Jesus Christ marching (as it were) north, south, east and west to the conquest of the world. "You will be my witnesses," his last words to them had been, "in Jerusalem, and in all Judea and Samaria, and to the ends of the earth" (Acts 1:8). Strategically, therefore, God has set Jerusalem "in the centre of the nations" (Ezek. 5:5). If Christ's witnesses had taught more clearly the Middle Eastern origins of Christianity, one wonders if the gospel would ever have

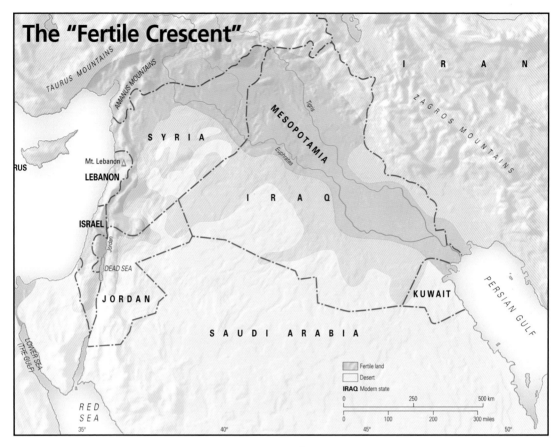

The "Fertile Crescent"

TAURUS MOUNTAINS

AMANUS MOUNTAINS

RUS

SYRIA

Mt. Lebanon △

LEBANON

ISRAEL

Jordan

DEAD SEA

JORDAN

LOWER SEA
(THE GULF)

RED
SEA

MESOPOTAMIA

Tigris

Euphrates

I R A N

ZAGROS MOUNTAINS

I R A Q

KUWAIT

SAUDI ARABIA

PERSIAN GULF

Fertile land

Desert

IRAQ Modern state

0   250   500 km

0   100   200   300 miles

35°   40°   45°   50°

become so closely associated in the minds of Africans and Asians with the white and the Western world.

"Palestine" – the word came originally from the Philistines who occupied a small western section of it – is itself only a part of the arena of Old Testament history. The wider scene has often been called the "Fertile Crescent," because it sweeps round in a semi-circle from Egypt to Mesopotamia, from the Nile valley to the alluvial plain watered by the Euphrates and Tigris rivers, enclosing the arid Arabian desert. In order to understand the history of God's people, one needs to keep this crescent in mind, and not least the two great rivers which form its extremities. For God called Abraham from Ur of the Chaldees, situated only nine miles from the River Euphrates in Southern Iraq, and Moses from Egypt where he had narrowly escaped drowning as a baby in the River Nile. The very words "Egypt" and "Babylonia" reminded

Israelites of the saving initiatives of their God, for these countries were the scenes of their two bitter captivities, from which their God had delivered them.

A good land

When God told Moses that he was about to bring them out of Egypt into Canaan, he described it as "a good and spacious land, a land flowing with milk and honey" (Exod. 3:8), adding later that it was "the most beautiful of all lands" (Ezek. 20:6, 15). And when the twelve spies or scouts, whom Moses had sent to explore the land, reported, they confirmed this description from their own experience. Joshua and Caleb said:

> The land we passed through and explored is exceedingly good . . . a land flowing with milk and honey. (Num. 14:7-8)

They were able, moreover, to supply evidence for their assertion, for they had brought back with them from the Valley of Eshcol (a little north of Hebron) a single cluster of grapes so heavy that it had to be slung on a pole and carried by two of them, with some pomegranates and figs as well (Num. 13:23-24).

Then, just before entering the land, after a delay of forty years because of Israel's disobedience and unbelief, Moses urged the people to keep God's commandments and added:

> For the LORD your God is bringing you
> into a good land – a land with streams
> and pools of water, with springs flowing
> in the valleys and hills; a land with
> wheat and barley, vines and fig trees,
> pomegranates, olive oil and honey; a
> land where bread will not be scarce and
> you will lack nothing; a land where the
> rocks are iron and you can dig copper
> out of the hills. When you have eaten
> and are satisfied, praise the LORD your
> God for the good land he has given you.
> (Deut. 8:7-10)

Although Palestinian farmers have to work hard to secure a good yield, this is still an accurate description of the country's fertility and produce. The country we are describing extends only about 200 miles from north to south and 100 miles from west to east. It is hemmed in by natural boundaries. To the north rises the mountainous mass of the Lebanon (meaning "white" because of its snows) and the Anti-Lebanon, the valley between being known as "the entrance to Hamath." To the west lies the Mediterranean or "the Great Sea," and to the east and south the forbidding deserts of Arabia and of Zin (see Num. 34:1-15).

Several popular expressions were used to refer to the whole country from north to south. One was "from the entrance to Hamath as far as the Sea of the Arabah" that is the Dead Sea (for example, 2 Kings 14:25). But the commonest was simply "from Dan to Beersheba" (for example, Judg. 20:1; 1 Sam. 3:20; 2 Sam. 3:10; 1 Kings 4:25), Dan being Israel's most northerly city, while Beersheba was its most southerly, situated at the edge of the desert of Zin, about halfway between the Mediterranean and the southern tip of the Dead Sea.

Visitors to the Holy Land, provided that they have an opportunity to explore it adequately, are struck by the great variety of its terrain. The contrast is nowhere greater than between the "seas" or "lakes" at the northern and southern ends of the Jordan River. For the colorful beauty of Galilee – with its blue lake surrounded by mountains, its carpet of springtime flowers and its distant backdrop of snow-capped Mount Hermon to the north – is a veritable paradise in comparison with the heat, the stench and the desolation of the Dead Sea and its surroundings.

The biblical record often alludes to the different "regions" into which Palestine is divided. For example, its inhabitants are described as living "in the Arabah, in the mountains, in the western foothills, in the Negev and along the coast" (Deut. 1:7). The "Arabah" is the deep gorge of the Jordan Valley running south to the Gulf of Aqabah. The "mountains" refer to the mountains of Judea, while the "western foothills" refer to the Shephelah district. The "Negev," meaning "the dry," is the great southern desert whose other name is the wilderness of Zin, and the "coast" lies along the Mediterranean.

Perhaps a simpler way to remember the map of Palestine is to visualize four strips of country running parallel from north to south. The most striking is the Jordan Valley. The river cuts its way deep between two mountain ranges – the central highlands which form the backbone of Palestine (its western slopes going down to the coastal plain) and the eastern tableland beyond which lies the desert. So the four strips between the sea and the desert are the coastland, the central highlands, the Jordan valley and the eastern tableland. We shall look at each in turn. See the map on p. 23.

Dan was Israel's most northerly city, in the shadow of snow-capped Mount Hermon.

The coastal strip

The coastal strip varies in breadth from a few hundred yards where Mount Carmel juts out into the sea (and the modern port of Haifa is situated) to some thirty miles at the southern end. This southern part was the ancient land of the Philistines. It is here that the five main Philistine cities were located – Gaza, the most southerly, on the great coastal road which runs up from Egypt about three miles inland, Ashkelon twelve miles north and on the sea, Ashdod eight miles farther north and on the road again, with Ekron farther north and more inland, and Gath in the middle of the plain.

The Shephelah, or foothills, lies immediately east of the Plain of Philistia. It is not surprising to read, therefore, that "the Philistines had raided towns in the foothills" (2 Chron. 28:18). Its sycamore trees were proverbial; so it could be said that Solomon made "cedar as plentiful as sycamore-fig trees in the foothills" (1 Kings 10:27).

Its slopes are, in fact, the foothills of the central plateau. They rise steadily from about 500 feet at Gath to 1,300 feet ten miles to the east.

Then the mountains proper begin, and a further ten miles east lies Hebron, at 3,300 feet the highest city in Palestine.

Going back to the coast, immediately north of the plain of Philistia is the plain of Sharon, whose main town and port is Joppa. In our day it is rich in citrus orchards. Precisely what it was like in biblical times is not certain, but it certainly supported flocks of sheep, since we read once or twice of "the pasturelands of Sharon" (1 Chron. 5:16; cf. 27:29). On the other hand, before modern drainage it must have been very marshy, so that "the splendor of . . . Sharon" (Isa. 35:2) probably refers to its luxuriant vegetation, and the "rose of Sharon" (to whom the bride likens herself in the Song of Solomon) may have been an emblem of exceptional beauty because it blossomed in such unpromising surroundings, like "a lily among thorns" (Song of Songs 2:1-2).

The central highlands

The central mountain range of Palestine begins in Galilee, whose hills and valleys were the background of Jesus' boyhood and of much of his public ministry. The peaks of Upper Galilee rise to just over 3,000 feet, and from the hills above Nazareth in Lower Galilee, although not much higher than 1,500 feet, the Mediterranean Sea is visible on a clear day only seventeen miles to the northwest.

South of Nazareth the ground slopes gently down to a broad alluvial plain, which runs in a southeasterly direction from the Mediterranean north of Mount Carmel to the River Jordan. Its western part is known as the Plain of Esdraelon; the eastern part is the narrower Valley of Jezreel, which lies between the formerly volcanic Hill of Moreh and the limestone Mount Gilboa. It was on the slopes of these two mountains that the Philistines and the Israelites encamped, facing each other across the valley, before the final battle in which King Saul died:

> Now the Philistines fought against Israel; the Israelites fled before them, and many fell slain on Mount Gilboa. . . . David took up this lament concerning Saul and his son Jonathan . . . : "Your glory, O Israel, lies slain on your heights. How the mighty have fallen! . . . O mountains of Gilboa, may you have neither dew nor rain, nor fields that yield offerings of grain. For there the shield of the mighty was defiled, the shield of Saul – no longer rubbed with oil."
> (1 Sam. 31:1; 2 Sam. 1:17, 19, 21)

At the southern edge of the middle of the plain of Esdraelon, on a prominent site at the foot of the Carmel range, lies the fortress town of Megiddo. For centuries it has guarded the entrance to the main pass through the mountains to the south. It was one of the cities which King Solomon rebuilt and fortified to accommodate his horses and chariots (1 Kings 9:15, 19). Here also two kings of Judah died, Ahaziah who was shot by Jehu (2 Kings 9:27), and Josiah who was killed while attempting to stop Pharaoh Neco of Egypt from going to the help of the Assyrians (2 Chron. 35:20-24; cf. 2 Kings 23:28-30).

South of the plain of Esdraelon lies the hill country of Manasseh and Ephraim, well cov-

Ashkelon, situated on the Mediterranean coast, was part of the ancient land of the Philistines.

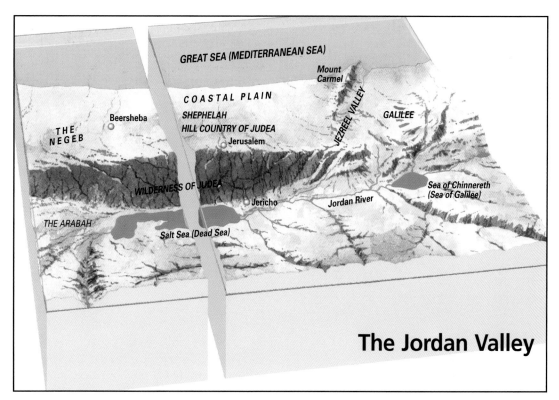

GREAT SEA (MEDITERRANEAN SEA)

Mount
Carmel

COASTAL PLAIN

SHEPHELAH

HILL COUNTRY OF JUDEA

Beersheba

THE
NEGEB

Jerusalem

JEZREEL VALLEY

GALILEE

WILDERNESS OF JUDEA

THE ARABAH

Jericho

Jordan River

Sea of Chinnereth
(Sea of Galilee)

Salt Sea (Dead Sea)

The Jordan Valley

ered with vineyards on their west-facing slopes, and still farther south the hill country of Judah. These two mountainous regions were the focal point of Israel's history during the period of the divided monarchy. For the capital of the northern kingdom was Samaria (in the land of Manasseh-Ephraim) and the capital of the southern kingdom was Jerusalem (in the land of Judah).

Jerusalem is built on a mountain surrounded by mountains. God's "holy mountain . . . beautiful in its loftiness," the psalmist could sing, was "the joy of the whole earth." Again, "as the mountains surround Jerusalem, so the LORD surrounds his people" (Pss. 48:1-2; 125:2). The Mount of Olives lies immediately to the east of Jerusalem, across the Kidron valley, and from this summit the road runs east through the most barren land imaginable, dropping more than 3,000 feet to Jericho and on to the Dead Sea. It was while making this two-day journey on foot that the traveler in Christ's parable was attacked by brigands and rescued by the Good Samaritan.

The whole area between Jerusalem and the

Dead Sea is known as the Wilderness of Judea, and it was somewhere in this scene of desolation that Jesus spent forty days following his baptism, fasting and being tempted by the devil.

The Jordan Valley

The Jordan Valley is part of the Great Rift Valley which stretches for 4,000 miles from Asia Minor through the Red Sea to the Rift Valley lakes of East Africa. But the River Jordan itself is only about eighty miles in total length, excluding its meanderings. It rises in Mount Hermon, a 9,000-foot shoulder of the Anti-Lebanon mass, and then maintains a steady descent ("Jordan" means "descender") through Lake Huleh and Lake Tiberias until it peters out in the Dead Sea. At Huleh it is still above sea level (about 230 feet), but Lake Tiberias is nearly 700 feet below, while its final descent takes it to about 1,300 feet below at the Dead Sea, whose bottom at over 2,500 feet is the deepest point on the surface of the earth.

Lake Huleh is known in the Bible as "the

Lake Tiberias, sometimes called "the Sea of Kinnereth" (or Gennesaret) but usually "the Sea of Galilee."

Waters of Merom" but does not feature prominently in the biblical narrative (only Josh. 11:5, 7). It has always been the haunt of birds rather than of men – purple herons still nest in its tall papyrus reeds – although recently most of it was drained for agricultural land.

Lake Tiberias is sometimes called in the Gospels "the Sea of Kinnereth" (or Gennesaret) but usually "the Sea of Galilee," although to Luke, the much-traveled evangelist who knew the Mediterranean firsthand, it is always merely a "lake." Indeed, he is right, for it is only twelve miles long and – at its widest point – only seven miles across. It is deep and full of fish, and the first disciples of Jesus, the two pairs of brothers, Andrew and Simon, James and John, were partners in a fishing business on the lake. Although it is almost surrounded by mountains, there were numerous villages round its northern and western shores, and these Jesus visited when he went about preaching, teaching and healing.

South of Lake Tiberias the Jordan River flows for a further sixty-five miles (though the mileage is more like 200 if all the meanderings are included) until it reaches the Dead Sea. For much of this distance it is unimpressive and muddy, so that one has some sympathy for Naaman the leprous Syrian general who had no desire to be cured by having to wash in it:

> Are not Abana and Pharpar, the rivers of
> Damascus, better than any of the waters
> of Israel? Couldn't I wash in them and be
> cleansed? (2 Kings 5:12)

More impressive was the thick jungle of the river valley, a famous haunt of wild animals, so that God could liken himself in his judgments to a "lion coming up from Jordan's thickets to a rich pastureland" (Jer. 49:19).

The exact site of the baptisms administered by John the Baptist is unknown, but it must have been at one of the fords a few miles from where the Jordan enters the Dead Sea. Thus:

> The whole Judean countryside and all the
> people of Jerusalem went out to him.
> Confessing their sins, they were baptized
> by him in the Jordan River. (Mark 1:5)

Relief map
of Palestine

△ Mt. Hermon
(9,232ft / 2,184m)

Tyre

PLAIN OF PHOENICIA

Dan

Lake Huleh

SYRIAN DESERT

Hazor

A R A M

Acco

*SEA OF CHINNERETH
(SEA OF GALILEE)*

Mt. Carmel
(1,732ft / 528m) △

Tiberias

GREAT SEA

(MEDITERRANEAN SEA)

Mt. Tabor
(1,929ft / 588m) △

Yarmuk

VALLEY OF JEZREEL

Megiddo

PLAIN OF SHARON

Mt. Gilboa
(1,630ft / 497m) △

G I L E A D

Pella

Jordan

Samaria

Mt. Ebal
(3,083ft / 940m) △

Shechem

Jabbok

△ Mt. Gerizim
(2,889ft / 881m)

I S R A E L

HILLS OF EPHRAIM

A M M O N

Joppa

Shiloh

THE ARABAH

Bethel

Lod

Gibeon

Gezer

Jericho

Heshbon

Mt. of Olives
(2,723ft / 830m) △

Jerusalem

△ Mt. Nebo
(2,630m / 802m)

Ashkelon

Bethlehem

SHEPHELAH

JUDAH

HILLS OF JUDEA

Lachish

Dibon

Gaza

Hebron

WILDERNESS OF JUDEA

SALT SEA (DEAD SEA)

Arnon

PLAIN OF PHILISTIA

M O A B

Beersheba

THE NEGEB

Zered

metres   feet
1,000   3,281
500   1,640
200   656
0   0
below sea below sea
level   level

THE ARABAH

0   25   50 km

0   10   20   30 miles

E D O M

Qumran, where the Essene monastic community lived before and during the time of Christ.

The whole of the Palestinian Rift Valley is called in the Old Testament "the Arabah," meaning "dry," and the Dead Sea is "the Sea of the Arabah" or "the Salt Sea." This is forty-eight miles long and a scene of almost unrelieved desolation. Its eastern shore is overlooked by the sheer cliffs of the mountains of Moab, while on the west are the barren slopes of the mountains of Judah. Here (at Qumran) lived the Essene monastic community before and during the time of Christ, and here in our time the Dead Sea Scrolls were found in some of the caves which honeycomb the hills.

The heat is so intense (up to 43° C, 110° F in the summer), the evaporation so great and the rainfall so small, that the water level of the Dead Sea remains constant despite the inflowing streams and the absence of all outflow. As a result, the chemical deposits in the water (especially salt, potash and magnesium) are highly concentrated, and no fish can survive (cf. Ezek. 47:1-12). It seems likely that Sodom and Gomorrah, "the cities of the plain," were situated in the area now covered by the southern tip of the Dead Sea. And it is not impossible that the "brimstone and fire" which the Lord "rained" on them, together with the "pillar of salt" into which Lot's wife was changed, were the results of an earthquake and eruption which God used to destroy them for their wickedness (Gen. 19:24-29).

The Arabah continues south of the Dead Sea until it reaches the Red Sea at the Gulf of Aqabah. Here was the port of Ezion Geber (the equivalent of the modern Eilat), giving Israel access by sea to the trade of Africa and Asia. For "King Solomon built a fleet of ships at Ezion-geber" (1 Kings 9:26 RSV). Copper was exported from the nearby mines which Solomon developed, while imports included such exotic items as "gold, silver and ivory, and apes and baboons" (1 Kings 10:22).

The eastern tableland

The fourth strip of Palestinian country we have to consider is the eastern tableland, between the Jordan Valley and the Arabian Desert. This was the area inherited by two and a half of Israel's twelve tribes:

Gad, Reuben and the half-tribe of Manasseh have already received their inheritance on the east side of the Jordan. (Josh. 18:7)

It is a vast plateau stretching for about 250 miles from north to south, divided by four rivers which have cut deep canyons on their way westwards into the River Jordan or the Dead Sea. The first is the River Yarmuq, which flows into the Jordan just south of Lake Tiberias. The second is the River Jabbok which reaches the Jordan approximately halfway between Lake Tiberias and the Dead Sea. It was here that "Jacob was left alone, and a man wrestled with him till daybreak" (Gen. 32:22-32). The River Arnon flows into the middle of the Dead Sea and the River Zered into its southern tip. These rivers formed natural frontiers for Israel's neighboring tribes, Ammon claiming the territory between the Jabbok and the Arnon, Moab that between the Arnon and the Zered (though often spilling over to the north), and Edom that south of the Zered.

Perhaps it is easiest, however, to visualize the plateau east of the Jordan by remembering the main divisions which Denis Baly describes in his *Geography of the Bible*. Bashan, the tableland east of Lake Tiberias, he calls "the land of the farmer," for though it was probably well wooded in Bible times it was famed for its corn crop and for its rams, lambs, goats and bulls, "all of them fattened animals from Bashan" (Ezek. 39:18; cf. Ps. 22:12).

South of Bashan was Gilead, a term covering virtually the whole of Transjordan between Lake Tiberias and the Dead Sea. This is the "land of the highlander." As the terrain rises to over 3,000 feet, the rainfall is considerable and brings fertility to both forest and vineyard. The grapes of Gilead were unrivaled throughout Palestine and "the balm of Gilead" (an aromatic spice of some king) was famous. The caravan of Ishmaelites to whom Joseph was sold by his brothers were "coming from Gilead. Their camels were loaded with spices, balm and myrrh, and they were on their way to take them down to Egypt" (Gen. 37:25).

Modern Eilat, the ancient port of Ezion Geber, which gave Israel access by sea to trade with Africa and Asia.

The ancient rock-hewn city of Petra, center of the Edomite (Idumean) trading kingdom.

Continuing our journey south in Transjordan, Moab comes next, occupying the mountainous territory east of the Dead Sea. Apart from the deep gorges of the River Arnon and of some smaller streams, most of Moab is a high plateau. Denis Baly calls it "the land of the Shepherd": "Everywhere . . . there are sheep, great flocks and converging lines of them, like the spokes of a limitless wheel, moving in clouds of golden dust to be given their water at the well" (see Gen. 37:25; cf. Jer. 8:22).

So, too, we read in the Bible:

Now Mesha king of Moab raised sheep,
and he had to supply the king of Israel
with a hundred thousand lambs and with
the wool of a hundred thousand rams.
(2 Kings 3:4)

It was from the mountains of Moab (Mount Nebo, to be precise) that Moses viewed the promised land before he died, and on the plains of Moab that the children of Israel encamped before crossing the Jordan to take possession of it (Deut. 32:49-50; 34:1-8; Num. 22:1).

The most southerly section of Transjordan is Edom. At its highest points it rises to about 3,500 feet, towering above the deserts to the west, east and south. Denis Baly names it "the land of the trader," for through it passed the great eastern trade route known as "the King's Highway." It was because of Edom's refusal to allow Israel to use this route on their way to the promised land that there was long-standing enmity between the two countries (Num. 20:14-21; 21:4).

Such is the "good land" which the Lord their God gave to Israel. It was a country for farmers, who kept livestock and cultivated the arable soil.

Agriculture and rainfall

Their livestock consisted mostly of sheep and goats, which roamed in huge mixed flocks over the hills and the steppe. The goats sup-

The soils of Palestine

- Alluvium
- Chalk
- Kurkar ridge of sandstone
- Limestone
- Marl and gravel
- Sand dunes
- Sandstone
- Volcanic deposit

The natural vegetation of Palestine

- Forest
- Scrub and grassland
- Desert
- Sand dunes
- Oasis

plied milk and the black hair of which Bedouin tents were made, while the sheep gave milk, meat and wool. Because Palestinian shepherds kept their sheep more for wool than for mutton, however, quite an intimate relationship grew up between them over the years. The shepherd would lead his sheep, not drive them. He would know them individually, and call them by name, while they for their part would know his voice and follow him. It seemed only natural that God should reveal himself as the "Shepherd of Israel" who "gathers the lambs in his arms and carries them close to his heart; he gently leads those that have young" (Ps. 80:1; Isa. 40:11), and indeed that the godly Israelite should be able to affirm:

The LORD is my shepherd, I shall not be in want. He makes me lie down in green pastures, he leads me beside quiet waters. (Ps. 23:1-2)

The Lord Jesus developed the metaphor further, calling himself "the Good Shepherd" and affirming that he would both lay down his life for the sheep and go out into the desert in search of only one that was lost (John 10:1-18; Luke 15:3-7).

Though many Israelite farmers kept livestock, even more cultivated the soil. The three main products of Palestine are bracketed together in many biblical passages. Before they entered the land, this was the reward which they were promised for their obedience:

The LORD your God . . . will bless . . . the crops of your land – your grain, new wine and oil. (Deut. 7:13)

When they had taken possession of it, they proved God's faithfulness in giving "wine that gladdens the heart of man, oil to make his face shine, and bread that sustains his heart" (Ps. 104:15). But when they rebelled against him he withheld these blessings – through famine or pestilence or locusts – until they repented and he could say to them:

I am sending you grain, new wine and oil, enough to satisfy you fully. (Joel 2:19; cf. Deut. 7:13; Ps. 104:15; Hos. 2:8).

The grain from which their bread came was mostly wheat and barley, while the wind came from the extensive vineyards, and the oil (principally for cooking) from the olive yards. Olive trees are particularly hardy, being able to survive in shallow soil and to withstand long periods of drought.

Other fruits of ancient Israel were pomegranates, and especially figs, so that the sweetest Israelite dream of peace and security in the Messianic kingdom was:

Every man will sit under his own vine and under his own fig tree, and no one will make them afraid. (Mic. 4:4)

For a good harvest the land was entirely dependent upon rain. The Israelite knew that there was no greater blessing of God. It was "the living God, who made heaven and earth and sea and everything in them" who gave "rain from heaven and crops in their seasons," thus bearing witness to his own faithfulness. And so great is his grace to all humankind, Jesus emphasized, that "he causes his sun to rise on the evil and the good, and sends rain on the righteous and the unrighteous" (Acts 14:15-17; Matt. 5:45).

Generally speaking, the Palestinian rainy seasons are predictable. The summer extends from May/June to September/October, and during these five months rain is virtually unknown, so that Samuel's prayer for rain during wheat harvest was a request for a miracle. Indeed, "snow in summer or rain in harvest" is as out of place as "honor . . . for a fool" (1 Sam. 12:16-18; Prov. 26:1). During this dry season there is only the dew to bring moisture, and the morning mist. But both dissipate speedily when the sun rises, and their disappearance is used as a picture of idolatrous Israel when the judgment of God falls:

They will be like the morning mist, like the early dew that disappears. (Hos. 13:3)

From about mid-October, however, the rain clouds begin to form, and when the rain finally comes, often accompanied by thunder, there is nothing to do but run for shelter. Denis Baly describes the scene:

Jesus quoted it as a well-known occurrence that a badly built house might collapse during the rainy season (Matt. 7:27) and, indeed, it is only when one has seen a storm sweeping in from the Mediterranean across the Palestinian hills or the torrents pouring down the precipitous slopes into the lake of Galilee that one knows quite what a concentrated fury is contained in those words, "and the rain fell, and the floods came, and the winds blew and beat against that house."

The beginning of the rainy season was usually termed "the early rains," and, far from being regarded as destructive, they were looked upon as beneficial, indeed indispensable. Without them plowing was impossible, for the sunbaked earth was hard as iron (Deut. 28:23). But once the rains had started and begun to soften the soil, especially if their arrival was late, the farmer must brave the weather and get on with his plowing if he was to be able to sow his fields in time for harvest. Jesus used this as a picture of Christian courage and perseverance:

No one who puts his hand to the plow and looks back is fit for service in the kingdom of God. (Luke 9:62)

If the "early rains" at the start of the rainy season (from November) were essential to plowing, the "latter rains" at its end (in March and April) were essential to reaping. Without them the corn would remain thin and desiccated; it was the rain which swelled and matured

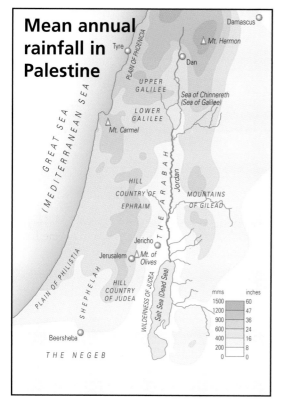

Mean annual rainfall in Palestine

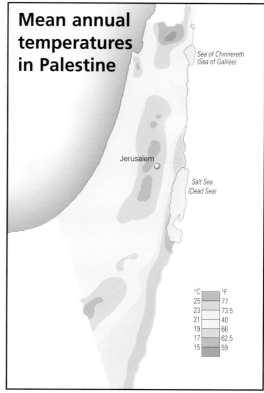

Mean annual temperatures in Palestine

the grain for the harvest. And when the fields were finally "ripe for harvest," the laborers would put in their sickles (John 4:35; Joel 3:13). The corn would then be tied into sheaves and carted by donkeys or camels to the threshing floor, a flat, hardened surface at the top of a local hillock. There it would first be threshed by animal hooves or a sledge (cf. Isa. 41:15) and afterwards winnowed. Tossed into the air with a pitchfork, the precious golden grain would fall to the earth to be garnered, while the wind would blow the chaff away. This separation of wheat from chaff became a common image for the divine judgment (for example, Ps. 1:4; Luke 3:17).

So "the early and the latter rain," sometimes called the "autumn rain and the spring rain," were a necessary prelude to a good harvest. God had himself linked the rain and the harvest together and promised them to his obedient people:

So if you faithfully obey the commands I am giving you today – to love the LORD your God and to serve him with all your heart and with all your soul – then I will send rain on your land in its season, both autumn and spring rains, so that you may gather in your grain, new wine and oil. (Deut. 11:13-14)

Wise farmers knew this and waited for "the valuable crop" of the earth, being patient over it until it receives "the autumn and spring rains" (Jas. 5:7). Consequently, when the rains were given, they were full of thanksgiving to God for his mercy. No more poetic account of his harvest blessings occurs in Scripture than in Psalm 65. Notice the reference both to the early rains which water the hard ground, "leveling its ridges, softening it with showers," and to the "crown" of the year some eight months later when "the valleys are mantled with grain":

You care for the land and water it;
    you enrich it abundantly.
The streams of God are filled with water

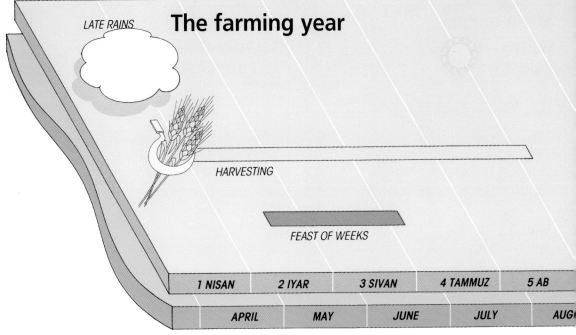

The farming year

LATE RAINS

HARVESTING

FEAST OF WEEKS

1 NISAN	2 IYAR	3 SIVAN	4 TAMMUZ	5 AB
APRIL	MAY	JUNE	JULY	AUG

to provide the people with grain,
for so you have ordained it.
You drench its furrows
and level its ridges;
you soften it with showers
and bless its crops.
You crown the year with your bounty,
and your carts overflow with abundance.
The grasslands of the desert overflow;
the hills are clothed with gladness.
The meadows are covered with flocks
and the valleys are mantled with grain;
they shout for joy and sing. (Ps. 65:9-13)

Palestinians still use old methods of reaping.

The three annual festivals

In the light of Israel's closeness to the soil as a farming community, it is not surprising that their three annual festivals had an agricultural as well as a religious significance. In them they worshiped the God of nature and the God of grace as the one God, Lord of the earth and of Israel.

The Feast of the Passover, followed immediately by the Feast of Unleavened Bread, commemorated primarily Israel's redemption from Egypt. But it also took place about the middle of April when the first sheaf of ripe barley could be waved humbly and gratefully before the Lord.

The second was the Feast of the Firstfruits or Harvest, also called the Feast of Weeks or Pentecost because it was celebrated seven weeks or fifty days after the Passover – that is, at about the beginning of June. It was a thanksgiving for the completed grain harvest – wheat as well as barley. Later it came to be regarded also as commemorating the giving of the law at Mount Sinai, perhaps because in connection with it Israel was told:

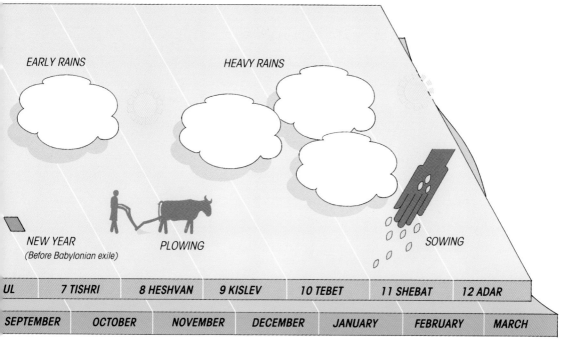

EARLY RAINS

HEAVY RAINS

NEW YEAR
(Before Babylonian exile)

PLOWING

SOWING

UL	7 TISHRI	8 HESHVAN	9 KISLEV	10 TEBET	11 SHEBAT	12 ADAR
SEPTEMBER	OCTOBER	NOVEMBER	DECEMBER	JANUARY	FEBRUARY	MARCH

Remember that you were slaves in Egypt, and follow carefully these decrees. (Deut. 16:12)

The last of the three annual festivals was the Feast of Booths or Tabernacles. For seven days the people had to dwell in booths made out of tree branches. God's purpose in requiring this was clear:

So your descendants will know that I had the Israelites live in booths when I brought them out of Egypt. (Lev. 23:43)

But this festival was also known as the Feast of Ingathering, for it took place in mid-October, six months later than the Passover, by which time each year the produce of vineyard and olive yard as well as grain field had been gathered in.

The observance of these three annual festivals was obligatory. God had said:

Three times a year you are to celebrate a festival to me. Celebrate the Feast of Unleavened Bread. . . . Celebrate the Feast of Harvest with the first fruits of the crops you sow in your field. Celebrate

A Palestinian woman uses a sickle to gather crops.

the Feast of Ingathering at the end of the year, when you gather in your crops from the field. (Exod. 23:14-16; cf. Deut. 16:16-17)

From one point of view these festivals commemorated the signal mercies of the covenant God of Israel who first redeemed his people from their Egyptian bondage, then gave them the law at Sinai and then provided for them during their wanderings in the wilderness. From another point of view the three feasts

A modern Jewish family celebrates Passover, remembering Israel's redemption from Egypt.

were all harvest festivals, marking respectively the beginning of the barley harvest, the end of the grain harvest, and the end of the fruit harvest.

So Israel was taught to honor Jehovah both as God of creation and as God of salvation. The two themes were brought together in what the people of Israel were to do when they had come into the land of promise:

> Take some of the first fruits of all that you produce from the soil of the land the LORD your God is giving you and put them in a basket . . . and say to the priest . . . ,
> "I declare today to the LORD your God that I have come to the land that the LORD swore to our forefathers to give us . . . and

now I bring the first fruits of the soil that you, O LORD, have given me." . . . and . . . you shall rejoice in all the good things the LORD your God has given to you and your household. (Deut. 26:1-11)

Here was rich symbolism indeed. The basket of fruit was a token of "all the good things" which God had given Israel. It was the fruit of the ground, fruit which God had caused to grow. But from what ground? From ground which God had also given them, as he had sworn to their fathers. The fruit was a sacrament of both creation and redemption, for it was the fruit of the promised land.

3. The Story of the Bible (Old Testament)

❖ *What kinds of events and people does the Bible focus on, and why?*

❖ *How do we see God's covenant to his people*
  and how he kept it expressed throughout the Old Testament?

❖ *What is the inter-testamental period,*
  and what significant things happened during it?

Christianity is essentially a historical religion. God's revelation, which Christians cherish and seek to communicate, was not given in a vacuum but in an unfolding historical situation, through a nation called Israel and a person called Jesus Christ. It must never be divorced from its historical context; it can be understood only within it.

This does not mean that the history recorded in the Bible is identical in every respect with the modern view of history. A historian today is supposed to give a full and objective account of all the facts of his period. The biblical historians, however, made no such claim. On the contrary, they were regarded as "the former prophets," for they were writing "sacred history," the story of God's dealings with a particular people, for a particular purpose. They were convinced that God had "done this for no other nation" (Ps. 147:20). So their record is more a testimony than a history. They were writing down their own confession of faith.

Therefore, they were selective in their choice of material and (the secular historian would add) unbalanced in their presentation of it. For example, ancient Babylonia, Persia, Egypt, Greece and Rome – each a mighty empire and a rich civilization – are included only as they impinge on the fortunes of Israel and Judah, two tiny buffer states on the edge of the Arabian desert, which hardly anybody had heard of. The great thinkers of Greece like Aristotle, Socrates and Plato are not so much as mentioned, nor are national heroes like Alexander the Great (except obliquely) and Julius Caesar.

Instead, the scriptural record concentrates on men like Abraham, Moses, David, Isaiah and the prophets to whom the word of God camel and on Jesus Christ, God's Word made flesh. For the concern of Scripture is not with the wisdom, wealth or might of the world, but with the salvation of God. Biblical history is *Heilsgeschichte*, the story of salvation.

The sweep of this sacred history is magnificent. Although it omits great areas of human civilization which would feature prominently in any history of the world written by men, yet in principle and from God's point of view it tells the whole story of man from start to finish, from the beginning when "God created the heavens and the earth" to the end when he will create "a new heaven and a new earth" (Gen. 1:1; Rev. 21:1, 5).

Christians divide history into BC and AD, indicating the periods before and after Christ, believing that Jesus Christ's coming into the world is the watershed of history. So too it is the life of Jesus Christ which divides the Bible into half, the Old Testament looking forward to his arrival and preparing for it, the New Testament telling the story of his life, death and resurrection and drawing out its implications as they began to emerge in the infant

SURREXIT ELIAS
PROPHETA QUASI
IGNIS ET VERBUM
IPSIUS QUASI FACULA
ARDEBAT (ECCLI. XLVIII. 1)

Political leaders such as Alexander and Augustus Caesar (*above*) are scarcely mentioned in Scripture.

The scriptural record concentrates on men such as Abraham, Moses, David and Elijah (*above*).

church and will one day reach fruition.

In this chapter I shall attempt to give an outline of the story of the Old Testament, and in the following chapter its sequel in the New Testament. Then, having looked at the Bible's geographical and historical setting, we shall be ready in chapter 5 to consider the message which God chose to give in it.

The Old Testament is a library of thirty-nine books. The order in which they are placed[1] is dictated neither by the date of their composition, nor even by the date of the subject matter they contain, but by their literary genre. Broadly speaking, there are three types of literature in the Old Testament: history, poetry and prophecy. The historical books (the five from Genesis to Deuteronomy forming the "Pentateuch" and then twelve more) do tell a continuous story. They begin with the creation of man in Genesis 1 and the call of Abraham in Genesis 12. They go on to tell the story of Israel, the birth of the nation (in the rest of the

Pentateuch), its varied fortunes during nearly seven centuries in the promised land (in the books of Joshua, Judges, Samuel, Kings and Chronicles), and its rebirth under the leadership of Ezra and Nehemiah. After these seventeen historical books come five books of Hebrew poetry or "Wisdom" – Job, Psalms, Proverbs, Ecclesiastes and the Song of Solomon – and finally the seventeen prophetical books, five "major" prophets (Isaiah, Jeremiah, Lamentations, Ezekiel and Daniel) and twelve "minor" ones (from Hosea to Malachi).

Any reconstruction of the Old Testament story is bound to be somewhat arbitrary. Scholars are still debating, for example, the date of the Exodus and the order in which Ezra and Nehemiah left their Babylonian exile in the fifth century in order to visit Jerusalem. I propose to tell the story according to what I believe is the consensus of most conservative scholars.

The creation

The Bible begins with a majestic account of the creation of the universe, of earth, of life and of man. It establishes from the outset that the God who later chose to reveal himself to Israel was not the God of Israel alone. Israel must not regard Yahweh[2] as the Moabites regarded Chemosh and the Ammonites their god Milcom or Molech, almost as a national mascot. For he was no petty godling or tribal deity, whose domain and interests were limited to the tribe and its territory, but the God of creation, the Lord of the whole earth.

It is true that the Genesis account of creation is earth-centered and man-centered, in the sense that it is deliberately told from the perspective of human beings on earth, but it is above all God-centered in the sense that the whole initiative in the creation lies with the one, true God:

In the beginning God created . . . and God said . . . God saw . . . God called . . . God blessed . . . God finished . . .

This simple, unadorned narrative, which ascribes wisdom, purpose, power and goodness to the creator God, is far removed from the fantastic and even disgusting creation stories which circulated in the ancient Near East. There are superficial similarities, in that both begin with chaos and end with some kind of cosmos. But the dissimilarities are far greater. The Near-Eastern stories are crude, polytheistic, immoral and grotesque; the biblical account is dignified, monotheistic, ethical and sublime.

Modern readers inevitably approach the early chapters of Genesis with some knowledge that during the last century they have been a battlefield between religion and science. We shall be wise, therefore, to learn a lesson from history, and to study them with caution born of humility. For in the past representatives of both sides have made rashly dogmatic assertions, which either they or their successors have later been obliged to repudiate.

Scientists need to distinguish between fact and theory, and Bible students between plain scriptural statement and fallible human interpretation. For our purposes in this book the latter is particularly important. The principle should be clear: what Scripture affirms God affirms and what God affirms is true. So what does God affirm in Scripture about creation?

In general, we can say with assurance that Genesis 1 begins with God ("in the beginning God created . . ."), continues with progressive stages ("and God said . . . and God said . . ."), and ends with man ("So God created man in his own image . . . male and female he created them"). How much further may we go than this? In particular, what may we say about the "how" of God's creative activity? Some Christians today defend the concept of a literal six-day creation, but the text does not demand it, and scientific discovery appears to contradict it. The biblical text presents itself not as a scientific treatise but as a highly stylized literary statement (deliberately framed in three pairs, the fourth "day" corresponding to the first, the fifth to the second, and the sixth to the third). Moreover the geological evidence for a gradual development over thousands of millions of years seems to many scientists conclusive.

Indeed, speaking for myself, I cannot see that at least some forms of the theory of evolution contradict or are contradicted by the Genesis account of creation. It is most unfortunate that some who debate this issue begin by assuming that the words "creation" and "evolution" are mutually exclusive. If everything has come into existence through evolution, they say, then biblical creation has been disproved, whereas if God has created all things, then evolution must be false. It is, rather, this naive alternative which is false. It presupposes a very narrow definition of the two terms, both of which in fact have a wide range of meanings, and both of which are being freshly discussed today. For example, although the great majority of scientists continue to believe that there was a long evolutionary process, the Darwinian theory of "natural selection" (or "the survival of the fittest") as its operational principle is being increasingly questioned, and instead of a single and gradual progression a theory is being developed which posits multiple changes, in fits and starts, and sometimes by inexplicable major leaps. Of course any theory of evolution which is presented as a blind and random process must be rejected by Christians as incompatible with the biblical revelation that God created everything by his will and word, that he made it "good," and that his creative program culminated in Godlike human beings. But there does not seem to me any biblical reason for denying that some kind of purposive evolutionary development may have been the mode which God employed in creating.[3]

To suggest this tentatively need not in any way detract from humankind's uniqueness. I myself believe in the historicity of Adam and Eve, as the original couple from whom the human race is descended. I shall give my reasons in chapter 7, when I come to the question of how we are to interpret Scripture. But my acceptance of Adam and Eve as historical is not incompatible with my belief that several forms of pre-Adamic "hominid" seem to have existed for thousands of years previously. These hominids began to advance culturally. They made their cave drawings and buried their dead. It is conceivable that God created Adam out of one of them. You may call them *homo erectus*. I think you may even call some of them *homo sapiens*, for these are arbitrary scientific names. But Adam was the first *homo divinus*, if I may coin the phrase, the first man to whom may be given the specific biblical designation "made in the image of God." Precisely what the divine likeness was, which was stamped upon him, we do not know, for Scripture nowhere tells us. But it seems to have included those rational, moral, social and spiritual faculties which made man unlike all other creatures and like God the Creator, and on account of which he was given "domination" over the lower creation.

When shall we date Adam, then? The chronology which was added in 1701 to the Authorized Version of the Bible (1611) was calculated by James Ussher, Archbishop of Armagh, from the biblical genealogies. By working backwards he reckoned that Adam was created in the year 4004 BC. But the genealogies never claim to be complete. For example, it is written in one of the genealogies of Jesus that Joram "begat" Uzziah, whereas we know from the Second Book of Kings that he was actually not his father but his great-great-grandfather. Three complete generations have been left out. And recent Near-Eastern studies have confirmed that such omissions were a regular practice in genealogies. Certainly the purpose of the biblical tables was more to establish the line of descent (for example, that Jesus was descended from David) than to provide a comprehensive family tree. If, then, they do not profess to be complete we have no ground for complaining about their omissions. Nor can we use them to calculate a detailed chronology.

The Genesis text gives us some better clues. The biblical account of Adam and his immediate descendants in chapters 3 and 4 seems to imply a Neolithic civilization. Adam is said to have been put in a garden to work it and take care of it. His sons Cain and Abel are described as having respectively worked the soil and kept flocks, while Cain also "built a city," which may not have been more than a fairly rudimentary village. These are significant expressions, since farming the land and domesticating animals (as opposed to foraging and hunting), together with primitive community life in villages, did not begin until the late Stone Age. Only a few generations later we read of those who played "the lyre and pipe" and those who forged "instruments of bronze and iron." Since the Neolithic age is usually dated from about 6000 BC, this would still suggest a comparatively late date for Adam.

The second chapter of Genesis tells us that work and leisure (six days' work and one day's rest), and monogamous marriage, are "creation ordinances" instituted by God for human benefit before sin entered the world. The entry of sin through Adam's "fall" or disobedience is described in Genesis 3, and in the

Charles Darwin, the English naturalist who introduced the theory of "natural selection" or "survival of the fittest."

following chapters the resulting deterioration of human beings and their society, and the inevitable judgments of God. The flood seems to have been a comparatively local – though widespread – disaster. The assertion that "all the high mountains under the entire heavens were covered" (Gen. 7:19) is not to be pressed with strict literalism, but rather understood from the perspective of the observer, just as the "God-fearing Jews from every nation under heaven" who were in Jerusalem for Pentecost (Acts 2:5) evidently refers to the known world of the Mediterranean basin. For Luke goes on to list fifteen such groups (vv. 8-11). He was not alluding to distant peoples like Eskimos, Australian Aborigines and Maoris. The flood is recorded as an object lesson of God's judgment on human wickedness and of his mercy both towards Noah's family and towards all subsequent generations in his solemn covenant that "as long as the earth endures, seedtime and harvest, cold and heat, summer and win-

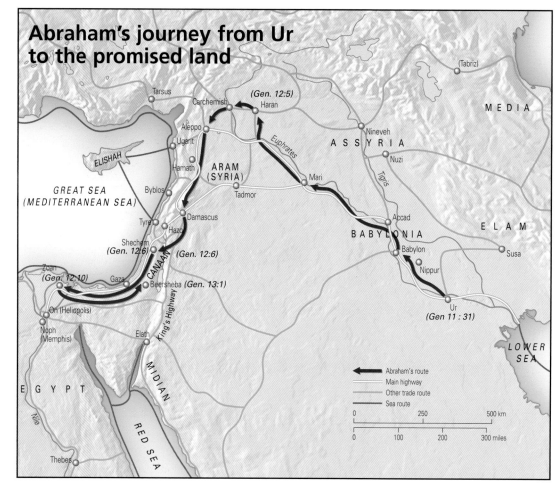

Abraham's journey from Ur to the promised land

ter, day and night will never cease" (Gen. 8:22). Similarly, the building of the tower of Babel, which may have been a Babylonian zig-gurat[4] or something similar, is recorded as an example of divine judgment on human pride, leading to the scattering of the nations (Gen. 11:1-9).

God's promise to Abraham

It was some time after the year 2000 BC that a new beginning of immense importance took place with God's call of Abraham. It seems to have come to him first in Ur of the Chaldees, then in Haran. It summoned him to leave his country and his people in exchange for anoth-er country and another people which God would later give him:

The LORD had said to Abram, "Leave

your country, your people and your father's household and go to the land I will show you. I will make you into a great nation and I will bless you; I will make your name great, and you will be a blessing. I will bless those who bless you, and whoever curses you I will curse; and all peoples on earth will be blessed through you." (Gen. 12:1-3)

Fundamentally, God's promise was "I will bless you." This was spelled out later:

I will establish my covenant . . . between me and you . . . to be your God and the God of your descendants after you. (Gen. 17:7)

This came to be recognized as the essence of

Mountains near Hebron. Abraham was a nomad; the only territory he possessed was a field near Hebron.

God's covenant with Israel, repeated again and again in the Old Testament: "I will be your God and you shall be my people." In addition to this covenant relationship, God promised Abraham both a land and a seed, a line of descent. It may truly be said without exaggeration that not only the rest of the Old Testament but the whole of the New Testament are an outworking of these promises of God. In Old Testament days Israel was the promised seed and Canaan the promised land. But the covenant included a reference to "all the families of the earth" and their blessing. Only now in Christ have these promises begun to be fulfilled. For Jesus Christ and his people are the true seed of Abraham. As Paul wrote to the Galatians:

If you belong to Christ, then you are Abraham's seed, and heirs according to the promise. (Gal. 3:29)

The final fulfillment lies beyond history.

Then Abraham's seed will be "a great multitude that no one could count," as many in fact as the stars in the sky and the sand of the seashore, and their inheritance will be the new Jerusalem, "the city with foundations, whose architect and builder is God" (Rev. 7:9; Gen. 22:17; Heb. 11:8-12, 16, 39-40).

God kept renewing his covenant with Abraham during his lifetime, and then confirmed it to his son Isaac and to his grandson Jacob.[5] The Palestine of their day was in the Bronze Age, but they never settled down to enjoy it. They were nomads. The only territory they possessed was a field near Hebron, which Abraham bought so that he could bury his wife Sarah in its cave (Gen. 23).

Jacob (whose other name was "Israel") had twelve sons. They were, in fact, the original "children of Israel." But these progenitors of Israel's twelve tribes all spent their declining years and died not in the promised land of Canaan, but in Egypt, to which famine had driven them. Joseph had become a very senior administrator in Egypt, perhaps even a kind of grand vizier. Such a promotion is not as improbable as some have thought, for the ruling Egyptian dynasty from about 1700 BC were the Hyksos, the so-called shepherd-kings, who were themselves Semitic in origin. But Joseph also died in exile, and the Book of Genesis ends with the words: "After they embalmed him, he was placed in a coffin in Egypt" (Gen. 50:26).

When the bald statement is made in Exodus 1:8 that "a new king, who did not know about Joseph, came to power in Egypt," one of the succeeding dynasties is meant. This is likely to have been the nineteenth, whose early Pharaohs built the cities Pithom and Raamses, the latter as a royal residence in the Delta area, where the Israelites had settled. It was convenient, therefore, to use Israelite slave labor. And as the years passed, the bondage of the Israelites became crueler and harder to bear, until their lives became "bitter with hard labor in brick and mortar and with all kinds of work in the fields" (Exod. 1:14).

The Egyptian exile lasted altogether 430 years (Exod. 12:40-41). What had become of God's promise?

The Exodus from Egypt

As the people of Israel groaned under the Pharaohs' oppressive regime, they cried to God for deliverance:

> God heard their groaning and he
> remembered his covenant with Abraham,
> with Isaac and with Jacob. (Exod. 2:24)

Indeed, already God was preparing the deliverer he had chosen. By a remarkable providence Moses had actually been brought up in the Egyptian court (Exod. 2:1-10) and learned "all the wisdom of the Egyptians." But he had had to flee for his life and was now in hiding in the Sinai peninsula (Exod. 2:15). Here, near Mount Horeb (or Sinai), where he would later receive the ten commandments for the newborn nation, God spoke to him from the burning bush:

> I am the God of your father, the God of Abraham, the God of Isaac and the God of Jacob. (Exod. 3:1-6)

Then God told Moses that he was about to rescue the people of Israel from their bondage and bring them at last into the land of promise. He further commissioned Moses to go to Pharaoh and demand his people's release.

At first Moses was full of apprehension. He was frightened of Pharaoh, and even more of the response he might get from his fellow Israelites. But God reassured him:

> Say to the Israelites, "The LORD, the God of your fathers – the God of Abraham, the God of Isaac and the God of Jacob – has sent me to you." (Exod. 3:15)

Moses obeyed. And the people of Israel accepted his leadership. But Pharaoh, probably Rameses II who reigned over Egypt for sixty-six years (1290-1224), demurred. In biblical language, he "hardened his heart." Not until the ten plagues had decisively demonstrated Yahweh's superiority over all the gods of Egypt did he finally consent (Exod. 4:27–13:16). The date would have been about 1280 BC.

"The Red Sea" which the escaping Israelites crossed was probably some water north of the northern tip of the Suez Gulf. The miracle lay not in the "strong east wind" which parted the waters, but in the fact that God sent it at the very moment when "Moses stretched out his hand over the sea" (Exod. 14:21). Israel never forgot their safe exodus from Egypt by the supernatural intervention of God. They sang of it in public worship as a signal example of God's power and mercy:

> He saved them for his name's sake,
>   to make his mighty power known.
> He rebuked the Red Sea, and it dried up;
>   he led them through the depths as
>   through a desert.
> He saved them from the hand of the foe;
>   from the hand of the enemy he redeemed
>   them. (Ps. 106:8-10)

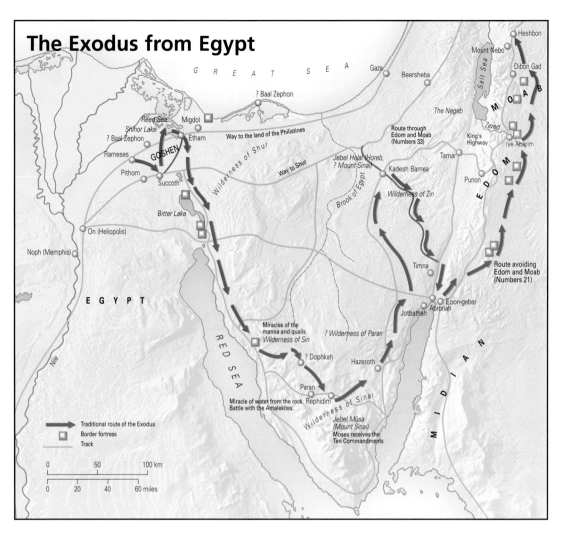

The Exodus from Egypt

Again,

Give thanks to the LORD, for he is good.
His love endures forever.
Give thanks to the God of gods. . . .
His love endures forever.
to him who struck down the firstborn of Egypt
His love endures forever.
and brought Israel out from among them
His love endures forever.
with a mighty hand and outstretched arm;
His love endures forever.
to him who divided the Red Sea asunder
His love endures forever.
and brought Israel through the midst of it,
His love endures forever.

(Ps. 136:1-2, 10-14)

The escaping Israelites, a large and ragged multitude, did not travel direct to the promised land along the coastal route known as "The Way of the Land of the Philistines." They turned southeast to meet their God at Mount Sinai, as he had directed Moses. It took them about three months to get there, and once encamped at the foot of the mountain, they stayed almost a year.

Here God gave Israel three precious gifts – a renewed covenant, a moral law and atoning sacrifices.

The renewal of the covenant came first. God called Moses up the mountain, and told him to say to Israel:

You yourselves have seen what I did to Egypt, and how I carried you on eagles' wings and brought you to myself. Now if you obey me fully and keep my covenant, then out of all nations you will be my treasured possession. Although the whole earth is mine, you will be for me a kingdom of priests and a holy nation. (Exod. 19:4-6)

Secondly, God gave them a moral law. Obedience to this law was to be Israel's part in the covenant. Its essence was the ten commandments. But these were supplemented both by further "statutes" ("you shall," "you shall not") and by "judgments" which form a body of case law ("When a man . . ."). The covenant was solemnly ratified by the blood of sacrifice when the people gave a public undertaking to keep God's law.

Thirdly, God made generous provision for the remedying of breaches of his law. He gave instructions for the building of a "tabernacle," a rectangular tent measuring about forty-five feet by fifteen, made of dyed linen curtains stretched over a frame and covered with goats' hair and waterproof skins. Inside were two rooms, "the holy place" and "the most holy place" or "holy of holies." This inner sanctuary was half the size of the bigger room, from which it was separated by a curtain known as "the veil." Outside the veil stood a golden lampstand, an incense altar and a table on which baked cakes were displayed. Beyond the veil was the sacred ark, a wooden chest containing the stone tablets on which the ten commandments were inscribed. Its golden lid, called the "mercy seat," was flanked by cherubim, figures of celestial creatures. In heathen temples these would have formed a kind of throne for the idol. But not in Israel's tabernacle, since the making of idols was forbidden. Instead, God manifested himself here in a kind of radiance. This was "the Shekinah," his abiding presence in the midst of his people (for example, Exod. 25:8; 40:34).

The tabernacle was pitched in a large courtyard. Outside its east-facing door stood a copper basin called the laver, where the priests washed their hands and feet, and the great altar on which the animal sacrifices were burned.

The tabernacle's fabric, furniture and con-

The barren wilderness near Mount Sinai, where the escaping Israelites met their God.

A modern full-size replica of the tabernacle, showing the great altar in the foreground.

Plan of the tabernacle

Holy of Holies

1

2

4

3

5

Holy Place

Entrance

Laver

Altar of Sacrifice

Entrance

struction are described in Exodus 25–27 and 35–40. The five standard sacrifices are explained in Leviticus 1–7, and full details for the dress, consecration and duties of the priests are given in Exodus 28–29 and the rest of the Book of Leviticus.

Specially significant is the ritual prescribed for the annual Day of Atonement (Lev. 16). The high priest was instructed to take two goats. He was to kill one as a sin offering, to take some of its blood "within the veil" and sprinkle it on the mercy seat. The blood stood for a life laid down in place of the sinner whose life was forfeit:

> For the life of a creature is in the blood,
> and I have given it to you to make
> atonement for yourselves on the altar; it
> is the blood that makes atonement for
> one's life. (Lev. 17:11)

1. Ark of the Covenant
2. Veil
3. Seven-branched lampstand
4. Altar of Incense
5. Table of Shewbread

The veil symbolizing God's inaccessibility to the sinner was to be penetrated on no other day than the Day of Atonement, by no other person than the high priest, and on no other condition than the shedding and the sprinkling of blood. Then:

> [Aaron] is to lay both hands on the head of the live goat and confess over it all the wickedness and rebellion of the Israelites – all their sins – and put them on the goat's head. He shall send the goat away into the desert. . . . The goat will carry on itself all their sins to a solitary place.
> (Lev. 16:21-22)

These symbolic acts – the shedding and sprinkling of blood, the penetration of the veil and the bearing of sin – all prefigure the atoning work of Jesus Christ our Savior.

The wilderness wanderings

The tabernacle was erected on the first anniversary of the Israelites' escape from Egypt (Exod. 40:17). A fortnight later the Passover was celebrated (Num. 9:1-3), and a fortnight later still a census taken of all the men of twenty years or older, who would be fit to fight (Num. 1:1-3). The development is striking. Israel is seen first as a disorganized rabble of freed slaves (Exod. 13:17-18), then as a holy nation in covenant with Yahweh, a "kingdom of priests" among whom he dwelt, but now (in Numbers) as fighting soldiers, an army encamped in battle array, ready to march to the promised land.

On the twentieth day of the second month of the second year the march began. The tabernacle was dismantled, only seven weeks after it had been erected. The pillar of cloud, symbol of God's guiding presence, began to move, and "the Israelites set out from the Desert of Sinai" (Num. 10:11-12).

It must have been an exciting moment. At last, seven centuries after it had been first made to Abraham, God's promise to give his people the land of Canaan was about to be fulfilled. "We are setting out," they said to one another, "for the place about which the LORD said, 'I will give it to you'" (Num. 10:29).

But their expectation was short-lived. First, the people complained about the shortage of food. Their mouth watered for the fish, the cucumbers, melons, leeks, onions and garlic they had enjoyed in Egypt (Num. 11:1-6). Then Miriam and Aaron, Moses' sister and brother, began to undermine his authority (Num. 12). Finally, the twelve scouts whom Moses sent out to reconnoiter the land of Canaan – although the fruit they brought back proved that it was indeed "a land flowing with milk and honey" – added that in their view its inhabitants were invincible:

> The people who live there are powerful, and the cities are fortified and very large. . . . The Amalekites live in the Negev; the Hittites, Jebusites and Amorites live in the hill country; and the Canaanites live near the sea and along the Jordan. . . . We can't attack these people; they are stronger than we are.
> (Num. 13:28-29, 31).

At this report the people wept and wailed. Two of the spies, Caleb and Joshua, pleaded with them not to disobey or disbelieve the Lord or fear the people of the land. But it was of no use. The majority spoke only of stoning them. So God's judgment fell upon his people for their inveterate rebellion. None of that adult generation would enter the land of promise, he said; only the faithful Caleb and Joshua.

Forty years were now to elapse between the exodus from Egypt and the entry into Canaan, instead of only one or two. Many of them seem to have been spent at the oasis of Kadesh-barnea in the Negev. But they were years of wandering, too, down south to Sinai again, then north and east through rugged Edomite territory south of the Dead Sea. From here they could have joined the famous "King's Highway" which ran from the gulf of

Mount Tabor, where Barak scored a notable victory over the Philistines, chasing them down the steep slopes.

Aqabah east of the Dead Sea right up into Syria. But the Edomites would not allow them to traverse their territory by this route, so they had to skirt round it further east (Num. 20:14-21). They did not fight the Edomites, for they were kinsmen. But north of them now were the Amorites, also blocking the King's Highway, under Sihon King of Heshbon and Og King of Bashan. Their defeat in battle, and the defeat of the King of Moab's attempts to overthrow Israel, first by hiring Balaam to curse them and then by immoral enticement, are described in Numbers 21–25.

Israel was now encamped on the plains of Moab close to the River Jordan, north of where it flows into the Dead Sea. Here Moses addressed the people for the last time; his words are preserved in the Book of Deuteronomy. He began by recalling the recent years of tragic wandering and its solemn lessons. He then reminded them of the Lord's covenant and of its conditions. He repeated the ten commandments and expounded them in terms of Israel's requirement to love the Lord their God with all their being and to prove their love by their obedience.

You are a people holy to the LORD your God. The LORD your God has chosen you out of all the peoples on the face of the earth to be his people, his treasured possession. . . . And now, O Israel, what does the LORD your God ask of you but to fear the LORD your God, to walk in all his ways, to love him, to serve the LORD your God with all your heart and with all your soul, and to observe the LORD's commands and decrees . . . ?
(Deut. 7:6; 10:12-13)

Moses went on to expound a number of laws in detail, applying them to the situation the people might expect in the promised land. Two or three times in the course of his exposition he placed before the Israelites the only alternatives:

See, I am setting before you today a blessing and a curse – the blessing if you obey the commands of the LORD your God . . . the curse if you disobey the commands of the LORD your God. . . .
See, I set before you today life and

prosperity, death and destruction. (Deut. 11:26-28; 30:15)

The death of Moses is recorded at the end of Deuteronomy. For forty years he had served God and the people of God with extraordinary patience and faithfulness. He had acted as lawgiver, administrator and judge. Above all he was a chosen spokesman of God, a prophet. Indeed the writer adds:

Since then, no prophet has risen in Israel like Moses, whom the LORD knew face to face. (Deut. 34:10)

Israel's settlement in Canaan

Already, before his death, Moses by divine command had appointed Joshua to succeed him and to lead the people into the promised land. Now therefore God's word came to Joshua:

Be strong and courageous, because you will lead these people to inherit the land I swore to their forefathers to give them. (Josh. 1:6)

The Israelites were able to cross the River Jordan, as they had crossed the Red Sea, by a supernatural act of God, although this time he seems to have used a landslide instead of a strong wind to stem the waters for them (Josh. 3:15-16). Before them stood the ancient walled city of Jericho; its destruction without a siege was their first victory in the land of promise. After an initial defeat at Ai, owing to the disobedience of Achan in stealing 'the devoted thing', the victorious Israelites turned south. They routed a confederate army led by five Amorite kings, and swept on to conquer the southern hill country up to the borders of Philistia.

Next they turned north, where a coalition commanded by Jabin King of Haor had gathered near Lake Huleh. Although this army was equipped with "very many horses and chariots," for Israel's settlement in Canaan coincided approximately with the beginning of the Iron Age, it too was decisively defeated:

So Joshua took this entire land: the hill country, all the Negev, the whole region of Goshen, the western foothills, the Arabah and the mountains of Israel with their foothills, from Mount Halak, which rises toward Seir, to Baal Gad in the Valley of Lebanon below Mount Hermon. (Josh. 11:16-17)

The rest of the Book of Joshua contains a description of the territories which were allocated by lot to the Israelite tribes as their inheritance (chapters 13–22). It ends with a stirring speech which Joshua delivered "a long time afterward," reminiscent of Moses' charge recorded in Deuteronomy, in which he reminded the people of their history and issued this challenge:

Now fear the LORD and serve him with all faithfulness. Throw away the gods your forefathers worshiped beyond the River and in Egypt, and serve the LORD. But if serving the LORD seems undesirable to you, then choose for yourselves this day whom you will serve, whether the gods your forefathers served beyond the River, or the gods of the Amorites, in whose land you are living. But as for me and my household, we will serve the LORD. (Josh. 24:14-15)

Although the children of Israel were now settled in the land which God had promised to give them they had not obeyed his command to exterminate its former inhabitants. There is no need for us to be offended by this divine decree. The reason for it can best be described as the need for radical surgery. Canaanite religion was characterized by both idolatry and immorality of the worst kind. The "baals" were fertility gods, supposed to be responsible for rainfall and harvest, and both ritual prostitution and sexual orgies defiled the "worship" of the local sanctuaries. So Moses said:

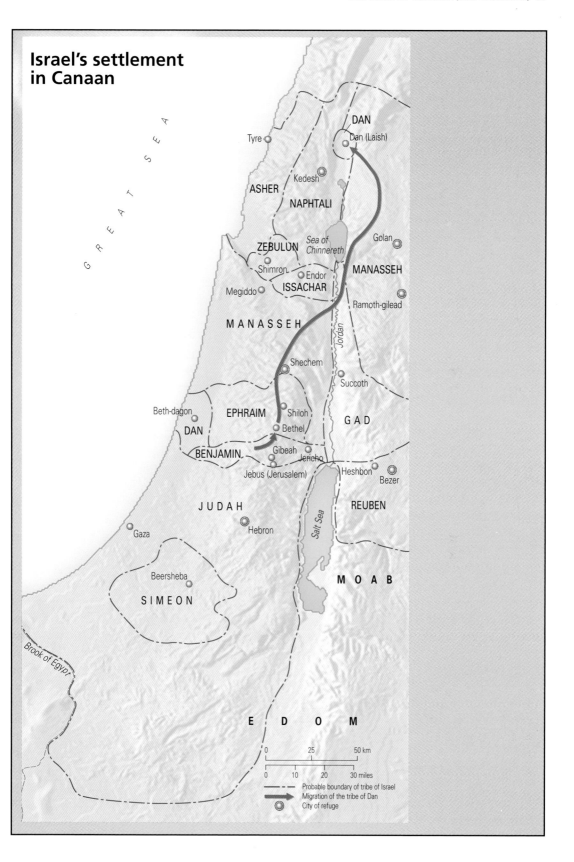

Israel's settlement in Canaan

GREAT SEA

Tyre

DAN
Dan (Laish)

Kedesh

ASHER

NAPHTALI

Golan

ZEBULUN
Sea of Chinnereth

Shimron

Endor

MANASSEH

Megiddo

ISSACHAR

Ramoth-gilead

MANASSEH

Jordan

Shechem

Succoth

Beth-dagon

EPHRAIM

Shiloh

GAD

DAN

Bethel

BENJAMIN

Gibeah

Jericho

Jebus (Jerusalem)

Heshbon

Bezer

JUDAH

REUBEN

Gaza

Hebron

Salt Sea

Beersheba

MOAB

SIMEON

Brook of Egypt

E   D   O   M

| 0 | 25 | 50 km |
| 0 | 10 | 20 | 30 miles |

Probable boundary of tribe of Israel
Migration of the tribe of Dan
City of refuge

It is on account of the wickedness of these nations that the LORD is going to drive them out before you. (Deut. 9:4)

Indeed so degraded were the practices of the heathen nations inhabiting Canaan, including the abomination of child sacrifice, that their ejection by Israel is sometimes portrayed in Scripture as the land "vomiting out its inhabitants" (Lev. 18:24-30).

Israel's failure to obey God's command resulted in the persistence of heathen culture within her territory and its penetration into her beliefs and practices. This is the situation throughout the period – nearly 200 years – described in the Book of Judges. The same cycle of backsliding, oppression and deliverance kept repeating itself. First the backsliding:

> Then the Israelites did evil in the eyes of the LORD and served the Baals. They forsook the LORD, the God of their fathers, who had brought them out of Egypt. They followed and worshiped various gods of the peoples around them. They provoked the LORD to anger because they forsook him and served Baal and the Ashtoreths. (Judg. 2:11-13)

Then came the judgment in form of a foreign oppression:

> In his anger against Israel the LORD handed them over to raiders who plundered them. He sold them to their enemies all around, whom they were no longer able to resist. (Judg. 2:14)

Finally the deliverance:

> Then the LORD raised up judges, who saved them out of the hands of these raiders. (Judg. 2:16)

But then it happened all over again:

> Yet they would not listen to the judges but prostituted themselves to other gods and worshiped them. Unlike their fathers, they quickly turned from the way in which their fathers had walked, the way of obedience to the LORD's commands. (Judg. 2:17)

These "judges" combined several functions. First and foremost they were military leaders, raised up to deliver Israel from her oppressors. Thus Ehud rescued Israel from the Moabites, Deborah from the Canaanites, Gideon from the Midianites, Jephthah from the Ammonites and Samson from the Philistines. Next they were spiritual leaders, men of the Spirit, though exhibiting different degrees of devotion to Yahweh. Thirdly, they were judges, as their title indicates, hearing cases referred to them and administering justice in Israel. Nevertheless, there appears to have been but little law and order throughout this period, which is well summed up by the last words of the book: "Everyone did as he saw fit."

Undoubtedly the greatest of the judges was Samuel. Unlike the others he displayed no military prowess. It was during his term of office that the unthinkable disaster occurred: the Philistines captured the ark of God and transferred it from Shiloh to Ashdod. Samuel relied on spiritual weapons to recover it – prayer and national repentance.

His reputation as a spiritual leader began early. Dedicated to the Lord before his birth, he was brought up at Shiloh under the tutelage of the high priest Eli. When he was still a young man, we are told, "all Israel from Dan to Beersheba recognized that Samuel was attested as a prophet of the LORD" (1 Sam. 3:20). He acted as a priest as well.

He also judged Israel, going on circuit every year from Ramah, his hometown, to Bethel, Gilgal and Mizpah (1 Sam. 7:15-17).

However, when he grew old and appointed his sons as judges, they did not walk in their father's ways, but "accepted bribes and perverted justice" (1 Sam. 8:1-3). So the elders of Israel came to Samuel at Ramah and demanded that he should appoint a king to govern them. As Samuel prayed about their request, it

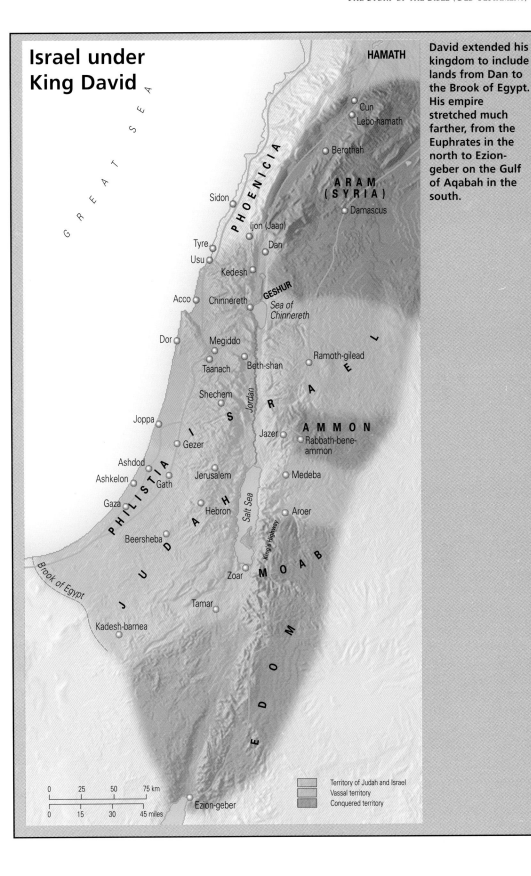

Israel under King David

David extended his kingdom to include lands from Dan to the Brook of Egypt. His empire stretched much farther, from the Euphrates in the north to Ezion-geber on the Gulf of Aqabah in the south.

HAMATH

Cun
Lebo-hamath

Berothah

ARAM (SYRIA)

Sidon

PHOENICIA

Damascus

Ijon (Jaan)

Tyre
Usu
Kedesh
Dan

GESHUR

Acco
Chinnereth
Sea of Chinnereth

Dor
Megiddo
Ramoth-gilead

Taanach
Beth-shan

I S R A E L

Shechem

Jordan

Joppa
Gezer

Jazer
AMMON
Rabbath-bene-ammon

Ashdod
Ashkelon
Gath
Jerusalem
Medeba

Gaza
Hebron
Aroer

J U D A H

PHILISTIA

Beersheba

Salt Sea

King's Highway

Zoar
M O A B

Tamar

Brook of Egypt

E D O M

Kadesh-barnea

GREAT SEA

	Territory of Judah and Israel
	Vassal territory
	Conquered territory

0   25   50   75 km
0   15   30   45 miles

Ezion-geber

became clear to him that they had rejected not him but God. For Israel had been a theocracy, a nation ruled by God since its beginning some 250 years before. Therefore Samuel remonstrated with them and warned them that future kings would oppress them. But the people refused to listen:

> "No!" they said. "We want a king over us. Then we shall be like all the other nations." (1 Sam. 8:19-20)

The establishment of the monarchy

Israel's first king, Saul the son of Kish, began his reign with great promise. He was rich, tall, handsome, young and popular. He was also a strong patriot, so that when he heard that Jabesh-Gilead was being besieged by Nahash the Ammonite he immediately mustered a large army and made a bold dash across the Jordan to rescue its inhabitants.

He was not so successful against the Philistines, however. They had garrisons on Israelite territory and were a source of constant humiliation to Israel. It was Saul's son Jonathan who one day routed a whole Philistine garrison single-handed, and the youth David (destined to be Saul's successor on the throne) who slew the Philistine giant Goliath. The people were enthusiastic over these daring exploits. But Saul's jealousy was aroused.

The major cause of Saul's downfall was his disobedience. Three times he disobeyed the plain commands of God – in not utterly destroying the Amalekites, in usurping the priestly prerogative of sacrifice and in consulting a medium. God's verdict through Samuel was inevitable:

> Because you have rejected the word of the Lord, he has rejected you as king. (1 Sam. 15:23)

Saul fell in battle against the Philistines, together with his three sons, and David was overcome with grief:

> Your glory, O Israel, lies slain on your heights. How the mighty have fallen! (2 Sam. 1:19)

David had already been designated heir to the throne during Saul's lifetime, but spent the latter years of Saul's reign a fugitive from the king's jealousy. He began his own reign in Hebron, where the men of Judah (his own tribe) anointed him king. But, seven years later, representatives of all the tribes of Israel came to Hebron to do homage to him, and he was anointed king for the second time. He then moved his capital to Jebus (captured only now from the Jebusites), changed its name to Jerusalem, "city of peace," and brought the ark there from Kiriath-jearim amid tumultuous rejoicing.

David's first achievement was to unify Israel and make the country safe from her enemies. He won victories over all Israel's traditional foes – the Philistines, Edomites, Moabites, Ammonites and Syrians – and ruled over the whole promised land from "the river of Egypt" (Egypt's frontier wadi) to the River Euphrates. In view of these conquests it was all the more humiliating that he should have to endure rebellion at home, first from his son Absalom and then from a worthless pretender named Sheba.

But David was far from being a warlord. He was artistic, being both a poet and a musician (he had often soothed Saul's melancholia with his lyre). He was also a sensitive spirit, magnanimous to his enemies and loyal to his friends.

Above all, he was devoted to his God. The psalms he wrote express a remarkable depth of spirituality, of penitence after his adultery with Bathsheba (Ps. 51) and of trust in the God of his salvation. For example:

> The LORD is my rock, my fortress and my
> deliverer;
> my God is my rock, in whom I take
> refuge,

The City of David Archaeological Garden, Jerusalem, preserves some of the oldest remains of the city.

my shield and the horn of my salvation.
He is my stronghold, my refuge and my
    savior –
    from violent men you save me. . . .

For who is God besides the LORD?
    And who is the Rock except our God?
It is God who arms me with strength
    and makes my way perfect. . . .

I love you, O LORD, my strength.
The LORD is my rock, my fortress and my
    deliverer;
    my God is my rock, in whom I take
    refuge.
    He is my shield and the horn of my
    salvation, my stronghold.
I call to the LORD, who is worthy of praise,
    and I am saved from my enemies. . . .
For who is God besides the LORD?
    And who is the Rock except our God?
It is God who arms me with strength
    and makes my way perfect.
(2 Sam. 22:1-3, 32-33; Ps. 18:1-3, 31-32)

Having built a palace for himself in Jerusalem, David was anxious also to build a house for the Lord. But through the prophet Nathan God forbade it, telling him that his son would be allowed to build the temple. Meanwhile God added:

The LORD declares to you that the LORD
himself will establish a house for you. . . .
Your house and your kingdom shall
endure forever before me; your throne
shall be established forever.
(2 Sam. 7:11, 16)

Israel never forgot God's everlasting covenant with David. Believers in Israel knew for certain that when Messiah came, he would be a son of David.

God began to fulfill his promise to David by setting his son Solomon on the throne, and during his reign the kingdom of Israel reached the zenith of its magnificence. It was not for nothing that Jesus referred to "Solomon in all his glory."

King Solomon had a genius for administra-

An artist's impression of Solomon's Temple, Jerusalem.

tion and building. Soon after his accession he prayed that God would give him wisdom.

> Give your servant a discerning heart to govern your people and to distinguish between right and wrong. (1 Kings 3:9)

Solomon's prayer was answered. He divided the country into twelve regions under twelve officers, whose responsibility was to make provision for the royal household, one each month of the year. He fortified cities, built up a standing army, and provided himself with 1,400 chariots and 40,000 horses. He was the father of Israel's navy, whose ships (kept in the Gulf of Aqabah) embarked on adventurous voyages for trade. He built palaces for himself and his queen, halls for assembly, justice and armory and above all the great Temple, made of hewn stone, cedar and cypress wood and gold. He was also a kind of patron of the arts, and himself the author of numerous songs and proverbs (1 Kings 4:32-34). His reputation for splendor,

The northern and southern kingdoms of Israel

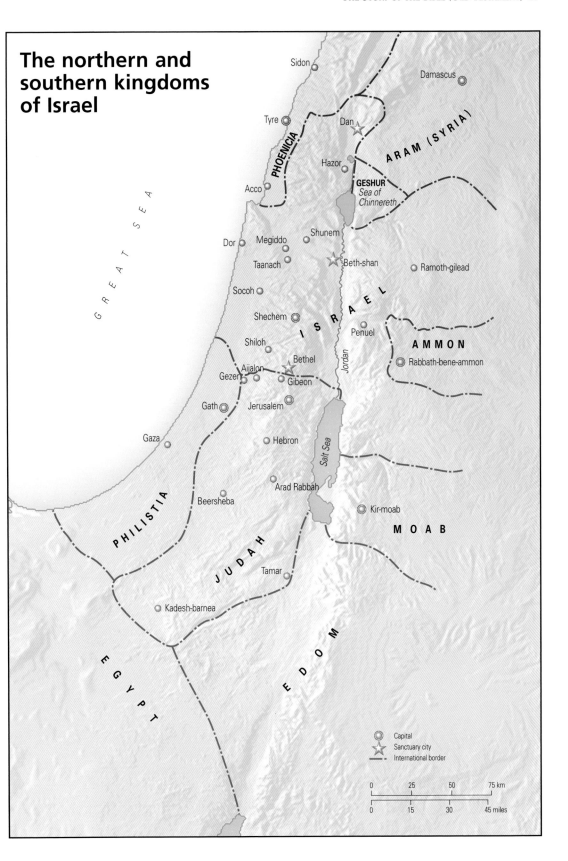

Sidon

Damascus

Tyre

Dan

PHOENICIA

ARAM (SYRIA)

Hazor

Acco

GESHUR
Sea of Chinnereth

G R E A T   S E A

Dor

Megiddo

Shunem

Taanach

Beth-shan

Ramoth-gilead

Socoh

Shechem

I S R A E L

Penuel

Shiloh

AMMON

Aijalon

Bethel

Jordan

Gezer

Gibeon

Rabbath-bene-ammon

Gath

Jerusalem

Gaza

Hebron

Salt Sea

Arad Rabbah

Beersheba

Kir-moab

M O A B

P H I L I S T I A

J U D A H

Tamar

Kadesh-barnea

E
G
Y
P
T

E
D
O
M

Capital
Sanctuary city
International border

0		25		50		75 km
0	15		30		45 miles	

wisdom and justice spread far and wide, and under his rule his people enjoyed peace and prosperity:

> The people of Judah and Israel were as numerous as the sand on the seashore; they ate, they drank and they were happy. . . . Judah and Israel, from Dan to Beersheba, lived in safety, each man under his own vine and fig tree.
> (1 Kings 4:20, 25)

All was not as well as it seemed on the surface, however. Solomon did not love the Lord his God with all his heart. Nor did he love his neighbor as himself. He kept a harem of foreign (heathen) princesses, in defiance of God's prohibition of such intermarriage, and they "turned his heart after other gods" (1 Kings 11:1-8). Also, he was able to maintain his building program and his grandiose lifestyle at court only by oppressive measures, including high taxation and a levy of forced labor numbering 30,000 men.

It is not surprising, therefore, that when the people came together to make Rehoboam king in succession to his father Solomon, they said to him:

> Your father put a heavy yoke on us, but now lighten the harsh labor and the heavy yoke he put on us, and we will serve you. (1 Kings 12:4)

The old king's counselor gave Rehoboam wise advice, which lies at the foundation of every modern constitutional monarchy's ideals of service:

> If today you will be a servant to these people and serve them . . . they will always be your servants. (1 Kings 12:7)

But Rehoboam made a rash and foolish mistake. He accepted instead the advice of young and inexperienced counselors, warned the people that he intended to add to their yoke, and so provoked the ten northern and eastern tribes to proclaim their independence from the dynasty of David.

Saul, David and Solomon had reigned over all Israel for forty years each, so that for the 120 years from approximately 1050-930 BC there had been a united kingdom. But now the kingdom was divided. The northern kingdom was Israel, with Jeroboam its first king and its capital city Shechem (later changed to Samaria). The southern kingdom was Judah, with Rehoboam its first king and its capital city Jerusalem. Israel had several changes of dynasty and lasted just over 200 years until the destruction of Samaria in 772 BC. Judah was more stable, retaining the dynasty of David throughout its longer history of about 350 years until Jerusalem was destroyed in 586 BC.

The story of the divided monarchy is not easy to follow, as we try to understand the relations between the two kingdoms, their involvement with the mighty empires to their north and south, and the intervention of the prophets who spoke boldly in the name of Yahweh to kings and commoners alike. The biblical story is further complicated by the fact that much of it is told twice, once in the Books of Kings and once in the Books of Chronicles, the chronicler (possibly Ezra) writing later with the clear object of emphasizing the importance of the southern kingdom, the Davidic dynasty and the temple cultus. It may be best to concentrate first on the story of Israel.

The northern kingdom of Israel

Jeroboam, the first ruler of the northern kingdom, had been one of Solomon's servants. Indeed, so high an opinion did Solomon form of his ability and industry that he put him in charge of a major part of the forced labor levy. Later Solomon had reason to suspect Jeroboam of treason, and Jeroboam fled for his life to Egypt where he was harbored by Shishak (i.e. Sheshonq I of the XXII Dynasty). He only returned after Solomon's death to challenge Rehoboam, as we have seen.

In order to wean the hearts of his subjects

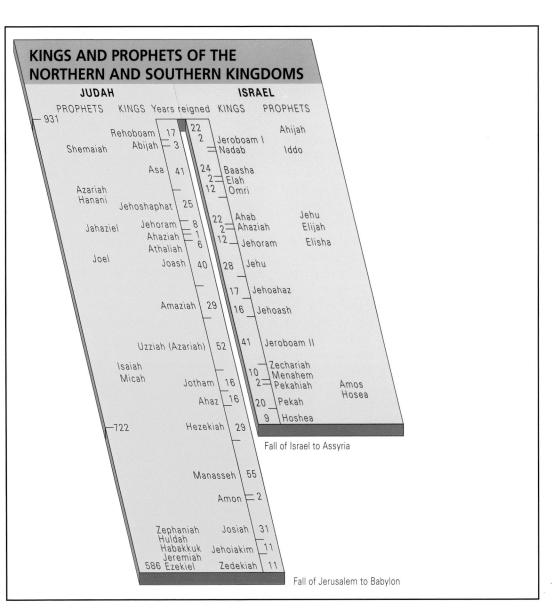

KINGS AND PROPHETS OF THE NORTHERN AND SOUTHERN KINGDOMS

JUDAH				ISRAEL	
PROPHETS	KINGS	Years reigned	KINGS	PROPHETS
931					
	Rehoboam	17	22		Ahijah
Shemaiah	Abijah	3	2	Jeroboam I	
				Nadab	Iddo
	Asa	41	24	Baasha	
			2	Elah	
Azariah			12	Omri	
Hanani					
	Jehoshaphat	25			
			22	Ahab	Jehu
Jahaziel	Jehoram	8	2	Ahaziah	Elijah
	Ahaziah	1	12	Jehoram	Elisha
	Athaliah	6			
Joel					
	Joash	40	28	Jehu	
			17	Jehoahaz	
	Amaziah	29	16	Jehoash	
	Uzziah (Azariah)	52	41	Jeroboam II	
Isaiah				Zechariah	
Micah			10	Menahem	
	Jotham	16	2	Pekahiah	Amos
	Ahaz	16	20	Pekah	Hosea
			9	Hoshea	
722	Hezekiah	29			

Fall of Israel to Assyria

	Manasseh	55			
	Amon	2			
Zephaniah	Josiah	31			
Huldah					
Habakkuk	Jehoiakim	11			
Jeremiah					
586 Ezekiel	Zedekiah	11			

Fall of Jerusalem to Babylon

from the house of David, Jeroboam was determined to stop them going on pilgrimage to Jerusalem. So he made two alternative sanctuaries, the one up north at Dan and the other down south at Bethel, installed in each a golden calf and said:

> Here are your gods, O Israel, who
> brought you up out of Egypt.
> (1 Kings 12:28)

It is for this reason that Jeroboam has come down to posterity as the one "who made Israel sin."

But Judah under Rehoboam was scarcely any better, for alongside the worship of Yahweh the people corrupted themselves with some of the abominations of the Canaanite fertility rituals. Rehoboam had only been king for four or five years when Shishak invaded Jerusalem and denuded the temple of the treasures with which Solomon had enriched it.

Jeroboam was succeeded on the throne of Israel by five kings of whom we know little. But in 881 BC, some 28 years after Jeroboam's death, the dynasty of Omri began. It was he who established his capital in Samaria, and made it almost impregnable on a well-fortified conical hill. But he brought great trouble to Israel by marrying his son Ahab (who soon succeeded him) to the Phoenician princess Jezebel. For she was not only herself a worshiper of Melqart ("Baal" in the biblical narrative), the main deity of Tyre, but insisted on maintaining at her own expense at court a retinue of "the prophets of Baal," and involved her husband the king in her idolatrous worship. She also killed the prophets of the Lord.

This brazen apostasy in the palace was the signal for the reawakening of ethical prophecy, which was destined to play a dominant part in Israel and Judah for the next three centuries and more. The first prophet of this noble line was Elijah, who came from Gilead in Transjordan. Austere in his private lifestyle and fearless in his public ministry, he accused Ahab of troubling Israel by his religious defection. He also challenged the prophets of Baal to a public contest on Mount Carmel, at the same time taunting the people with double-mindedness, wavering between two opinions (1 Kings 18:21). When Baal's prophets had failed to elicit any response from their god, Elijah prayed:

> O Lord, God of Abraham, Isaac and
> Israel, let it be known today that you are
> God in Israel, and that I am your servant.
> (1 Kings 18:36)

The outcome was an incontrovertible vindication of the living God.

Elijah had a social as well as a religious conscience. He knew that Yahweh was as displeased with the king's oppression of his subjects as with his apostasy. Next to a palace which belonged to Ahab on the plain of Jezreel there was a desirable vineyard owned by a man named Naboth. Ahab coveted it for himself but Naboth refused to sell his fathers' inheritance. So Jezebel, doubtless with Ahab's connivance, had Naboth assassinated and proceeded to annex his property. Here Elijah met him:

> Have you not murdered a man and seized
> his property? . . . In the place were dogs
> licked up Naboth's blood, dogs will lick
> up your blood – yes, yours!
> (1 Kings 21:19)

Naboth's innocent blood was avenged by Jehu, an Israelite army commander who was now anointed king on the authority of the prophet Elisha. With brutal thoroughness he liquidated the house of Ahab and rid the land of Baal worship.

The dynasty of Jehu lasted nearly a hundred years (c. 841-753 BC), almost half the total duration of the northern kingdom. During the early years of the dynasty there was virtually continuous war with Syria, which wrested the whole of Transjordan from Jehu. But it began to be recovered by his grandson, and his great-grandson Jeroboam II completed the process.

It was under Jeroboam II (782-753 BC) that the northern kingdom of Israel reached its zenith of power:

> He . . . restored the boundaries of Israel
> from Lebo Hamath to the Sea of the
> Arabah. (2 Kings 14:25)

Peace brought prosperity, prosperity luxury, and luxury license. True, the local sanctuaries were thronged with pilgrims, and to all appearances Israel was experiencing a religious boom. But the prophets had eyes only for the injustice and immorality of the nation's leaders. Amos, the first great prophet of the eighth century BC,[6] was a simple shepherd from the south, but the compulsion of God's word drove him into the northern kingdom to denounce Israel's hypocrisy:

> This is what the Lord says:
> "For three sins of Israel,
>   even for four, I will not turn back my
>   wrath.
> They sell the righteous for silver,
>   and the needy for a pair of sandals.
> They trample on the heads of the poor
>   as upon the dust of the ground

Israelite remains at Samaria, capital of the northern kingdom of Israel.

and deny justice to the oppressed.
Father and son use the same girl
    and so profane my holy name.
They lie down beside every altar
    on garments taken in pledge.
In the house of their god
    they drink wine taken as fines."
(Amos 2:6-8)

He knew that religion divorced from morality was an abomination to Yahweh:

. . . I hate, I despise your religious feasts;
    I cannot stand your assemblies.
Even though you bring me burnt offerings
    and grain offerings,
    I will not accept them.
Though you bring choice fellowship offerings,
    I will have no regard for them.
Away with the noise of your songs!
    I will not listen to the music of your harps.
But let justice roll on like a river,
    righteousness like a never-failing stream!

(Amos 5:21-24)

To Hosea the word of the Lord came through the agony of his wife's unfaithfulness. For Israel had similarly broken her marriage covenant with Yahweh and gone after her "lovers," the baals of the local shrines. It was not outward religious devotion God wanted from Israel, but faithfulness to the covenant:

I desire mercy, not sacrifice,
    and acknowledgement of God rather than
    burnt offerings.
(Hos. 6:6)

When the dynasty of Jehu came to an end, the northern kingdom had only about thirty years left. A succession of military rulers occupied the throne. But the new factor in international politics was the rise of the great Assyrian empire. Already in the middle of the previous century both Ahab and Jehu had paid tribute to King Shalmaneser III. Now the King of Assyria was Tiglath-Pileser III (745-727 BC), called Pul in the biblical narrative, and he embarked on a

Assyrian relief of deportations during one of Tiglath Pileser III's campaigns. Clerks are recording events.

series of expansionist campaigns. When he reached Israel, he was bought off by King Menahem with a thousand talents of silver.

A few years later (in 735 BC) the "colonel" who was ruling Israel, Pekah the son of Remaliah, entered into an alliance with Rezin King of Syria to throw off the Assyrian yoke. When Ahaz King of Judah refused to join them, they invaded his territory. Ahaz was thrown into a panic, but the prophet Isaiah sought to calm him with a word from God:

Be careful, keep calm and don't be afraid.
Do not lose heart because of these two
smoldering stubs of firewood. . . . If you
do not stand firm in your faith, you will
not stand at all. (Isa. 7:4, 9)

Ahaz did not believe. Instead, he appealed to Tiglath-Pileser for help, with devastating results. Syria was overthrown. The Galilean and Transjordanian territories of Israel were depopulated. And Ahaz paid homage to Tiglath-Pileser with silver and gold from the temple, and even to Ashur, Assyria's god.

When Tiglath-Pileser died, Samaria defiantly withheld tribute from Assyria. This reckless act sounded Israel's death knell. The new King Shalmaneser V laid siege to Samaria, which capitulated three years later (probably in 722) to his successor Sargon II. The people of Israel were largely deported, and their country was colonized with Syrians and Babylonians. The resulting mixed population was the origin of the Samaritans.

So the northern kingdom came to an ignominious end. It had lasted just over two centuries. Israel had regarded God's covenant as rendering her immune to his judgment, but the prophet Amos had taught otherwise:

You only have I chosen
of all the families of the earth;
therefore I will punish you
for all your sins. (Amos 3:2)

The southern kingdom of Judah

So far we have been following the rise and fall of the northern kingdom. The Books of Kings

Hezekiah secured Jerusalem's water supply by building a tunnel from a spring outside the walls.

resolutely removed from his kingdom all the paraphernalia of Assyrian idolatry which his father Ahaz had introduced.

These reforms were certainly the fruit of the faithful witness of Isaiah and Micah, who had been denouncing idolatry, empty ritual and social injustice and calling the people to repentance during both the preceding reigns, while Amos and Hosea were proclaiming God's word to the northern kingdom. Here is one of Micah's great oracles:

> With what shall I come before the LORD
>   and bow down before the exalted God?
> Shall I come before him with burnt
>   offerings,
>   with calves a year old?
> Will the LORD be pleased with thousands of
>   rams,
>   with ten thousand rivers of oil?
> Shall I offer my firstborn for my
>   transgression,
>   the fruit of my body for the sin of my
>   soul?
> He has showed you, O man, what is good.
>   And what does the LORD require of you?
> To act justly and to love mercy
>   and to walk humbly with your God.
> (Mic. 6:6-8)

and Chronicles also give some account of the southern kingdom during the same period. But its history was not so colorful, and the names of its earlier kings are not so well known, except perhaps for Jehoshaphat, Ahab's contemporary.

Now, however, the southern kingdom was to continue alone for a further 135 years. Its period of independence was ennobled in particular by two great religious reforms. The first was promoted by King Hezekiah, with the encouragement of the prophets Isaiah and Micah. The second reforming king was Josiah, who was encouraged by his distant cousin the prophet Zephaniah and by the young prophet Jeremiah.

At the very beginning of his reign Hezekiah repaired and reopened the temple. Then he

Sargon King of Assyria was killed in action in 705 BC and succeeded by his son Sennacherib. This seems to have been the signal for Hezekiah's revolt against Assyrian suzerainty. Not until 701 BC, however, did Sennacherib reach the rebel kingdom of Judah. Having taken its fortified cities, he laid siege to Jerusalem, shutting Hezekiah up (to use his own expression) "like a bird in a cage." Fortunately, Hezekiah had taken the precaution of securing the city's water supply by building his famous tunnel from a spring outside the walls to the Pool of Siloam. Even so, the situation appeared desperate. As Isaiah described it:

> The Daughter of Zion is
>   left like a shelter in a vineyard,

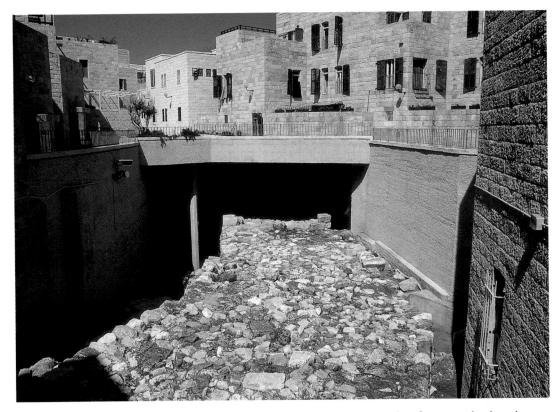

An excavated section of the "broad wall" built by Hezekiah to protect Jerusalem from Assyrian invasion.

like a hut in a field of melons,
   like a city under siege.
(Isa. 1:8)

The Assyrian commander taunted the inhabitants of the beleaguered city:

Do not listen to Hezekiah, for he is misleading you when he says, "The LORD will deliver us." Has the god of any nation ever delivered his land from the hand of the king of Assyria? Where are the gods of Hamath and Arpad? Where are the gods of Sepharvaim, Hena and Ivvah? Have they rescued Samaria from my hand? (2 Kings 18:32-34)

King Hezekiah consulted Isaiah, and the prophet replied:

This is what the LORD says: Do not be afraid of what you have heard – those words with which the underlings of the king of Assyria have blasphemed me. (2 Kings 19:6; cf. Isa. 37:33-35)

The central doctrine of Isaiah's theology was the sovereignty of God. His call to the prophetic office came to him in a vision of the Lord as king, reigning from his exalted throne. He believed that God was king of the nations and used them as instruments of his own purpose.

So Sennacherib's siege of Jerusalem was lifted. According to the biblical record, "that night the angel of the LORD went out and put to death a hundred and eighty-five thousand men in the Assyrian camp" (2 Kings 19:35; cf. Isa. 37:36). It is possible that Herodotus is referring to this incident when he describes a night invasion of the Assyrian camp by field mice. But he says the mice rendered the soldiers defenseless by eating their bowstrings, quivers and shield straps, where in reality they may rather have been carriers of bubonic plague.

By whatever means it was accomplished, Israel regarded it as an outstanding divine deliverance:

God is our refuge and strength,
    an ever-present help in trouble. . . .
  "Be still, and know that I am God;
    I will be exalted among the nations,
    I will be exalted on the earth."
The LORD Almighty is with us;
    the God of Jacob is our fortress.
  (Ps. 46:1, 10-11)

The half-century following Hezekiah's death was a time of religious apostasy. His son Manasseh, an abject vassal of Assyria, adopted a policy of religious syncretism and reintroduced the abomination of Canaanite and Assyrian worship which Hezekiah had destroyed. The astral cult, spiritism, Baal worship and even the horrors of child sacrifice defiled the land. Amon his son, who reigned only two years, seems to have been no better.

But good King Josiah, who reigned from 639 to 609 BC, turned the scales again and inaugurated even more thoroughgoing reforms than his great-grandfather Hezekiah. He ascended the throne of Judah as a boy of eight. When he was still a youth of sixteen, "he began to seek the God of his father David," which presumably means that he reformed himself and his immediate entourage of court. Four years later "he began to purge Judah and Jerusalem of high places, Asherah poles, carved idols and cast images" (2 Chron. 34:3), and the following year Jeremiah received his call to be a prophet.

It was not until five years later still that, as a young man of twenty-six, Josiah led the radical reform of the whole nation. It was the result of the discovery during repairs in the temple of "the Book of the Law," which appears to have been some edition or part of the Book of Deuteronomy. The king summoned the people, "both great and small," to a large public assembly and himself read to them the rediscovered law book. He then renewed the nation's covenant with God, had all idolatrous objects of Assyrian and Canaanite worship removed from the city and the provinces, closed down the local sanctuaries, prohibited spiritism and human sacrifice and ordered the Passover to be celebrated in Jerusalem.

Neither before nor after Josiah was there
a king like him who turned to the LORD
as he did – with all his heart and with all
his soul and with all his strength, in
accordance with the Law of Moses.
(2 Kings 23:25)

We may be sure that, behind the scenes, Jeremiah was encouraging this reformation. At the same time the prophet deplored what he saw to be its comparative superficiality. He drew the people's attention to the fate of faithless Israel, and added:

"In spite of all this, her unfaithful sister
Judah did not return to me with all her
heart, but only in pretense," declares the
LORD. (Jer. 3:10)

Jeremiah often referred to the "stubbornness" of the evil human hearts, "deceitful above all things and beyond cure," and looked forward to the days of the new covenant when God would put his law within men and "write it on their hearts" (Jer. 7:24; 17:9; 31:33).

In any event, Jeremiah was proved right. The results of Josiah's reform did not last, and his son Jehoiakim quickly succeeded in undoing his good work. The new king seems to have used slave labor to build a luxurious palace for himself, and so brought upon his head one of Jeremiah's fiercest denunciations:

"Woe to him who builds his palace by
  unrighteousness,
  his upper rooms by injustice,
making his countrymen work for nothing,
  not paying them for their labor."
He says, "I will build myself a great palace
  with spacious upper rooms."
So he makes large windows in it,
  panels it with cedar

and decorates it in red.
Does it make you a king,
   to have more and more cedar?
Did not your father have food and drink?
   He did what was right and just,
   so all went well with him.
He defended the cause of the poor and
needy,
   and so all went well.
Is that not what it means to know me?"
   declares the LORD.
"But your eyes and your heart
   are set only on dishonest gain,
   on shedding innocent blood
   and on oppression and extortion."
(Jer. 22:13-17)

Such outspoken talk was not calculated to establish Jeremiah in King Jehoiakim's favor. So when a scroll containing Jeremiah's warnings of the coming judgment upon Judah was read to the king as he sat in his winter house before a brazier, he cut it up with a penknife and threw it bit by bit into the fire (Jer. 36:21-23).

During these years the international scene underwent some important changes. For the past 200 years the Assyrians had been the dominant power in the Near East, and the countryside of Israel and Judah had been repeatedly overrun by their armies. But in 616 BC Assyria was invaded by Nabopolasser, the founder of the Babylonian dynasty, and in 612 Nineveh (the Assyrian capital) fell after a siege of two and a half months. No tears were shed over her downfall. The Book of Jonah illustrates how reluctantly an Israelite would contemplate Nineveh's repentance and forgiveness, and the prophet Nahum expresses the widespread reaction to Nineveh's oppression:

Woe to the city of blood,
   full of lies,
full of plunder,
   never without victims! . . .
"I am against you," declares the LORD
   Almighty. . . .
Everyone who hears the news about you
   claps his hands at your fall,

for who has not felt
   your endless cruelty? (Nah. 3:1, 5, 19)

Even after the fall of Nineveh, Assyria did not immediately concede defeat. In 609 Pharaoh Necho of Egypt went to her aid, but was himself defeated in 605 by the Babylonians at the Battle of Carchemish on the Euphrates. Now Babylon was supreme, and Judah transferred her homage from Necho to Nebuchadnezzar.

When Nebuchadnezzar's army failed to defeat Necho at the Egyptian border in 601, King Jehoiakim withheld his tribute money. This was tantamount to a rebellion. But Jehoiakim died in 598 before Nebuchadnezzar had had time to quell the revolt, and his son Jehoiachin was left to bear the punitive wrath of Babylon. It fell upon him the following year. Jerusalem was besieged and captured. Three thousand members of the nobility were taken captive to Babylon, and so were the temple treasures. Among the exiles was Ezekiel, who was both a prophet and a priest, and who foretold the departure of God's glory from the temple because of Judah's inveterate sin.

Nebuchadnezzar appointed Zedekiah to the throne of Judah, yet another of King Josiah's sons. He was a weak and indecisive character. His counselors advised him to look to Egypt for help, but Jeremiah insisted that Judah's only hope of survival was to submit to Babylon. Himself a firm patriot, Jeremiah found it very hard to witness his country's humiliation, and even harder because of his policies to be suspected of treason. His was a voice crying in the wilderness. He stood and suffered alone.

Unfortunately, Zedekiah "did not humble himself before Jeremiah the prophet, who spoke the word of the LORD" (2 Chron. 36:12). In 589 BC he openly rebelled against Babylon. None of the hoped-for help from Egypt was forthcoming, and Jerusalem had to endure a second siege, this time for eighteen months. The famine conditions were appalling. Jeremiah continued to urge surrender, bringing upon himself first imprisonment and then an attempt on his life.

In 587-586 BC a breach was made in the walls and the city fell. The city walls were broken into rubble and Solomon's magnificent temple was burned to the ground.

The tiny remnant who were left were put in the charge of Gedaliah, and Jeremiah went on urging them to submit to the authority of Babylon. But Gedaliah was assassinated, and the survivors fled to Egypt, dragging the hapless Jeremiah with them.

The best way to feel Israel's despair when her temple had been destroyed and her people exiled is to read the Book of Lamentations:

> How deserted lies the city, once so full of
>   people!
> How like a widow is she,
>   who once was great among the nations!
> She who was queen among the provinces
>   has now become a slave. . . .
> All the splendor has departed
>   from the Daughter of Zion.
> Her princes are like deer
>   that find no pasture;
> in weakness they have fled
>   before the pursuer. . . .
> "Is it nothing to you, all you who pass by?
>   Look around and see.
> Is any suffering like my suffering
>   that was inflicted on me,
> that the LORD brought on me
>   in the day of his fierce anger?
> (Lam. 1:1, 6, 12)

Yet the godly were not taken by surprise. They knew that God's covenant with Israel was founded not only on his promise to be their God but on their undertaking to obey. From the beginning Moses had warned them of the consequence of disobedience, and the prophets had gone on insisting that judgment was inevitable if the nation did not repent:

> The LORD, the God of their fathers, sent
> word to them through his messengers
> again and again, because he had pity on
> his people and on his dwelling place.
> (2 Chron. 36:15)

The restoration from Babylonian captivity

The Babylonian captivity lasted about fifty years. Although the exiles had been forcibly deported from their homes, they seem to have enjoyed considerable freedom. Jeremiah had written a letter to the first contingent of exiles, telling them to "build houses and settle down," "plant gardens and eat what they produce" and "marry and have sons and daughters" (Jer. 29:5-6).

Their hardest trial was religious, for they felt spiritually lost in their separation from temple and sacrifice. But Ezekiel was among them to guide them. He still spoke to them the word of the Lord. He even claimed to have seen the glory of the Lord "among the exiles by the Kebar River" (Ezek. 1:1) – the very same glory which had dwelt in the temple – so God could not after all have entirely abandoned them.

In the year 559 BC Cyrus II ascended the throne of the nearby Persian kingdom. Nine years later, by overcoming the Median army he became King of Media as well, and "the Medes and Persians" (a familiar expression to readers of the Book of Daniel) became united. But this was only the beginning of Cyrus' brilliant military career. In 546 BC he defeated that byword of wealth, Croesus King of Lydia, and all Asia Minor was added to his empire.

The Jewish exiles must have heard of the exploits of Cyrus with growing expectation that their own deliverance from Babylon would not be long delayed. They knew that God was going one day to redeem them, for their prophets had always' added visions of hope to their warnings of doom. In these promises of Yahweh the exiles put their trust.

The clearest and most immediate of such promises of salvation are to be found in Isaiah 40–55. There is a continuing debate among biblical scholars whether these chapters were really written 150 or 200 years previously by Isaiah or came from the pen of some anonymous contemporary prophet. If the authorship is in dispute, however, the message is not.

Yahweh is not like the heathen idols. He is the living God, the Creator of the world, and he rules in the kingdoms of men. Even heathen rulers are the instruments of his power. It is he who had raised up Cyrus to deliver his people.

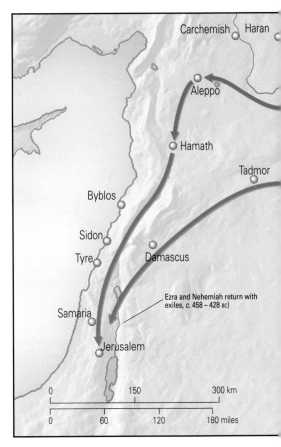

> Who has stirred up one from the east,
>   calling him in righteousness to his service?
> He hands nations over to him
>   and subdues kings before him.
> He turns them to dust with his sword,
>   to windblown chaff with his bow. . . .
> Who has done this and carried it through,
>   calling forth the generations from the
>   beginning?
> I, the LORD – with the first of them
>   and with the last – I am he. (Isa. 41:2, 4)

> This is what the LORD says to his anointed,
>   to Cyrus, whose right hand I take hold of
> to subdue nations before him
>   and to strip kings of their armor,
> to open doors before him
>   so that gates will not be shut:
> I will go before you
>   and will level the mountains;
> I will break down gates of bronze
>   and cut through bars of iron. . . .
> For the sake of Jacob my servant,
>   of Israel my chosen,
> I call you by name
>   and bestow on you a title of honor,
>   though you do not acknowledge me.
> I am the LORD, and there is no other;
>   apart from me there is no God.
> I will strengthen you,
>   though you have not acknowledged me.
> (Isa. 45:1-2, 4-5)

In the year 539 BC the longed-for salvation was given. Belshazzar King of Babylon saw the handwriting on the wall, and that very night Babylon fell into the hands of the Persians. Immediately Cyrus issued two decrees, authorizing the Jewish exiles to return home and to rebuild their temple. The actual text of the second decree, including the materials and measurements of the temple to be built, has been preserved in Ezra 6:3-5. That Cyrus should have issued such an edict is fully consistent with his known policy. As Professor F. F. Bruce has written:

> Cyrus' conception of empire was widely different from Assyria's. The Assyrians imposed the worship of their chief gods on their subjects, and boasted in the subjugation of their subjects' gods. Cyrus . . . had no intention of offending his subjects' religious susceptibilities by such a policy; on the contrary, he would conciliate their suscepti-bilities by playing the part of a worshipper of their various gods.[7]

It is hard to imagine the relief, the joy, the exultation of the Jewish exiles when the news of their deliverance reached them:

> When the LORD brought back the captives
>   to Zion,

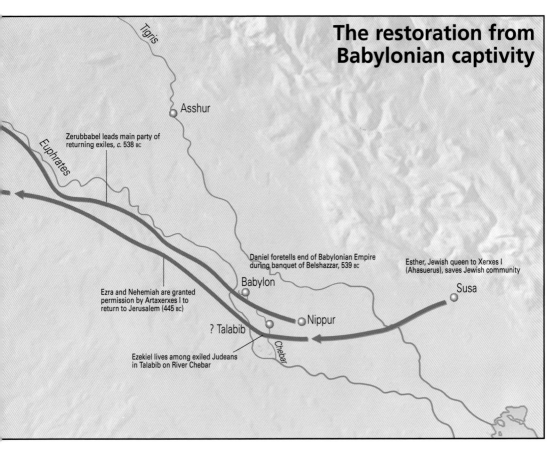

The restoration from Babylonian captivity

Asshur

Tigris

Euphrates

Zerubbabel leads main party of returning exiles, *c.* 538 BC

Ezra and Nehemiah are granted permission by Artaxerxes I to return to Jerusalem (445 BC)

Daniel foretells end of Babylonian Empire during banquet of Belshazzar, 539 BC

Babylon

? Talabib

Chebar

Nippur

Esther, Jewish queen to Xerxes I (Ahasuerus), saves Jewish community

Susa

Ezekiel lives among exiled Judeans in Talabib on River Chebar

we were like men who dreamed.
Our mouths were filled with laughter,
    our tongues with songs of joy.
Then it was said among the nations,
    "The LORD has done great things for
    them."
The LORD has done great things for us,
    and we are filled with joy. (Ps. 126:1-3)

Indeed, as the Israelites reflected on their past history and on the steadfast love of their covenant God, they linked together three outstanding examples of his mercy. In each case he took the initiative in his sovereign grace, and in each case he called his people to the land of promise. In the first he brought Abraham from Mesopotamia, in the second the twelve tribes from Egypt, and in the third the exiles from Babylon.

Not that all the exiles took advantage of Cyrus' decree and accepted repatriation. A large number remained. The Book of Esther

tells a dramatic story about some of them during the reign of Ahasuerus (Xerxes I), who ruled the Persian empire from 486-465 BC.

The restoration took place in three clearly defined stages. Not all scholars agree about the order of events, but I give the traditional view. First, Zerubbabel left (538 BC) to restore the temple, then Ezra (458 BC) to restore the laws and lastly Nehemiah (445 BC) to restore the city wall.

The first and main party of Jews left Babylon for home in 538 BC, a year or so after Cyrus' edict. They were led by Zerubbabel, grandson of King Jehoiachin, and Joshua the high priest. No sooner had they arrived in Jerusalem than they built the altar of burnt offering and laid the foundations of the temple. But then the Samaritans, on being refused the opportunity to collaborate, began to oppose the reconstruction. And the work ceased for about fifteen years.

That it restarted was due largely to the

encouragement of the prophets Haggai and Zechariah. Haggai reproved the people that they had built their own houses, while the Lord's house still lay in ruins:

> "Who of you is left who saw this house in its former glory? How does it look to you now? Does it not seem to you like nothing? But now be strong, O Zerubbabel," declares the LORD. "Be strong, O Joshua son of Jehozadak, the high priest. Be strong, all you people of the land," declares the LORD, "and work. For I am with you," declares the LORD Almighty. (Hag. 2:3-4)

Zechariah added his word of exhortation:

> The hands of Zerubbabel have laid the foundation of this temple; his hands will also complete it. (Zech. 4:9)

So the work began again in the year 520 and was finished in 515, some seventy years after the destruction of its predecessor.

We now jump nearly seventy-five years in the story to the second stage in the reconstruction of Israel's national life after the exile. This was led by Ezra, who was a priest and a scribe, and (as several scholars have described him) a kind of "Secretary of State for Jewish Affairs" in Babylonia. He was sent to Jerusalem by the Persian King Artaxerxes I (465-423 BC), with royal instructions "to inquire about Judah and Jerusalem with regard to the Law of your God" (Ezra 7:14). It was his task to regulate Israel's religious and moral responsibilities in accordance with the law.

Thirteen years later came Nehemiah, also sent by Artaxerxes, with authority to rebuild the city, and in particular its walls. On arrival he lost no time, but said to the local officials:

> You see the trouble we are in: Jerusalem lies in ruins, and its gates have been burned with fire. Come, let us rebuild the wall of Jerusalem, and we will no longer be in disgrace. (Neh. 2:17)

In spite of opposition and threats, the task was accomplished in 52 days. Then a great public assembly was held, at which Ezra and the Levites read God's law aloud and expounded it to the people. There followed a public confession of national sin and a renewal of the covenant to keep God's law in the future. Finally the rebuilt wall was dedicated amid much rejoicing, and "the sound of rejoicing in Jerusalem could be heard far away" (Neh. 12:43).

Unfortunately, as with previous national reformations, not all the undertakings of the people were kept. For when Nehemiah paid a second visit to Jerusalem a little later he found several sad irregularities, such as a failure to pay tithes, keep the Sabbath and avoid intermarriage with the heathen. But Nehemiah dealt faithfully with these matters according to God's law.

It may well be that the prophecy of Malachi belongs to this period, for reference is made in it to identical or very similar malpractices – for example, mixed marriage and divorce, laxity in the payment of tithes and the offering of blemished sacrifices to God.

The inter-testamental period

Israel had to wait another 400 years before her Messiah was born. This is called "the inter-testamental period," since no book of either the Old or the New Testament was written during it. The voice of prophecy was known to be silent. The author of the First Book of the Maccabees, which belongs to the Apocrypha[8] and describes the events of 175-134 BC, mentions this several times. He refers to a time of great affliction for Israel as being "worse than any since the day when prophets ceased to appear among them" (1 Macc. 9:27) and says that Simon was confirmed as leader and high priest in perpetuity "until a true prophet should appear" (1 Macc. 14:41).

Nevertheless, there are references to this period in the Book of Daniel, which is certainly one of the most difficult books in the Bible. Questions regarding its authorship, composition and interpretation continue to perplex scholars. It contains several remarkable dreams and visions, some of which are explained, while others are left wholly or partially without explanation.

In general, these predict the rise and fall of the great empires, especially as they affect the people of God. The best-known is Nebuchadnezzar's dream of a vast image of colossus, whose head was made of gold, breast and arms of silver, belly and thighs of bronze, legs of iron and feet of mixed iron and clay. Then (in the dream) a stone hit the feet, and the whole image was smashed to pieces. Daniel interpreted the dream as referring to successive empires. Traditionally, these have been understood as Babylon ("You are the head of gold"), Medo-Persia (the breast and arms), Greece, the kingdom which "will rule over all the earth," and Rome, which became "a divided kingdom" and did not stand. If this is right, then the stone, "cut out, but not by human hands," is the kingdom of the Messiah, of which Daniel says:

Alexander the Great, who defeated Persia in 331 BC.

> The God of heaven will set up a kingdom
> that will never be destroyed. . . . It will
> . . . endure forever. (Dan. 2:44)

These great empires did follow one another. They provided the setting within which God's drama of redemption was acted out. The Babylonian kingdom lasted from 605 to 539 BC, the Medo-Persian from 539 to 331, the Greek from 331 to 63, and the Roman from 63 on into the Christian era.

Later chapters of the Book of Daniel are more explicit. His vision recorded in chapter 8 is of a powerful ram, charging west, north and south, with no beast able to stand before it. Being two-horned, it represents the Medo-Persian empire (v. 20). Then "a goat . . . came from the west, crossing the whole earth" (v. 5). This is "the king of Greece" (v. 21), that is to say, the rise of the Greek empire under Philip of Macedon. The goat from the west "had a prominent horn" between its eyes, with which it struck the ram and broke its two horns. This prominent horn will be Philip's son, Alexander the Great, who after a series of dashing victories against Asia Minor, Tyre, Gad and Egypt, defeated the Persian army in 331 BC.

"The goat became very great" (v. 8), referring perhaps to the continuance of Alexander's campaign through Afghanistan as far as India. "But at the height of his power his large horn was broken off;" for he died in 323 BC in Babylon, and in its place four prominent horns grew up, for Alexander's empire was divided into four major regions under his generals – Macedonia and Greece, Thrace or West Asia, Syria and Babylonia (under Seleucus) and Egypt (under Ptolemy).

Of these the last two dominated the fortunes of Israel for the next 300 years. "They brought untold miseries upon the world" (1 Macc. 1:9). As in earlier centuries Palestine was a buffer territory between the Assyrian-Babylonian-Persian empires to the northeast and the Egyptian to the southwest, so now Judea was caught between the Seleucids ruling

Syria and the Ptolemies ruling Egypt. The former are termed "the king of the north" in Daniel 11 and the latter "the king of the south." Both dynasties lasted until the middle of the first century BC, and relations between them varied from uneasy coexistence to active hostility and warfare. Judea kept coming under the control now of the one, now of the other.

Returning to Daniel's vision of the he-goat, whose one conspicuous horn had been replaced by "four prominent horns," the vision developed as follows:

> Out of one of them came another horn,
> which started small but grew in power to
> the south and to the east and toward the
> Beautiful Land. It grew until it reached
> the host of the heavens. . . . It set itself up
> to be as great as the Prince of the host; it
> took away the daily sacrifice from him,
> and the place of his sanctuary was
> brought low . . . and truth was thrown to
> the ground. (Dan. 8:9-12)

This "little horn" is interpreted as "a stern-faced king" who "will cause astounding devastation and . . . will destroy the mighty men and the holy people" (Dan. 8:23-24). He seems without doubt to be Antiochus Epiphanes (175-163 BC), who is further designated "a contemptible person" in Daniel 11:21.

In 167 BC Antiochus Epiphanes ordered the suspension of the temple sacrifices, the destruction of the Scriptures, and the discontinuance of circumcision, Sabbath observance and the food laws. The climax came in December, when a new altar was dedicated to Zeus, "the Lord of heaven" (of whom Antiochus claimed to be an incarnation), and unclean animals were offered upon it. Thus the continual burnt offering was taken away and the sanctuary profaned by "the abomination that causes desolation" (Dan. 11:31).

The king's edict applied to the provinces as well as to Jerusalem, on pain of death. Many complied. Many others resisted, welcoming death rather than defilement. The most fearful tortures and massacres took place, some of which are described in the Books of the Maccabees. The martyrs died "by sword and flame, by captivity and plunder" (Dan. 11:33 RSV). It is probably to them that the author of the Letter to the Hebrews was referring when he wrote:

> Others were tortured and refused to be
> released, so that they might gain a better
> resurrection. Some faced jeers and
> flogging, while still others were chained
> and put in prison. They were stoned; they
> were sawn in two; they were put to death
> by the sword . . . the world was not
> worthy of them. (Heb. 11:35-38)

Organized resistance was sparked off by the high priest Mattathias who took it upon himself to kill both a Jewish traitor and the king's officer who was inviting them to sacrifice. This led to a period of guerrilla warfare, in which pagan altars were demolished, Jewish children forcibly circumcised and compromisers slain.

Mattathias died in 166 and was succeeded in turn by three of his sons – Judas who was surnamed Maccabaeus, an epithet meaning probably "the hammer" or "the eradicator" (166-161 BC), Jonathan (161-143 BC) and Simon (143-135 BC). The details of their revolt against Gentile rule and of their extraordinary military exploits are recorded in the Books of the Maccabees.

Probably the most triumphant moment in their history came in 164 BC when, under the leadership of Judas Maccabaeus, the temple area was purified and the temple itself restored, a new altar was constructed and dedicated, and the sacrifices began to be offered again.

> On the anniversary of the day when the
> Gentiles had profaned it, on that very
> day, it was rededicated, with hymns of
> thanksgiving, to the music of harps and
> lutes and cymbals. (1 Macc. 4:54)

Israel under the Maccabees

Tyre

PHOENICIA

Antiochia

Gischala

Seleucia

Ptolemais

Sea of Galilee

Gabara

Sepphoris

Hippos

Ditum

Geba

Mount Tabor

Philoteria

Abila

Dora

GALILEE

Gadara

GILEAD

Strato's Tower

Scythopolis

Pella

SAMARIA

Samaria

Gerasa

Apollonia

Shechem

Mount Gerizim

Jordan

Joppa

Arimathea

PEREA

Lydda

Philadelphia

JUDEA

Jamnia

Jericho

Emmaus

Samaga

Azotus

Jerusalem

Ascalon

Medeba

Anthedon

Beth-zur

Marisa

Gaza

Hebron

Orda

Gerar

En-gedi

IDUMEA

Dead Sea

MOAB

Raphia

Beersheba

Malatha

PARALIA

MEDITERRANEAN SEA

Rhinocorura

NABATAEA

Zoar

Independent Judea after Jonathan's campaigns, 142 BC
Land conquered by Simon, 142-135 BC
John Hyrcanus I, 128-104 BC
Aristobulus I, 104-103 BC
Alexander Jannaeus, 103-76 BC
Boundary of Hasmonean kingdom, 76 BC
Hellenistic city

0   25   50 km

0   10   20   30 miles

Some Old Testament dates to remember

c. 1280	The Exodus from Egypt
c. 1050	The Monarchy established under King Saul
c. 1010	King David ascends the throne
c. 930	King Solomon dies. The Divided Monarchy begins – Israel lasting until 722 and Judah until 586
722	The Fall of Samaria and the end of the Northern Kingdom
701	Jerusalem besieged by Sennacherib
612	The Fall of Nineveh, Assyria's capital
597	The Fall of Jerusalem. The Babylonian captivity begins
586	Jerusalem is destroyed
539	The Edict of Cyrus. The first exiles return about a year later
515	The restored Temple is opened
458	Ezra arrives in Jerusalem
445	Nehemiah arrives in Jerusalem
323	Alexander the Great dies
167	Antiochus Epiphanes profanes the Temple. The Maccabean revolt begins
63	Pompey reaches Jerusalem; Judea becomes a Roman protectorate

Great Empires of Old Testament times

The dates BC are related to each empire's sovereignty as it affected Israel.

845–612	Assyrian
612–605	Egyptian
605–539	Babylonian
539–331	Persian
331–63	Greek (including Seleucids and Ptolemies)
63–	Roman

The war of independence continued for many years, and political autonomy was not secured until 128 BC under John Hyrcanus, Simon's son. He was priest and leader, and some said prophet and king as well. He and his sons annexed a good deal of the territory surrounding Judea.

But in 63 BC the Roman general Pompey entered Jerusalem, and penetrated even into the holy of holies, to the horror of the priests. Judea became a Roman protectorate, and Jewish independence was lost again.

In 40 BC Herod, who had already been mili-tary prefect of Galilee and later joint tetrarch of Judea, was made by the Roman senate "King of the Jews." Gradually he reconquered his kingdom and in the year 37 BC besieged and took Jerusalem, executing Antigonus, the last of the Maccabean priest-rulers. Herod was always unpopular as an Edomite foreigner (although a Jew by religion). Nevertheless he reigned for thirty-three years. It was under his sponsorship that in 19 BC the great reconstruction of the temple began. The work continued almost until AD 70, when the temple was again and finally destroyed, this time by the Roman army.

Throughout the uneasy period of Maccabean rule, important movements were developing in the Jewish community which later hardened into the various religious parties of our Lord's day.

The revolt of the Maccabees was first and foremost a religious protest, a defiant refusal to compromise with Hellenizing influences. Nothing aroused the indignation of the Maccabees more than the time-serving high priests, installed by favor of the Seleucid kings. They and their followers are the "renegade Jews" of the Books of the Maccabees, who wanted even to remove the marks of circumcision and so to ape Greek ways as to wear Greek dress and to build themselves a Greek stadium in which to compete in the games.

The Jews who avoided all contamination from Hellenizing influences were the *Hasidim*, or pious ones. They were thorough- going separatists; the ancestors of the Pharisees, concerned for religious rather than political freedom.

The Hasmoneans (the Maccabees' family name) were not content with religious freedom; they wanted national independence too. They got involved in all kinds of political intrigue, and their successors were the Sadducees.

The political extremists, wanting to continue the Maccabean struggle for independence, were the Zealots. They were revolutionary firebrands, determined at all costs to wrest their freedom from Rome.

When, in the fullness of time, Jesus Christ came, the people once tried "to come and make him king by force" (John 6:15). But he withdrew from them. He had to explain that,

although he was indeed a king, his kingdom was "not of this world" (John 18:33-38). The freedom he offered was freedom from the tyranny of sin.

> If you hold to my teaching, you are really my disciples. Then you will know the truth, and the truth will set you free. (John 8:31-32)

NOTES

1. The order in which the Old Testament books are placed is different in the Hebrew and the Christian Bibles. The Christian Church followed the arrangement in the Septuagint, the Greek translation made in the second century BC.

2. Although less familiar than "Jehovah," this is probably the correct rendering of the Hebrew name YHWH, whose significance was revealed to Moses. See Exodus 3:13-15. It is usually translated "the LORD" in English versions.

3. I have more to say on the whole question of biblical interpretation in chapter 7.

4. A temple-tower constructed of brick in the shape of a terraced pyramid and set on an artificial mound.

Ziggurats are known to have been built in Babylonia as early as c. 3000 BC.

5. For example, to Abraham, Gen. 15:16; 17:1-8; 22:15-18; to Isaac, 26:1-5; to Jacob, 28:13-15 and 35:9-12.

6. Some, however, would date both Jonah and Joel earlier than Amos.

7. F. F. Bruce, *Israel and the Nations* (Paternoster, 1963, illustrated edition, 1969), p. 100.

8. The "Apocrypha" is an expression given to certain books which were not part of the Hebrew canon of the Old Testament. Some contain material which Christians read for ethical rather than doctrinal instruction.

4. The Story of the Bible (New Testament)

❖ *In what ways are the four Gospels different from one another, and in what ways are they similar?*

❖ *In what different ways did people respond to Jesus, from his birth to his ascension?*

❖ *How does the New Testament show that God's covenant with Israel has been extended to the world?*

The previous chapter sketched the story of the Old Testament, covering several thousands of years. In this chapter an outline of the New Testament story will be given, covering less than a century. It is a fascinating tale of the words and deeds of Jesus of Nazareth, first of what he "began to do and teach" during his life on earth and then of what he continued to do and teach through his chosen apostles after he had returned to his Father and constituted his church.

The four Gospels

Although there are a few scattered references to Jesus in contemporary secular writings, especially in Tacitus and Suetonius, the main source of our information about him remains the four "Gospels." They are rightly so called. For strictly speaking they are not biography, but testimony. They bear witness to Christ and to the good news of his salvation. Therefore their authors select, arrange and present their material according to their purpose as "evangelists." This gives us no ground to doubt their trustworthiness, however. On the contrary, we should approach the Gospels with confidence, not suspicion. There are many reasons for doing so.

• First, the four evangelists were certainly Christian men, and Christian men are honest men to whom truth matters.

• Second, they give evidence of their impartial-ity by including incidents which they would clearly have preferred to omit. For example, although by that time Peter was a highly respected church leader, neither his boastfulness nor his denial of Jesus is suppressed.

• Third, they claim either to be themselves eyewitnesses of Jesus or to report the experience of eyewitnesses. Although it seems likely that no Gospel was actually published earlier than AD 60, we must not imagine that there was an empty gap between the ascension of Jesus and that date. This was the period of "oral tradition," in which the words and deeds of Jesus were used in Christian worship, evangelism and the teaching of converts, and so began to be collected in writing. Luke says he drew on "many" such compilations (Luke 1:1-4).

• Fourth, Jesus seems to have taught like a Jewish rabbi. He gave his instruction in forms (for example, parables and epigrams) which a tenacious oriental memory would have had no difficulty in learning by heart, and in addition he promised that the Holy Spirit would stimulate the apostles' memory (John 14:25-26).

• Fifth, if God said and did something absolutely unique and decisive through Jesus, as Christians believe, it is inconceivable that he would have allowed it to be lost in the mists of antiquity. If he intended future generations to benefit from it, he must have made provision for it to be reliably reported, in order to make the good news available to all men in all times and places. What he decided to do was to pre-

The Parthenon, Athens. Luke is the only Gentile among the New Testament authors and traveled widely as one of Paul's companions.

sent the one gospel in four Gospels.

As we read the Gospels it becomes clear that they tell the same story, yet differently. The first three (Matthew, Mark and Luke) are usually known as the "synoptic" Gospels because their stories run parallel and present a "synoptic" (that is, similar) account of Jesus' life. Matthew and Luke appear to have known Mark's Gospel and to have incorporated most of it in theirs. They also have some additional common material, generally known as "Q" (the first letter of the German word *Quelle*, a source), though each has independent information as well. Scholars are not agreed how far the Synoptic Gospels were known or used by John, but most believe that his Gospel was the last to be published.

The Gospel of Mark is the shortest and probably the earliest of the four. The style is terse, the stories are vivid and the tone is exciting, with everything happening "immediately" after something else. The apostle Peter referred to Mark as his "son" (1 Pet. 5:13; cf. Acts 12:11-12), and the second-century fathers

Papias and Irenaeus described him as Peter's interpreter. It may well be, therefore, that Peter's memoirs or preaching or both have been preserved in Mark's Gospel, which has obvious similarities to Peter's First Letter.

It is possible that Matthew's name became attached to the first Gospel because "Q," consisting largely of the sayings of Jesus, was his collection. We know he was a tax collector (Matt. 9:9), so that he would have been used to making notes and keeping records. Certainly, according to Papias, "Matthew compiled the *logia* – sayings – in Hebrew (that is, Aramaic, the language spoken by Jesus), and everybody translated them as he was able."[1] His Gospel is very Jewish and reveals his special interest in the fulfillment of prophecy.

Luke is the only Gentile among the New Testament authors. He had himself traveled widely and as one of Paul's companions would have absorbed the apostle's teaching about God's grace to the Gentiles. Consequently, he emphasizes the universal scope of Christ's love, as illustrated in his care for the despised

Luke describes how Mary traveled south with Joseph to Bethlehem, where Jesus was born.

"outsiders" of contemporary Judaism – women and children, publicans and sinners, leprosy sufferers, Samaritans and Gentiles.

Every reader of John's Gospel is immediately struck by the differences between it and the Synoptic Gospels in subject matter, theological emphasis, literary style and vocabulary. Its tone is more "philosophical," as Jesus is presented as the Logos ("Word") of God and the Light of the World, and his offer is more of eternal life than of the kingdom. His claims to deity are more outspoken. And the Gospel's framework consists of a series of "signs," interspersed with and interpreted by long and involved speeches. So great have these differences seemed to many scholars that they have written at length about "The Problem of the Fourth Gospel." Some deny that it was written by the apostle John, and even attribute it to the second century AD. At the same time, recent writers have drawn attention to the "Jewishness" of this Gospel and have demonstrated that its author was familiar with contemporary Palestinian geography and culture, and is a historically reliable witness. Without doubt the distinctive emphases of the Fourth

Gospel enrich the diversity of the New Testament.[2]

John had evidently meditated long and deeply on the teaching of Jesus. His own thought and language became so completely assimilated to his Lord's that it is not always easy to tell when the one's words end and the other's begin. He leaves us in no uncertainty about the purpose of his Gospel, for he himself defines it for us. He as, he says, recorded a number of the "signs" which Jesus did, so that readers will believe in him as the Christ, God's Son, and so receive eternal life (John 20:30-31). True to his avowed purpose he assembles a variety both of signs and of witnesses, in order to demonstrate the unique "glory" of Jesus.

The birth and youth of Jesus

Each evangelist begins his story at a different place. Mark plunges almost immediately into Jesus' public ministry, heralded as it was by John the Baptist. John goes to the other extreme and reaches back into a past eternity to the pre-incarnate existence of Jesus Christ.

As "the Word" he was with God in the very beginning. Indeed, he was himself God, and was active in the creation of the universe. Long before he actually "came" into the world by becoming flesh, he was continually "coming into the world" as the true light (though unrecognized) to enlighten every man with the light of reason and of conscience (John 1:1-14).

It is Matthew and Luke who tell us the actual story of Jesus' birth. Luke tells it through the eyes of the Virgin Mary (perhaps even from her own lips), while Matthew tells it from Joseph's point of view.

Luke records the angel's announcement to Mary that both her conception and the boy to be born will be supernatural:

> The angel answered, "The Holy Spirit will come upon you, and the power of the Most High will overshadow you. So the holy one to be born will be called the Son of God." (Luke 1:35)

Luke goes on to describe how Mary shared her secret with her cousin Elizabeth who was shortly to give birth to John the Baptist; how

Joseph (whose painful dilemma over Mary's pregnancy Matthew describes) traveled south with her from Nazareth to Bethlehem, their ancestral home, in order to comply with the requirements of the imperial census; and how it was in the stable of a Bethlehem inn that Jesus was born and laid, by his mother, in a manger.

Although the world's Savior was born in such lowliness, and received no public acclaim, there were those who came to pay homage to him. Luke tells of certain shepherds who learned the good news from angels, and Matthew of mysterious Magi – astrologer-priests from Persia – who were guided to him by a star. There seems to have been a deliberate providence in bringing these two contrasting groups. For the shepherds were Jewish, untutored and poor, while the Magi were Gentile, cultured and rich. Yet the barriers of race, education and social rank were transcended by their common worship of the infant Christ. They foreshadow the colorful diversity of Christ's followers.

Not everybody worshiped him, however. Herod the Great, who in the course of his reign murdered every possible rival, was

Jesus was brought up in the hilltop town of Nazareth in Galilee, in a home that was far from affluent.

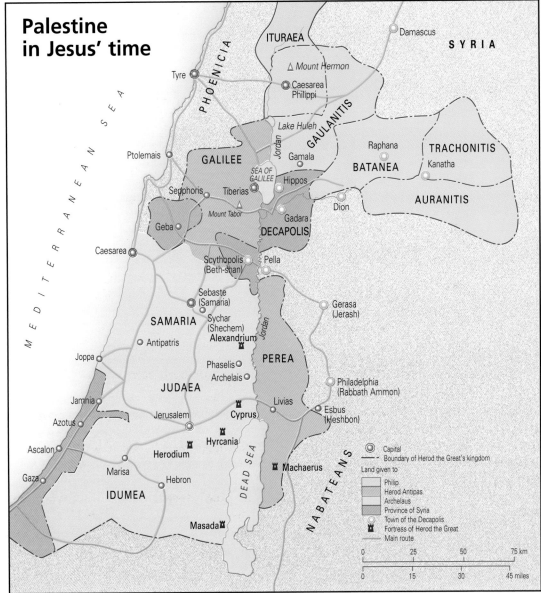

Palestine in Jesus' time

SYRIA

ITURAEA

Damascus

PHOENICIA

△ Mount Hermon

Tyre

Caesarea Philippi

Lake Huleh

GAULANITIS

Ptolemais

GALILEE

Jordan

Gamala

Raphana

TRACHONITIS

BATANEA

Kanatha

SEA OF GALILEE

Sepphoris

Tiberias

Hippos

AURANITIS

Mount Tabor △

Dion

Geba

Gadara

DECAPOLIS

Caesarea

Scythopolis (Beth-shan)

Pella

Sebaste (Samaria)

Gerasa (Jerash)

SAMARIA

Sychar (Shechem)

Antipatris

Alexandrium

Jordan

Joppa

Phaselis

PEREA

Archelais

Philadelphia (Rabbath Ammon)

JUDAEA

Livias

Jamnia

Jerusalem

Cyprus

Esbus (Heshbon)

Azotus

Hyrcania

DEAD SEA

Ascalon

Herodium

Machaerus

Gaza

Marisa

Hebron

NABATEANS

IDUMEA

Masada

○ Capital
- - Boundary of Herod the Great's kingdom
Land given to
  Philip
  Herod Antipas
  Archelaus
  Province of Syria
○ Town of the Decapolis
⚏ Fortress of Herod the Great
— Main route

| 0 | 25 | 50 | 75 km |
| 0 | 15 | 30 | 45 miles |

alarmed to hear the Magi say they had come to honor the King of the Jews. For *he* was the king of the Jews. So who was this? Warned by God of Herod's resolve to destroy the child, Joseph and Mary fled with him to the safety of Egypt, and the one who was born to rule became a refugee.

Jesus was brought up in Nazareth in Galilee. His home must have been far from affluent, for when presenting their firstborn son to the Lord, Joseph and Mary brought a pair of pigeons as their offering, prescribed in the law

for those who could not afford a lamb. But it would have been a happy home, shared (as the years passed) by other children of the family. Joseph worked as a carpenter and taught his trade to Jesus, while Mary would have nurtured him in godliness and righteousness by teaching him to read the Scriptures and to pray. In the beautiful countryside around he would have become familiar with the lilies of the field and the birds of the air, to which he later referred, and with the living God who clothes and feeds them.

The traditional site of John's baptisms in the Jordan river. Jesus persuaded John to baptize him in the Jordan.

The only incident from Jesus' boyhood which is recorded in the Gospels took place when he reached the age of twelve and was taken up to Jerusalem for the Passover, to prepare at thirteen to become a "son of the commandment." After the festival he was accidentally left behind. His parents found him "sitting among the teachers, listening to them and asking them questions." These Jewish leaders were "amazed at his understanding and his answers," and his parents were perplexed when he asked them: "Didn't you know I had to be in my Father's house?" (Luke 2:49). His sense of communion with God as Father and of compulsion to do his will were to remain with him throughout his later ministry.

Apart from this story, recorded in Luke 2:41-51, the verses which immediately precede and follow it tell us all we need to know about Jesus' youth. Both are bridge verses, verse 40 spanning the twelve years from his birth and verse 52 the remaining eighteen or so years before his public ministry began. Both tell us that during these years Jesus was developing naturally, yet per-fectly, in body, mind and spirit. Here is verse 52:

And Jesus grew in wisdom and stature,
and in favor with God and men.

Although the evangelists are not concerned to give us a strictly chronological account of the Lord's public ministry, it appears from John's Gospel to have lasted approximately three years.[3] We can call the first the year of obscurity, the second the year of popularity and the third the year of adversity.

The year of obscurity

All four Gospels tell something of the ministry of John the Baptist. He was an ascetic, wearing nothing but a camel's hair cloak with a leather girdle, and eating an austerity diet of locusts and wild honey. Through his lips, after a silence of several centuries, the authentic voice of prophecy was again heard, as he summoned the people to repentance and to his baptism of repentance in preparation for the coming of the Messiah. Large crowds flocked to the River Jordan to listen to his preaching and to be baptized.

When Jesus presented himself for baptism John protested, for he had pronounced himself unworthy even to stoop down and undo the sandal strap of the one coming after him. But Jesus was resolved to fulfill all righteousness and, though he had no sins of his own to confess, to identify himself with the sins of others. So he persuaded John to baptize him. At that moment the Holy Spirit came upon him like a dove, and the Father's voice was heard proclaiming him, in words of Old Testament Scripture, both his beloved Son and his suffering servant (Matt. 3; cf. Ps. 2:7 and Isa. 42:1).

Immediately after his baptism, the same Spirit who descended upon him "drove" him into the Judean desert. There he fasted for forty days in order no doubt to seek strength through prayer for the ministry to which he had just been commissioned. During this period he was also savagely tempted to compromise with the devil by trying to attain right ends by wrong means. But the Lord's hidden years of Scripture meditation stood him in good stead. He was able to counter every diabolical suggestion with an apt biblical rejoinder. For he was determined to live according to Scripture and so obey his Father's will.

It appears that after the temptation Jesus returned to the River Jordan and gave the two brothers Andrew and Simon Peter a kind of preliminary call to his service. They left John the Baptist and began to follow Jesus (John 1:35-42).

Returning north to Galilee, Jesus performed his first miracle, changing water into wine at a wedding in Cana. It symbolized his claim to introduce a new order, and by it he revealed his glory, and his disciples put their faith in him (John 2:1-11).

Next he went up to Jerusalem for the Passover and boldly ejected from the temple courts the merchants and money changers who had profaned it. When challenged about his action, he replied enigmatically:

Destroy this temple, and I will raise it again in three days. (John 2:19)

It was another dramatic claim about the new order. For he was alluding not only to his physical body which would be raised from death in three days, but to his spiritual body, the church, which would live in the power of the resurrection. His church would also be a new and spiritual temple, God's dwelling place, to replace Herod's material temple which would be destroyed.

One man who was deeply impressed by the early teaching and miracles of Jesus was a leading Jewish rabbi called Nicodemus. He came under cover of dark for a private interview, to be told by Jesus that the indispensable condition for seeing and entering God's kingdom was a new birth from above by the power of the Holy Spirit. Some time later, on his way north again into Galilee, Jesus repeated this message or something very similar, though not now to a Jewish man, but to a Samaritan woman. She needed "living water," he said, an inner "spring of water welling up to eternal life:' which would quench her thirst and which only he could supply.[4]

Other details of the first year of Jesus' ministry are not recorded. Most of it seems to have been spent in Judea. It was a transition period, during which his ministry overlapped with the ministry of his forerunner, John the Baptist. The disciples of Jesus were also baptizing. And gradually those following Jesus came to outnumber those following John, which John accepted with beautiful humility, saying: "He must become greater; I must become less" (John 3:30).

But this situation was the signal for Jesus to leave Judea for Galilee. Soon afterward, John was arrested and imprisoned, and the Galilean ministry, the year of popularity, began (John 3:24; 4:1-3; Mark 1:14).

The year of popularity

Attending the synagogue service one Sabbath day in his hometown Nazareth, Jesus was given the scroll of Isaiah from which to read:

Remains of the 3rd century AD synagogue at Capernaum. Jesus made his headquarters at Capernaum after being forced to leave Nazareth.

The Spirit of the Lord is on me,
  because he has anointed me
  to preach the good news to the poor.
He has sent me to proclaim freedom for the
  prisoners
  and recovery of sight for the blind,
  to release the oppressed,
  to proclaim the year of the Lord's favor.
  (Luke 4:18-19)

During the sermon which followed, Jesus dared to claim that he was himself the fulfillment of this Scripture. At first the congregation was amazed at his gracious words. But when he went on to suggest that his ministry, like that of the prophets Elijah and Elisha, would be more acceptable to the Gentiles than to Israel, they were so infuriated that they drove him out of the city and tried even to push him over the nearby cliff. It was a foretaste of his coming rejection, and forced him to move his home and headquarters from Nazareth to Capernaum on the northwest shore of the lake.

From Capernaum during the rest of this second year Jesus made innumerable journeys throughout Galilee. Matthew sums up what form his ministry took:

Jesus went through Galilee, teaching in
their synagogues, preaching the good
news of the kingdom, and healing every
disease and sickness among the people.
(Matt. 4:23; cf. 9:35)

First, he preached. Mark says that the topic of his preaching was "the gospel of God," summarized in these words:

The time has come. . . . The kingdom of
God is near. Repent and believe the good
news! (Mark 1:14-15)

This divine kingdom was the personal reign of God in the lives of human beings, and he (Jesus) had come to inaugurate it. Its arrival was in fulfillment of Old Testament expectation, and in order to "receive," "enter" or "inherit" the kingdom people must repent and believe, humbly accepting its privileges and submitting to its demands like little children.

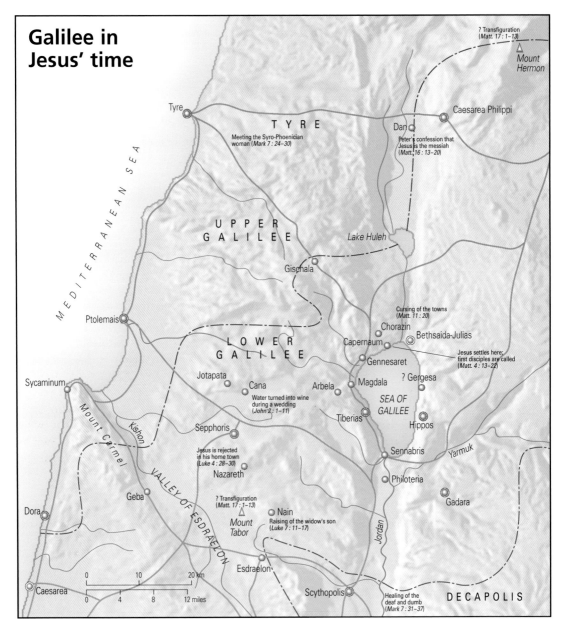

Galilee in Jesus' time

? Transfiguration (Matt. 17 : 1–13)

Mount Hermon

Tyre

Caesarea Philippi

T Y R E

Dan

Meeting the Syro-Phoenician woman (Mark 7 : 24–30)

Peter's confession that Jesus is the messiah (Matt. 16 : 13–20)

MEDITERRANEAN SEA

U P P E R
G A L I L E E

Lake Huleh

Gischala

Cursing of the towns (Matt. 11 : 20)

Chorazin
Ptolemais

Bethsaida-Julias

Capernaum

Jesus settles here; first disciples are called (Matt. 4 : 13–22)

L O W E R
G A L I L E E

Gennesaret

Jotapata

Sycaminum

Cana

Arbela

Magdala

? Gergesa

Water turned into wine during a wedding (John 2 : 1–11)

SEA OF GALILEE

Mount Carmel

Kishon

Sepphoris

Tiberias

Hippos

Jesus is rejected in his home town (Luke 4 : 28–30)

Sennabris

Yarmuk

VALLEY OF ESDRAELON

Nazareth

Philoteria

Geba

Gadara

Dora

? Transfiguration (Matt. 17 : 1–13)

Nain

Mount Tabor

Raising of the widow's son (Luke 7 : 11–17)

Jordan

Esdraelon

0   10   20 km
0   4   8   12 miles

Caesarea

Scythopolis

Healing of the deaf and dumb (Mark 7 : 31–37)

D E C A P O L I S

Next, he taught. That is, he did more than announce the gospel of the kingdom and call people to enter it; he went on to teach his disciples the law of the kingdom. Of this we have no better summary than the "Sermon on the Mount," perhaps consisting of instruction given over a protracted period. Its integrating theme is the call to his disciples to be different from both pagans and Pharisees. They must not try (like the casuists) to dodge the law's demands, or (like the hypocrites) to practice their piety before men, but realize that God sees in secret and looks on the heart. His disciples must be quite different from the Gentiles as well, in their love, their prayers and their ambition. They must love their enemies as well their friends, renounce vain repetitions in prayer for an intelligent but childlike approach to their Father, and seek first, as the supreme good, not their own material necessities but the rule and the righteousness of God.

The people were astounded by Jesus'

authority, for he taught neither like the scribes (who invariably quoted their authorities), nor even like the prophets (who spoke in the name of Yahweh), but with his own authority and in his own name, declaring "truly, truly, I say to you."

Moreover, he enforced his teaching with unforgettable parables, which illustrated the love of God for sinners (for example, the prodigal son), the necessity of humble trust in God's mercy for salvation (for example, the Pharisee and the publican), the love which we ought to have even for those who have no claim on us (for example, the good Samaritan), the way God's Word is received and God's kingdom grows (for example, the sower and the mustard seed), the responsibility of disciples to develop and exercise their gifts (the pounds and the talents), and the judgment of those who reject the gospel (for example, the wheat and the weeds).

Thirdly, he healed. He performed other miracles too, exhibiting his power over nature by stilling a storm on the lake, walking on water and multiplying loaves and fishes. But his commonest miracles were healing miracles, effected, now by a touch of the hand, now by a bare word of command. From one point of view, the sufficient explanation of his healing ministry is his love, for he was moved to compassion by the sight of every form of suffering. But, in addition, his miracles were "signs" both of God's kingdom and of his own deity. They signified that the Messiah's reign had begun, as the Scriptures had foretold. It was with this evidence that Jesus sought to reassure the doubts of John the Baptist in prison:

Go back and report to John what you have seen and heard: The blind receive their sight, the lame walk, those who have leprosy are cured, the deaf hear, the dead are raised, and the good news is preached to the poor. (Luke 7:22)

Similarly the miracles were signs that the forces of evil were in retreat before the advancing kingdom of God:

But if I drive out demons by the finger of God, then the kingdom of God has come to you. (Luke 11:20)

The miracles were also signs that Jesus was the Son of God, for each was an acted parable, dramatizing one of his divine claims. The feeding of the 5,000 set forth visibly his claim to be the bread of life, his healing of the man born blind his claim to be the light of the world, and his raising of the dead his claim to be the resurrection and the life.

In this threefold work of preaching, teaching and healing, Jesus also involved the Twelve. He seems to have chosen and called them early in this second year of his public ministry and, by surnaming them "apostles," to have indicated the work to which they were being commissioned. I shall enlarge on this in a later chapter when we consider their unique authority. In human terms they were a motley and unpromising group, including four fishermen, one tax collector, at least one political zealot and another who proved to be a traitor. Yet he kept them with him, training them by what they saw and heard, and sent them out two by two, endowed with his authority to preach and to heal like him.

During the Galilean ministry the crowds kept growing. The whole countryside became tense with excitement and expectation:

Crowds of people came to hear him and to be healed of their sicknesses.
(Luke 5:15)

The high tide of Jesus' popularity seems to have been reached at the time of the feeding of the 5,000. It took place just after the beheading of John the Baptist, an ugly omen of the turn of the tide. Since the 5,000 were all men, apart from women and children (Matt. 14:21), the total crowd must have been more than double that number. When the hunger of all had been satisfied as a result of the miraculous multiplication of five barley loaves and two pickled fish, the buzz of excitement reached fever pitch. The word began to go round the

Niches for images of classical deities at Banias, biblical Caesarea Philippi, near Mount Hermon.

crowd, "Surely this is the Prophet who is to come into the world." And as the rumor spread, the people made up their minds. They were determined to come and make him king by force, that is, their national leader to liberate them from the dominion of Rome. But Jesus caught wind of it, and "withdrew again to a mountain by himself" (John 6:14-15).

The year of adversity

Having returned to Capernaum on the other side of the lake, Jesus preached a sermon in the synagogue, using the miracle of the loaves and fishes as his text. He had not come to be a political revolutionary. He was the bread of life, he said. Anyone who came to him and believed in him would never again be hungry or thirsty. And the bread he would give for the life of the world was his flesh. Immediately a dispute broke out among the Jews:

How can this man give us his flesh to eat?

Even his disciples found it a hard saying, and many of them turned back and no longer followed him (John 6:52, 66). The tide had turned.

So now Jesus again "withdrew" and made more distant expeditions, beyond the boundaries of Galilee. He went to Tyre and Sidon in the northwest (Mark 7:24), and to the Decapolis, a region southeast of the lake (Mark 7:31). Then later he traveled north again, this time to Caesarea Philippi, in the foothills of Mount Hermon (Mark 8:27). Here a very important incident took place, which forms a kind of watershed in the Gospel narrative. Jesus asked the Twelve who people were saying he was, and they gave him the answers of popular speculation, that he was John the Baptist, Elijah or one of the prophets. But who did the Twelve say he was? Immediately Peter replied, "You are the Christ."

Our Lord's rejoinder comes as a shock to many readers, for he commanded them to tell no one about him (Mark 8:30). But the next verse explains the riddle:

He then began to teach them that the Son of Man must suffer many things and be rejected by the elders, chief priests and teachers of the law, and that he must be killed and after three days rise again. He spoke plainly about this. (Mark 8:31-32)

Jerusalem in Jesus' time

Josephus' Third Wall

Kidron Valley

N

Sheep Pool
(Pool of
Bethesda)

Tower Gate

Fish Gate

1. Triumphal entry
of Jesus

Antonia
Fortress

Israel Pool

3. Return to
Bethany

Sheep
Gate

Golden
Gate

Tyropoeon Valley

Temple

Mount of
Olives

Golgotha

8. Crucifixion

Warren's
Gate

Beautiful
Gate

2. Cleansing
of the
Temple

*Garden of
Gethsemane*

5. Arrest of Jesus

Barclay's
Gate

Court
of the
Gentiles

Ophel

Pinnacle of
the Temple

Gennath
Gate

? Palace of
Herod Antipas

7. Trial by Pontius
Pilate

Hulda
Gates

Herod's
Palace

Aqueduct

UPPER CITY

Valley
Gate

Gihon
Spring

Tyropoeon Valley

Kidron Valley

From Bethany

*Hezekiah's
Tunnel*

6. Night hearing
before the high
priest

? House of
Caiaphas

4. Last Supper

Upper
Room

ESSENE QUARTER

LOWER CITY

Aqueduct

Gate of the
Essenes

Pool of
Solomon

Pool of
Siloam

Aqueduct

Water
Gate

Valley of Hinnom

Area of the city at the time of Jesus
Modern city wall
Route of Jesus' last days

| 0 | 250 | 500 metres |
| 0 | 250 | 500 yards |

Jesus' command to silence, repeated after several of the miracles, was due to his desire to keep his Messiahship secret so long as the people misunderstood its nature, as exemplified in their attempt to make him a king by force. But now that Peter had clearly confessed his faith, Jesus "began" to teach the necessity of his sufferings and to do so "plainly" – that is, openly. At first Peter could not accept this truth. But Jesus insisted on it and added that the same pattern of glory through suffering or life through death would be the experience of his followers as well (Mark 8:34-38).

Six days later according to the synoptic evangelists Jesus took Peter, James and John with him up a "high mountain" (perhaps Hermon?) and was transfigured before them, his face and clothing becoming suffused with a bright light. It was a preview of his glory, the glory of his kingdom and of his resurrection body, the glory to which he would one day come through suffering.

When Jesus returned to Galilee it was for a largely private visit, since he was continuing to teach the disciples about his coming sufferings, and subsequent resurrection (Mark 9:30-31). Soon after he began his journey south (Mark 10:1). Indeed, he "resolutely set out for Jerusalem" (Luke 9:51), and on the way continued to emphasize the same things (for example, Mark 10:32-24, 45). Luke supplies a number of details about this journey and its accompanying instruction which the other evangelists do not record (see Luke 9:51–18:14). He tells us that Jesus referred to a baptism of suffering which he had to undergo and to his sense of distress until it was accomplished (Luke 12:50). Later he said:

We are going up to Jerusalem, and everything that is written by the prophets about the Son of Man will be fulfilled. (Luke 18:31)

The approach to Jerusalem was through Jericho, an oasis not far from where the Jordan flows into the Dead Sea. Here Jesus gave sight to blind Bartimaeus and salvation to Zacchaeus the shady tax collector (Luke 18:35–19:10). Then came the steep ascent along the desert road towards the holy city.

The impression conveyed by the synoptic evangelists is that Jesus went straight to Jerusalem and to the events of his last week. We know from John's Gospel, however, that he spent about another six months in Judea, which included visits to Jerusalem for the Feast of Tabernacles in October and the Feast of Dedication in December (John 7:2, 10, 14; 10:22-23). Exactly where he was staying during this period is not clear, but sometimes it was in the wilderness of Judea and sometimes even the other side of the Jordan near the scene of his baptism (John 10:40; 11:54).

When he appeared in public for the festivals, his claims (attested by his signs) became clearer and bolder. He was the bestower of living water, he said, the light of the world (as evidenced in giving sight to a man born blind), the great "I am" who lived eternally before Abraham, the good shepherd who would lay down his life for his sheep and (when he raised Lazarus from death) both the resurrection and the life (John 7:37-39; 8:12; 9:5; 8:58; 10:11; 11:25-26). The Jewish leaders found these claims increasingly provocative, and it is several times recorded that they tried to arrest and kill him (John 5:18; 7:30, 32; 8:59; 10:39; 11:53, 57).

Already during his Galilean ministry, although the crowds gave him tumultuous support, he did not escape the carping criticisms of the scribes and Pharisees. Mark assembles a series of four "controversy stories" in which Jesus was accused first of blasphemy (for daring to forgive a man's sins), then of fraternizing with sinners, thirdly of religious laxity in failing to fast and lastly of breaking the Sabbath (Mark 2:1-28). In defending himself against these charges Jesus had only made matters worse in his critics' eyes by claiming to be the Son of Man with authority to forgive, the physician who come to heal sick sinners, the bridegroom in whose presence the wedding guests could not fast, and the Lord even of the Sabbath.

As time passed he had gone further. He had

The Old City of Jerusalem and Temple Mount area, viewed from the green slopes of the Mount of Olives.

condemned the Pharisees for their hypocrisy (for example, Luke 11:37-52) and for exalting their human traditions above God's commandments (Mark 7:1-13), and was later to rebuke the Sadducees for their ignorance of God's Word and God's power (Mark 12:18-27). Gradually the tension grew. The Jewish leaders were jealous of his reputation with the people, wounded by his exposure of their superficiality and put to shame by his own transparent integrity. It was only a matter of time before the final collision.

When Jesus approached Jerusalem for the last time and reached the point on the road round the Mount of Olives where the city came into view, he could not restrain his tears. He wept and said:

If you, even you, had only known on this day what would bring you peace – but now it is hidden from your eyes.
(Luke 19:41-42)

Nevertheless, despite what it seemed would be the city's certain rejection, he issued one last appeal. By a careful prearrangement he was able to ride into Jerusalem on a borrowed donkey, in order deliberately to fulfill the prophecy of Zechariah:

Rejoice greatly, O Daughter of Zion!
    Shout, Daughter of Jerusalem!
See, your king comes to you,
    righteous and having salvation,
    gentle and riding on a donkey,
    on a colt, the foal of a donkey.
(Zech. 9:9; Matt. 21:5)

The crowds that were accompanying him were eager to acclaim him. They cut branches from the trees and took off their cloaks to make a carpet for him to ride over. They waved palm branches in the air and shouted their Hosannas. For this was his "triumphal entry" into Jerusalem. But his triumph was not shared by the authorities, and it was short-lived. He antagonized them by cleansing the temple for the second time (Mark 11:15-19), and during the next three days, from Monday to Wednesday, their hostility to him became increasingly intense. They engaged him in controversy, theological and political, although they could not fault him in argument (Mark 12). He for his part castigated the Pharisees for their religious pretense in a series of devastating "woes" (Matt. 23), and warned his apostles of the coming destruction of Jerusalem and of the opposition they must expect before his return would bring history to its end (Matt. 24; Mark 13; Luke 21).

The death and resurrection of Jesus

The Thursday of this last week was by one reckoning the eve of the Passover and by another the Passover itself. Jesus knew that his "hour," which he had repeatedly said was "not yet," had at last come. It was to be an hour of unparalleled suffering, and yet also the hour of his "glorification" by which he would be most fully revealed and the salvation even of the Gentiles would be accomplished (John 12:20-33).

He spent his final hours of liberty privately with the Twelve in a furnished, first-floor room lent him by a friend. Here they ate the Passover meal together. During supper he performed a slave's work, which evidently none of them had been willing to do, for he went round washing their feet. He told them that they must humble themselves and love one another in the same way. During and after supper he also gave them bread and wine as emblems of his body and blood which were to be offered for their salvation, and commanded them to eat and drink in his memory. Then he strengthened and encouraged them by profound instruction about the new and intimate relationship with him which the coming Holy Spirit would make possible, and he prayed for them that the Father would keep them what they were, a distinct people, who no longer belonged to the world but were to continue living in it as his representatives.

It must have been late when they left the Upper Room, walked through the deserted city streets, crossed the Kidron Valley and began to climb the Mount of Olives. In the Garden of Gethsemane Jesus prayed with an agony of desire that he might be spared having to drink "this cup," an Old Testament symbol of God's wrath upon sin. But he ended each prayer with a fresh surrender of his will, and emerged with a quiet, unshakable resolve to drink it. At that very moment the temple soldiers arrived to arrest him, carrying torches and weapons, and Judas betrayed him to them.

There now followed a grueling series (that night and the following morning) of six separate trials, three in Jewish courts, one before Herod and two before Pontius Pilate. When false witnesses accused him, Jesus was silent, but when the high priest challenged him whether he was "the Christ, the Son of God," he boldly acknowledged that he was and was immediately condemned to death for blasphemy. This travesty of justice was made the more bitter for him by the brutality of those who struck him and spat in his face, and by the cowardly denials of Peter in the courtyard outside.

Since by Roman law the Jews were not permitted to carry out the death sentence, it was necessary for them to get it ratified by the procurator. Pontius Pilate is known to have been an efficient administrator, but ruthless. He quickly saw through the political charge of which the Jews accused Jesus, namely that he had forbidden the payment of tribute to Caesar and had made claims to be a king himself. A few questions about Jesus' kingship satisfied him that the prisoner was no revolutionary agitator. But Pilate was a man ruled more by expedience than by principle. He wanted both to release Jesus and to satisfy the Jews simultaneously. So he tried various compromise arrangements. Would they be content if Jesus received a scourging, or a trial by Herod, or the customary Passover clemency? But the Jews would not allow him to escape a decision. When they hinted that if Pilate released Jesus he would forfeit Caesar's favor, his mind was made up. He washed his hands publicly in feigned innocence and handed Jesus over to them to be mocked, flogged and crucified.

Crucifixion was a horrible form of execution. To the Romans it was a shameful thing; they reserved it for slaves and the worst criminals. It was a sadistic kind of torture too, for it deliberately prolonged the pain and postponed death sometimes even for days.

How Jesus viewed and endured his ordeal is shown by the seven "words" which he spoke from the cross. The first three indicate that he was able so to forget his own suffering as to concern himself entirely with the welfare of others. He prayed that his tormentors might be forgiven; he commended his mother to John's care, and John to his mother's; and he assured the penitent brigand who was being crucified at his side that he would be with him that very day in paradise (Luke 23:34; John 19:26-27; Luke 23:43). After this Jesus seems to have been silent for several hours, while a strange darkness overshadowed the land. Then he uttered four cries, perhaps in quick succession, which give us some idea of the nature and purpose of his sufferings (John 19:28; Mark 15:33-34; John 19:30; Luke 23:46). First, "I am thirsty," betraying his physical anguish. Then "My God, my God, why have you forsaken me?" This cry of dereliction was framed as a question not because he did not know the answer, but because he was quoting Psalm 22:1. And he quoted it (as he always quoted Scripture) because he believed he was fulfilling it. The God-forsakenness which he experienced was the divine judgment which our sins deserved. He was drinking the "cup" of God's wrath. Almost immediately came a loud cry of triumph, the single word "Finished," expressing his accomplishment of the sin-bearing work he had come to do. Finally, he commended his spirit to the Father, to show that his death was a voluntary, self-determined act:

Father, into your hands I commit my spirit. (Luke 23:46)

About thirty-six hours later God raised him from the dead, as a decisive proof that he had

The Garden of Gethsemane, where Jesus prayed that he might be spared having to drink "this cup."

This "Tomb of the Herods" in Jerusalem has a rolling stone similar to the stone sealing Jesus' tomb.

not died in vain. At first light of dawn on Easter Day, Mary Magdalene and some other women came to Joseph of Arimathea's tomb, in order to complete the burial rites which the onset of the Sabbath had interrupted. But they found that the stone had been rolled aside from the mouth of the tomb and that the tomb itself was empty. Hearing the news, Peter and John raced to the sepulchre. Looking in, they discovered not only that the Lord's body was gone, but that his graveclothes were still there, lying in an undisturbed condition. It was clear circumstantial evidence that the body had not been touched by human hands but raised from death by God. They "saw and believed."

Then the risen Lord began to appear to people. First individually to Mary Magdalene and to Peter. Then to two disciples on the road from Jerusalem to Emmaus. Then to the apostles the same evening, and again the following Sunday when Thomas (absent the previous week) was with them. Next, when they had returned to Galilee, he appeared to them there also, both on a mountain and on the lakeshore. At every appearance he gave them

evidence that it was he himself, the same person as before his death, though now marvelously changed, and he commissioned them to go into the whole world and to make all nations his disciples.

These appearances continued for forty days. The last one took place on the Mount of Olives. Having promised them power to be his witnesses once the Holy Spirit had come upon them, and having blessed them, he was "taken up . . . into heaven." There is no need to doubt the literal nature of his ascension, so long as we realize its purpose. It was not necessary as a mode of departure, for "going to the Father" did not involve a journey in space and presumably he could simply have vanished as on previous occasions. The reason he ascended before their eyes was rather to show them that this departure was final. He had now gone for good, or at least until his coming in glory. So they returned to Jerusalem with great joy and waited – not for Jesus to make another resurrection appearance, but for the Holy Spirit to come in power, as had been promised.

The infant church

The disciples had only ten days to wait. Then suddenly, while they were praying together for the promise to be fulfilled, it happened. Accompanied by the noise of wind and the appearance of fiery flames, the Holy Spirit came and filled them all. It was the culminating event of Christ's saving career, for, as Peter explained in his sermon that same morning, it was Jesus Christ who brought the significance of his birth, death, resurrection and ascension to its climax by pouring out his Spirit from heaven.

Pentecost must also be understood fundamentally as a missionary event. The miracle of the foreign languages which the disciples spoke symbolized the international Christian community which was about to be brought to birth by the gospel.

Three thousand people were converted, baptized and added to the church that day:

They devoted themselves to the apostles'
teaching and to the fellowship, to the
breaking of bread and to prayer.
(Acts 2:42)

One marvels at the clarity and forcefulness of the early preaching of the apostles. Luke gives us four sample sermons by Peter – on the Day of Pentecost, after the healing of the cripple outside the temple's Beautiful Gate, before the Jewish Council and to the household of Cornelius (Acts 2:14-40; 3:12-26; 5:29-32; 10:34-43). Although of course he supplies only a précis of each, it is enough to show the content and pattern of Peter's proclamation.

Peter preached Jesus Christ, his life, death and resurrection. During his life he was divinely attested by miracles. His death was due both to the purpose of God and to the wickedness of men (Acts 2:23). Though men denied and killed him, God vindicated him by raising him from the dead. And now he is exalted as Lord, Christ, Savior and Judge. Moreover, all this is doubly confirmed by the testimony of Old Testament Scripture and of the apostolic eye-witnesses. Therefore, let them repent of their sins, believe in the name of Jesus Christ and be baptized, for then they will receive the blessing promised to Abraham's seed, namely the forgiveness of sins and the gift of the Spirit.

It must not be imagined, however, that the infant church had no problems. No sooner had Jesus Christ through his Spirit launched his offensive to conquer the world than the devil mounted a powerful counterattack. The devil's strategy was threefold.

First, he tried the crude weapon of persecution (Acts 3–5). When Peter and John started "teaching the people and proclaiming in Jesus the resurrection of the dead" (Acts 4:1-2), they were arrested and brought to trial before the Sanhedrin. Here they witnessed to Jesus with wonderful boldness, declaring him to be the only Savior. The Council was deeply impressed, knowing them to be uneducated men, but forbade them to "speak or teach at all in the name of Jesus" (4:18). Peter and John replied that they must obey God not men, and that in any case they simply could not help speaking of what they had seen and heard. Then, after they had been further threatened, they were let go. The apostles went straight to their Christian friends and together they prayed to the sovereign Lord of nature, scripture and history, not for their safety and protection, but that they might be given courage to go on speaking his word. So the preaching went on. They were again arrested, and now imprisoned, but an angel of the Lord released them and told them to go and preach the gospel in the sacred precincts of the temple itself Once more they were arrested and brought to trial, but this time the Jewish Council, cautioned by the Pharisee Gamaliel that they might be found opposing God, did no more than beat them and repeat the injunction not to speak in the name of Jesus. The reaction of the apostles?

The apostles left the Sanhedrin, rejoicing because they had been counted worthy of suffering disgrace for the Name. Day after day, in the temple courts and from house to house, they never stopped teaching and proclaiming the good news that Jesus is the Christ. (Acts 5:41-42)

The other weapons which the devil wielded against the church were more subtle. Unable to crush it by external pressure, he tried to undermine it from within. First by hypocrisy.

The generosity of the early Christians had led many of them to sell their lands and bring the proceeds to the apostles for the relief of those in need. A married couple called Ananias and Sapphira decided to do the same, but then kept back part of the money for themselves while pretending to surrender it all. Their property was entirely at their own disposal both before and after the sale, as Peter later made clear. They were under no obligation to give any of it away. Their sin was that they wanted the credit for giving everything, without the cost. If they had succeeded in their deceit, hypocrisy would have begun to seep into the Christian community. Peter detected their lie, however, and they paid for their duplicity with their lives (Acts 5:1-11).

The third satanic weapon was the most indirect. It was to preoccupy the apostles with social administration (to be precise, the care of Christian widows) and so divert them from the teaching role to which Jesus had called them. But the apostles were alert to this danger. So they delegated the task. They instructed the body of the disciples to choose seven "deacons" (as they are usually called) to take over the church's welfare work, so that they could devote themselves to their God-given priority, namely "to prayer and the ministry of the word."

When the devil's initial three-pronged counteroffensive had failed, Luke was able to write:

So the word of God spread. The number of disciples in Jerusalem increased rapidly. (Acts 6:7)

One of the seven was Stephen, a Christian man full of grace, faith, wisdom and power. Accused of speaking against the law of Moses and the temple, he was brought before the Council. His defense, recorded in Acts 7, is a masterly narrative of God's dealings with Israel, designed to demonstrate that God is tied to no place or building but only to the people whose God he is. He ended his speech by accusing his accusers. They were stiff-necked, he said, always resistant to the Holy Spirit, and now guilty of murdering the Christ. At this they rushed on him, threw him out of the city and stoned him to death.

But in the providence of God the death of the first Christian martyr helped rather than hindered the spread of the gospel. For the persecution of Christians which followed it scattered them throughout Judea and Samaria, and wherever they went they preached the word (Acts 8:1-4). Among them was Philip, who was another of the seven "deacons." He was given conspicuous success in evangelizing Samaritans, who for centuries had been repudiated by the Jews. So the apostles (who had stayed behind in Jerusalem) sent Peter and John to investigate and endorse what had happened, thus avoiding a continuance within the church of the Jewish-Samaritan schism. Philip also explained the good news of Christ crucified to an Ethiopian state official who was on his way back home from Jerusalem (Acts 8:5-40).

This outreach to Samaria and Ethiopia was only the prelude to the Gentile mission which soon began. Luke introduces it in Acts with two significant conversions, of Saul of Tarsus and (through Peter's witness) of the Roman centurion Cornelius. These events indicate the vital part played by the leading apostles Paul and Peter in opening the gates of the church to Gentiles.

Saul of Tarsus is first mentioned as the man who minded the clothing of those who were stoning Stephen. It is conjectured that he never forgot the courage and love of this first Christian martyr who prayed for the forgiveness of his enemies. But he continued to stifle the voice of conscience and savagely to persecute the church, until that memorable day (described no fewer than three times in Acts) when Jesus Christ appeared to him on the road

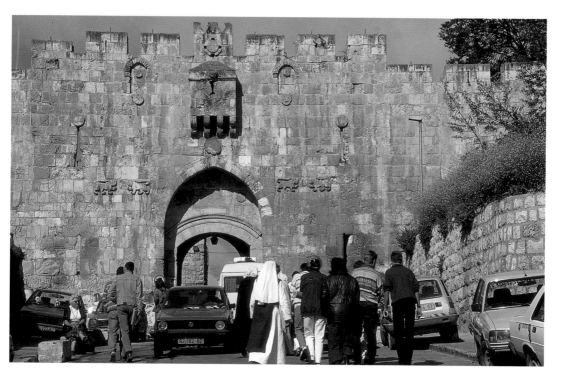

The Lion Gate, Jerusalem, by tradition the site of Stephen's martyrdom.

to Damascus and (as he later put it) "apprehended" him. After reaching Damascus he learned from Ananias that he had been called to be an apostle as well as a disciple, and to be Christ's chosen instrument to carry his name before Gentiles and well as Jews (Acts 9:15). His conversion must have taken place between three and five years only after the crucifixion.

Almost two complete chapters of Acts are devoted to the story of Cornelius' conversion, so important an event did Luke consider it (Acts 10–11). For Cornelius, although a "God-fearer" on the fringe of the synagogue, was still a Gentile outsider. It took a special vision to convince Peter that he should enter Cornelius' house and preach the gospel to him, and it took a special repetition of Pentecost (as I think we may describe it) to convince him that God now made no distinction between Jews and Gentiles but granted his cleansing and his Spirit to all believers without discrimination (Acts 10:47; 11:17; 15:7-11). It was an immense leap forward.

Some of those who left Jerusalem after Stephen's martyrdom traveled north to Antioch, which was the capital of Syria and the third most renowned city in the Empire. They preached the Lord Jesus to the Greeks, and a great number believed. Hearing about this, the Jerusalem church sent Barnabas to Antioch, and he in his turn fetched Paul to help him. For a whole year these two men taught the converts. Here (in Antioch) the first Gentile church was established, for the first time the disciples were called Christians, and the first missionary expedition was launched (Acts 11:19-26; 13:1-3). The date was now about AD 47.

The first missionary journey

The missionaries chosen, set apart by the church in obedience to the Spirit's leading, were Barnabas and Paul, who then invited Mark (Barnabas' cousin) to accompany them. They sailed to Cyprus, Barnabas' home country, and then northwest to land on Asian soil at Perga in Pamphylia. By this time Mark had had enough and returned to Jerusalem. Perhaps he was scared of the swamps of Pamphylia where (con-

The theater, Perga, the site of Paul's first landfall in Asia Minor during his initial missionary journey.

jecturally) Paul caught malaria which damaged his eyesight. At all events, when they had climbed the plateau and reached Galatia, Paul seems to have had some disfiguring eye disease (Gal. 4:13-15). The first Galatian city he visited was Pisidian Antioch, where he preached in the synagogue and many Jews were converted. But when the unbelieving Jews contradicted Paul's message, he took a bold step (which in the future he would often repeat) and turned to the Gentiles. Driven out of the city by opposition, Paul and Barnabas moved on to three more Galatian towns, Iconium, Lystra (where pagans nearly worshiped them as gods and Jews stoned Paul as a blasphemer) and Derbe. Then, retracing their steps, they strengthened the new converts and in every church appointed elders to care for them.[5]

Back in Antioch they gathered the church together and reported what God had done, especially "how he had opened the door of faith to the Gentiles" (Acts 14:27). But the church's rejoicing soon gave place to controversy, for there arrived in Antioch from Jerusalem a group of so-called "Judaizers,"

who started teaching that unless Gentile converts were circumcised and kept the law of Moses they could not be saved (Acts 15:1-5). Paul engaged them in a vigorous debate. And when even Peter, in a temporary lapse due to fear rather than conviction, withdrew from fellowship with Gentile Christians, Paul had to rebuke him publicly (Gal. 2:11-14).

It appears that the insidious influence of the Judaizers had penetrated even to the Galatian churches. This prompted Paul to write the first of his many letters. In his Letter to the Galatians he defended his apostolic authority as derived from Christ, assured them that there was no discord between him and the Jerusalem apostles, rejected the Judaizers' gospel as being no gospel at all, emphasized that salvation is by God's grace alone through faith alone without the addition of circumcision or the works of the law or anything else, and begged his Galatian readers to stand fast in their Christian liberty.

The church of Antioch decided to send Paul and Barnabas to Jerusalem to settle the issue which had been raised by the Judaizers, and

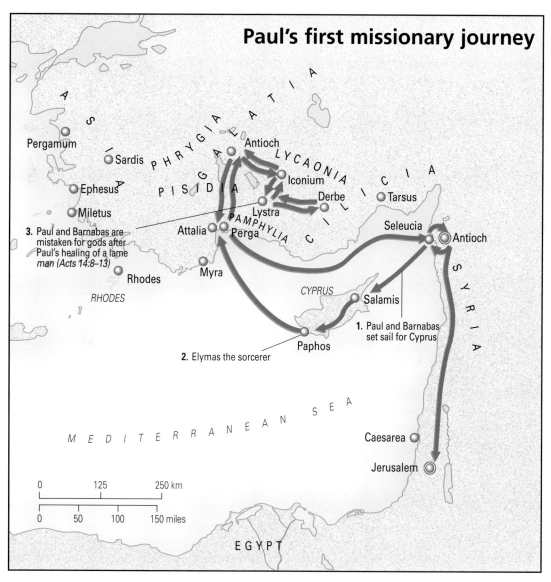

Paul's first missionary journey

3. Paul and Barnabas are mistaken for gods after Paul's healing of a lame man (Acts 14:8–13)

2. Elymas the sorcerer

1. Paul and Barnabas set sail for Cyprus

0   125   250 km

0   50   100   150 miles

this led to "the Council of Jerusalem" (described in Acts 15) in about AD 49 or 50. After much debate Peter (who by now had recovered from his lapse) recounted the conversion of Cornelius. Then Paul and Barnabas told what God had done through their ministry among the Gentiles. Finally, James, the Lord's brother, clinched the argument from Old Testament Scripture. Gentile converts, he concluded, did not need to be circumcised in order to be saved. Nevertheless, in order to respect the scruples of weak Jewish consciences and so promote Gentile-Jewish fellowship within the church, they were to be

asked voluntarily to follow certain Jewish food and marriage regulations.[6]

The second missionary journey

Armed with a letter from the Jerusalem apostles and elders, containing the decisions of the Council, Paul set out on his second missionary journey, this time accompanied by Silas.[7] They revisited the Galatian churches, delivering the Council's decree. At Lystra Paul invited Timothy to accompany them. Because he had a Gentile father, Paul even circumcised him out of deference to local Jews, for now that the

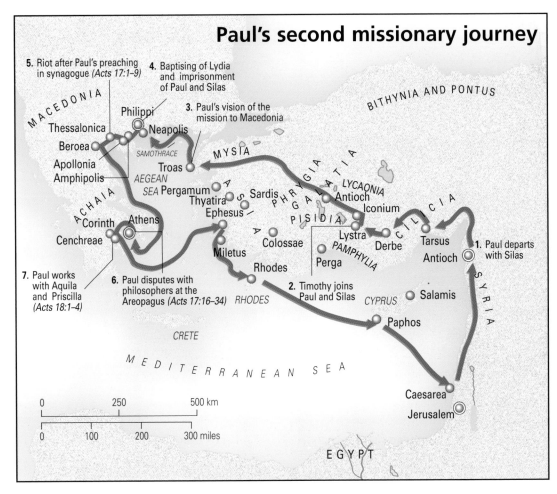

Paul's second missionary journey

5. Riot after Paul's preaching in synagogue (*Acts 17:1–9*)

4. Baptising of Lydia and imprisonment of Paul and Silas

3. Paul's vision of the mission to Macedonia

MACEDONIA

Philippi
Thessalonica
Neapolis
Beroea
SAMOTHRACE
Apollonia
Amphipolis
AEGEAN
SEA
Troas

BITHYNIA AND PONTUS

MYSIA

PHRYGIA
GALATIA
LYCAONIA

ACHAIA
Pergamum
Thyatira
Sardis
Antioch
Iconium
Ephesus
CILICIA

Corinth
Athens
PISIDIA

Cenchreae
Colossae
Lystra
Derbe
Tarsus
Miletus
PAMPHYLIA
Antioch

1. Paul departs with Silas

7. Paul works with Aquila and Priscilla (*Acts 18:1–4*)

6. Paul disputes with philosophers at the Areopagus (*Acts 17:16–34*)
RHODES

Rhodes
Perga

2. Timothy joins Paul and Silas
CYPRUS
Salamis

SYRIA

CRETE

Paphos

MEDITERRANEAN SEA

Caesarea
Jerusalem

0   250   500 km
0   100   200   300 miles

EGYPT

---

principle of salvation by grace alone had been established he was ready to make such a policy concession (Acts 16:1-4; cf. 1 Cor.9:19-20).

Forbidden by the Holy Spirit (in ways not explained) to journey either southwest towards Ephesus or due north into Bithynia, Paul and his companions were restricted to going in a northwesterly direction and so arrived at Troas on the Aegean coast. Here Paul had a dream in which a Greek begged him to go over to Macedonia and help them. He and his friends interpreted the vision as a call from God to take the gospel into Europe. And Luke, the author of Acts, by using the pronoun "we" for the first time in his narrative, quietly indicates that he sailed with them.

Macedonia was the northern province of Greece, and the missionary team preached the gospel in three of its principal towns – Philippi

(where Paul and Silas spent a memorable night in prison, with their feet in the stocks), Thessalonica (where during a three-week mission a great many believed) and Berea. Paul then moved on to Achaia, the southern province of Greece, visiting its two chief cities, Athens and Corinth.

There is something very moving about the picture of Paul in Athens, the Christian apostle alone amid the glories of ancient Greece. As he walked through the city it was not the beauty which struck him, however, but the idolatry. This stirred him deeply, and first in the synagogue with the Jews, then in the marketplace with passersby, and finally before the famous Council of the Areopagus with the Stoic and Epicurean philosophers, he faithfully preached Jesus, the resurrection and the judgment to come.

The Stoa, Athens, probable site of Paul's debate with the famous Council of the Areopagus.

Timothy joined him while he was in Athens, but Paul was so concerned to discover how the Thessalonian church was faring under persecution that he sent him off again at once to find out and to encourage them to stand firm (1 Thess. 3:1-5). By the time Timothy returned, Paul had moved on to Corinth (1 Thess. 3:6; Acts 18:5). The good news Timothy brought was the occasion of Paul's First Letter to the Thessalonians, with the Second Letter following it soon afterwards. In these letters Paul rejoices over the Thessalonians' faith, love and stead-fastness, and over the example which they are setting to all the believers in Macedonia and Achaia (1 Thess. 1). He goes on to defend his personal integrity against his Jewish detractors (1 Thess. 2–3). Then he exhorts his readers to earn their own living and not to give up work (which some seem to have done on the supposition that the Lord's return was imminent); to take courage in their bereavement because the living will not take precedence over the dead when Jesus comes; and to live lives of sexual purity. Perhaps he had these three categories in his mind when he wrote: "Warn those who are idle, encourage the timid, help the weak" (1 Thess. 5:14).

Paul stayed in Corinth for the best part of two years. He followed his normal custom of bearing witness to the Jews first, and won a notable convert in Crispus, the ruler of the synagogue. But when the Jews opposed and abused him, he again turned to the Gentiles and received support in his policy from an unexpected quarter, the proconsul of Achaia called Gallio. It was a truly wonderful triumph of God's grace that a Jewish-Gentile church should arise in such a cesspool of vice as Corinth was.

The third missionary journey

Paul's voyage back to Antioch was interrupted by a brief visit to Ephesus, the principal city of the Roman province of Asia. He must have been so impressed by its strategic importance, that he went almost straight there at the beginning of his third missionary journey.[8] After three months' preaching in the synagogue he broke fresh ground in evangelistic method. He

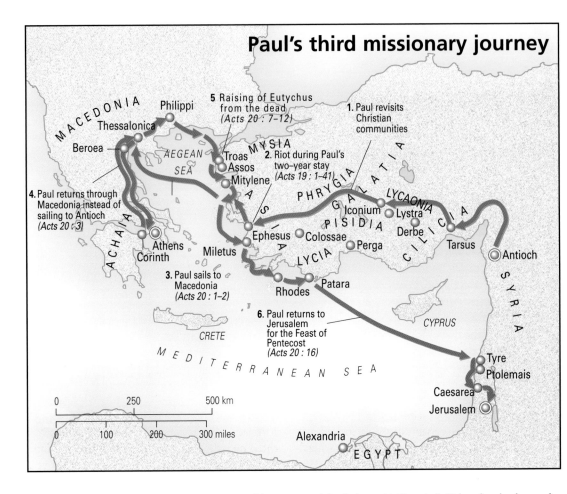

Paul's third missionary journey

1. Paul revisits Christian communities

2. Riot during Paul's two-year stay (Acts 19 : 1–41)

3. Paul sails to Macedonia (Acts 20 : 1–2)

4. Paul returns through Macedonia instead of sailing to Antioch (Acts 20 : 3)

5 Raising of Eutychus from the dead (Acts 20 : 7–12)

6. Paul returns to Jerusalem for the Feast of Pentecost (Acts 20 : 16)

MACEDONIA · Philippi · Thessalonica · Beroea · AEGEAN SEA · MYSIA · Troas · Assos · Mitylene · PHRYGIA · GALATIA · LYCAONIA · Iconium · Lystra · PISIDIA · Derbe · CILICIA · Tarsus · Antioch · Ephesus · Colossae · Perga · LYCIA · Athens · Corinth · Miletus · ACHAIA · Rhodes · Patara · CRETE · CYPRUS · SYRIA · MEDITERRANEAN SEA · Tyre · Ptolemais · Caesarea · Jerusalem · Alexandria · EGYPT

0   250   500 km
0   100   200   300 miles

hired "the hall of Tyrannus," presumably a secular school or lecture hall, and here every day for two years, according to some manuscripts "from the fifth hour to the tenth" (that is, from 11 AM to 4 PM), he argued the gospel. Assuming that he worked a six-day week, this represents 3,120 hours of gospel argument. It is not surprising that as a result "all the Jews and Greeks who lived in the province of Asia heard the word of the Lord" (Acts 19:8-10).

While he was in Ephesus, the Corinthian church gave him much cause for anxiety on both doctrinal and moral grounds. His first letter to them (mentioned in 1 Cor. 5:9) has been lost. However, on receiving disquieting news from some Corinthian travelers, who also brought with them a number of questions from the church, Paul wrote them a second letter which is our First Corinthians. In it he is able to thank God for the gifts with which Christ has

enriched them (1 Cor. 1:4-9) but he deplores the factions into which the church has been split and their false view of the ministry which lies behind the factions (1 Cor. 1:10–4:21). He also expresses indignant horror at the immorality and litigation which they are tolerating among their members (1 Cor. 5–6), and at the irregularities they are permitting in public worship (1 Cor. 11). In answer to their questions he writes about marriage (1 Cor. 7), about the eating of food offered to idols (1 Cor. 8–10), and about the use and abuse of spiritual gifts (1 Cor. 12–14). He then summarizes his gospel and emphasizes particularly the resurrection of Christ and of Christians (1 Cor. 15). This letter evidently failed to have its desired effect, for Paul decided to visit Corinth personally. He later referred to this as a "painful visit" (2 Cor. 2:1), because apparently one of the church leaders openly defied his authority. So serious was

This is all that now remains of the celebrated Temple of Diana (Artemis) at Ephesus.

this challenge that on leaving Paul wrote them yet another letter (usually referred to as the "severe letter"), insisting that the offender be punished. This letter also seems to have been lost, unless (as some scholars believe) it has somehow found its way into 2 Corinthians 10–13. At all events, the severe letter was heeded and the offender was duly disciplined. Paul was overjoyed to hear from Titus of their loyalty (2 Cor. 7:12-14) and immediately wrote to them again.

In this letter, our Second Corinthians, he begs them now to "forgive and comfort" the rebel, who has received a sufficient punishment (2 Cor. 2:5-11). He goes on to write of the glory, problems and responsibilities of the Christian ministry (2 Cor. 3–6), devotes two chapters to the appeal that he has launched to the churches of Macedonia and Achaia to raise money for the impoverished church of Judea (2 Cor. 8–9), and concludes with of his apostolic authority (2 Cor. 10–13).

He mentioned in this letter his intention to pay them a third visit (2 Cor. 12:14; 13:1), which came to pass in this way. Ephesus boasted a magnificent temple to the goddess Artemis (or Diana), which was one of the seven wonders of the world. As the number of Ephesian converts from idolatry grew, the silversmiths saw a strong threat to their trade in shrines or souvenirs of the goddess (Acts 19:23-41). A serious riot ensued, and Paul left the city for Macedonia and then Achaia (Acts 19:21-22; 20:1-2), including Corinth.

It appears that the apostle stayed about three months in Corinth in the home of Gaius, and that from here he wrote his great Letter to the Romans (Rom. 16:23; 1 Cor. 1:14). In it he tells the Christians in Rome how eager he is not only to visit and encourage them, but also to preach the gospel in the world's capital city (Rom. 1:8-15) and then to travel on into Spain (Rom. 15:18-29). So he takes the opportunity to unfold at length this gospel which is committed to him and to which he is committed. He describes the terrible degradation of humankind, and argues that there is no distinction between Jew and Gentile in the fact of their sin and guilt. Neither is there any distinction between them regarding the offer of salvation:

For there is no distinction between Jew and Gentile – the same Lord is Lord of all and richly blesses all who call on him. (Rom. 10:12-13; 1:16; 3:22-23)

This salvation is a free gift offered by God's

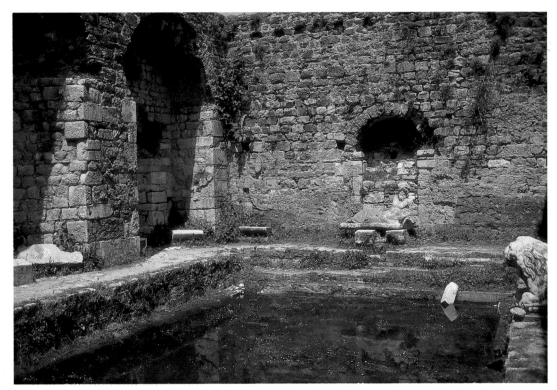

The Baths of Faustina, Miletus, the port from which Paul returned to Jerusalem at the end of his third journey.

grace, grounded upon Christ's death and – as the Old Testament itself makes plain – received by faith not earned by works (Rom. 3:21–5:21). Faith not only justifies the sinner, but unites him to Christ. And "in Christ," that is, joined to Christ by faith (invisibly) and by baptism (visibly), the Christian begins an altogether new life of freedom. He is free from the dominion of sin through slavery to God (Rom. 6), free from the bondage of the law through the indwelling Spirit (Rom. 7:1–8:13) and free from all fear of evil, whether in life or in death, through the assurance of being God's child forever (Rom. 8:14-39).

Next Paul wrestles with a problem which troubled him deeply: How is it that the Jews, God's specially privileged people, have not accepted Jesus as their Messiah? It is certainly not that God's word of promise has failed. The strange phenomenon of their unbelief can be understood in the light partly of the mysterious process of God's election (Rom. 9), partly of their own rebellion as "a disobe-dient and obstinate people" (Rom. 10, especially v. 21) and partly of a broad historical perspective that one day "the fullness" of Jews as well as Gentiles will come in and "so all Israel will be saved" (Rom. 11, especially vv. 12, 25-26).

After this exposition Paul comes back to the life of practical holiness which, because of "the mercies of God," all his people should lead – in mutual service (Rom. 12), in conscientious citizenship (Rom. 13), and in the brotherly love which accepts even the weak believer who has an overscrupulous conscience (Rom. 14–15).

Leaving Corinth, Paul and his companions began their long journey to Jerusalem (Acts 20:3–21:16), taking with them the now completed collection for the Judean church. Among the ports at which they called were Troas (where Paul's sermon lasted till midnight and their fellowship till daybreak!) and Miletus (where Paul gave a moving address to the elders of the Ephesian church).

Paul's arrest and journey to Rome

When at last they reached their destination, they had not been in Jerusalem a week before some Asian Jews started maliciously alleging that Paul had undermined Moses' law by his teaching and defiled the temple by bringing Greeks into it. A riot broke out, and Paul was rescued from being lynched by the prompt action of the military tribune (Acts 21:17–22:29).

During the next two years and more the apostle was held a prisoner. During the same period Luke was at liberty in Palestine, no doubt gathering material for his Gospel and the Acts. Paul had to undergo a series of trials in Jerusalem and Caesarea before the Sanhedrin (Acts 22:30–23:10), before the procurator Felix (Acts 24:1-21), before his successor Festus (Acts 25:1-12) and before King Agrippa and his wife Bernice (Acts 25:13–26:32). But since as a Roman citizen he had exercised his right to appeal to Caesar, he was eventually sent to Rome for trial.

The long and perilous sea voyage included the exciting escape from shipwreck on the island of Malta, which Luke tells with graphic detail (Acts 27:1–28:10), and at last Paul reached the Rome of his dreams. The Christians welcomed him, and the Jews came to visit him and hear the gospel from his lips.

Luke has now traced the spread of the gospel from Jerusalem, the capital of Jewry, to Rome, the capital of the world. He ends his narrative with a picture of his hero, the apostle Paul, who although under house arrest was still an indefatigable evangelist:

> Paul . . . welcomed all who came to see him. Boldly and without hindrance he preached the kingdom of God and taught about the Lord Jesus Christ. (Acts 28:30-31)

It was not only by spoken witness, however, that the apostle exploited his two years' imprisonment in Rome. He also spent time writing to various churches, and the so-called

Remains of piles from the ancient Roman harbor at Caesarea Maritima, Palestine.

"prison epistles" which belong to this period are the letters to the Ephesians (probably a circular letter to Asian churches of that region), to the Colossians, to Philemon (a personal letter instructing him to receive back as a brother his runaway slave, now converted) and to the Philippians (though some think this letter was written earlier from a supposed imprisonment in Ephesus). It is not easy to give a summary of the message of these letters, for each was occasioned by a different local situation. Yet if there is one truth which stands out in them all, it is the greatness of Jesus Christ. The very fullness of God, Paul writes, was pleased both to dwell in him and to work through him, on the one hand creating the universe and on the other reconciling all things to himself. He has now been exalted to God's right hand, far above all principalities and powers, and has been given the preeminent name, so that every knee should bow to him and every tongue confess him Lord. This cosmic Christ is also the head of the church, whose members are called to be what they are – a holy, united and victorious people.

The supremacy of Christ is also the theme of a very different New Testament book, the Letter to the Hebrews. Both its author and its destination are unknown, for neither is named in it. But its purpose is to prevent certain Jewish Christians from relapsing into Judaism by emphasizing the finality of Jesus Christ. In him all priesthood and sacrifice have been fulfilled, and by him an eternal redemption has been won.

After the Acts of the Apostles

Since Luke concludes the Acts with Paul's arrival and ministry in Rome, we are left somewhat in the dark about the following years. But it seems certain that Paul was released from custody (as he expected) and that he resumed his travels for another year or two. He visited Crete and left Titus there (Titus 1:5). Soon afterwards he wrote his Letter to Titus to remind him of his responsibilities. He must appoint suitable elders in every town who would be able to combat false teaching. He himself should also be a

teacher and emphasize the kind of Christian conduct which is appropriate in those who have embraced "the sound doctrine" of the gospel of salvation.

Paul then went on to Ephesus, where he left Timothy for similar reasons (1 Tim. 1:3). In his First Letter to Timothy he gives him instructions on how to deal with false teachers, conduct public worship, select candidates for the pastorate, exercise his own ministry in such a way that his comparative youth will not be despised, arrange for the care of Christian widows, give balanced advice about money and behave like a man of God. It is a truly "pastoral epistle" (as the letters to Timothy and Titus are usually known), containing much practical wisdom for church leaders today.

Then Paul journeyed on, perhaps to Colosse (Philem. 22), then to Macedonia (1 Tim. 1:3) and then across Greece to Nicopolis (Titus 3:12), the capital of Epirus on the Adriatic. Perhaps it was his intention when winter ended to sail from there for Spain. Whether he succeeded we may never know, though early tradition says he did. In any case, at some point he was rearrested. It may have been at Troas, so that he had to leave his personal possessions behind, including a cloak and some books and parchments (2 Tim. 4:13). This time his prison in Rome was not the comparative liberty of a house arrest, but probably a dismal underground dungeon.

From such an imprisonment he wrote his Second Letter to Timothy. He felt keenly his loneliness, for only Luke was with him. He begged Timothy to come and visit him soon, and in any case before the winter would make sailing impossible. But his great concern was not for himself but for the gospel, the precious "deposit" which he had committed to Timothy and which Timothy must now hand on to faithful men who would pass it to others also. Timothy must persevere in it himself and guard it from every falsification. He must be prepared, if need be, to suffer for it. Above all, he must preach it urgently and faithfully. Paul himself had preached the gospel fully during the first hearing of his case, so that "all the Gentiles,"

Paul's voyage to Rome

5. Paul preaches under house arrest for two years while awaiting trial before Caesar

Rome

ITALIA

ADRIATIC SEA

Puteoli

AEGEAN SEA

Rhegium

SICILIA

Athens

LYCIA *PAMPHYLIA* *CILICIA*

Tarsus

Cnidus

Myra

Antioch

4. Shipwrecked on Malta after storm at sea (Acts 28)

Syracuse

MALTA

Phoenix

Fair Havens

CRETE

RHODES

CYPRUS

Salmone

SYRIA

CAUDA

Lasea

2. Trials before Felix and Festus; Paul appeals to Caesar (Acts 24, 25)

Sidon

3. Strong winds make navigation difficult (Acts 27)

Caesarea

Antipatris

M E D I T E R R A N E A N   S E A

Jerusalem

1. Paul arrested (Acts 21 : 33)

Alexandria

SYRTIS

| 0 | 250 | 500 km |

| 0 | 100 | 200 | 300 miles |

crowded into the place of his trial, had heard it (2 Tim. 4:17). It was a fitting conclusion to his life of testimony. Now at last he could say:

> I have fought the good fight, I have finished the race, I have kept the faith. Now there is in store for me the crown of righteousness, which the Lord, the righteous Judge, will award to me on that day. (2 Tim. 4:7-8)

Tradition says that Paul was beheaded (as a Roman citizen would have been) on the Ostian Way. His execution was probably a part of the persecution which broke out in Rome in AD 64 when Nero tried to deflect responsibility for the great fire from himself to the Christians.

This same Neronian persecution forms the background to the First Letter of Peter. He wrote it from Rome and addressed it to Christians in the northern parts of Asia Minor to whom, he anticipated, the persecution was

Sculpted head of the Emperor Nero.

about to spread. He calls it a "painful trial" (1 Pet. 4:12). They are not to be surprised by it as something strange, nor to be afraid, but rather to rejoice at their privilege of sharing Christ's sufferings (1 Pet. 4:13). Indeed, the patient endurance of undeserved suffering is an inescapable part of the Christian calling, since Christians are followers of Christ, the suffering servant of the Lord (1 Pet. 2:18-25). The apostle Peter had soon to put his own instruction into practice, for he too (like Paul) was executed during the Neronian persecution, according to tradition by being crucified upside down.

The New Testament ends as the Acts begins, namely with satanic attacks on the church from within and from without. The three letters of John, written some time after the martyrdoms of Paul and Peter, warn the churches in the neighborhood of Ephesus of a particular kind of heresy. The heretics concerned were a Gnostic[10] group, which denied that Jesus was "the Christ come in the flesh," claimed to enjoy an experience of God without having to be righteous, and made arrogant pretensions to a superior enlightenment which led them to despise the unenlightened. Over against them John emphasized the truth of the divine-human person of Christ, the necessity of moral obedience and the centrality of love. The Second Letter of Peter and the Letter of Jude were also written to counter the promoters of "antinomianism," false teachers who degraded Christian liberty into license (cf. 2 Pet. 2:19). God's judgment would fall upon them.

The background to the Book of Revelation is probably the more severe and widespread persecution which was initiated by the Emperor Domitian (AD 81-96). Because of his faithful testimony John finds himself exiled to the little island of Patmos, some miles off shore from Ephesus (Rev. 1:9). Here he is given an "apocalypse" or unveiling. In a sense the books of Acts and of Revelation are complementary. For Acts portrays the beginning of the church's mission and persecution as they appeared on the stage of history, whereas Revelation enables us to peep behind the scenes and glimpse the unseen spiritual battle which is raging between Christ and Satan.

John's visions are full of weird symbolism. Satan appears as "an enormous red dragon with seven heads and ten horns," who declares war on the church. His three allies are two fearful monsters and a gaudy prostitute. The "beast coming out of the sea" represents the persecuting power of the state, the second "beast coming out of the earth" (also called "the false prophet") represents the cult of emperor-worship and indeed all erroneous teaching, while "the great prostitute" clothed in scarlet and decked with jewels, whose name is "Babylon," represents the sinful enticements of worldliness. Persecution, error and evil are still the three major weapons which the devil wields in his fight against the church. But he will not prevail against it.

For the Book of Revelation is supremely a revelation of Jesus Christ as the Lamb who fights and conquers the Dragon. He is seen in other guises too, now patrolling and supervising his church, now sharing the Father's throne, now riding forth on a white horse as King of kings and Lord of lords to judge the nations, now coming as the Bridegroom to claim his bride. The whole book summons hard-pressed Christians to lift up their hearts and take courage. For Christ Jesus has died to ransom his people for God out of every nation. He is reigning now from his heavenly throne. And he is coming soon to judge and to save.

The church's prayer, with which the Bible ends, is "Come, Lord Jesus." And the church's assurance throughout its tribulation is that, until he comes, "the grace of the Lord Jesus Christ" is sufficient to sustain all his people (Rev. 22:20-21).

The chronology of the New Testament period is difficult to determine with precision, although some dates are known. In areas of uncertainty, however, scholars differ from one another only by a year or two. One of the more commonly accepted reconstructions of events is given in the chart opposite.

Some New Testament dates to remember

BC

c. 5	Birth of Jesus
4	Herod the Great dies

AD

30	The death, resurrection and ascension of Jesus Pentecost
c. 33	Saul of Tarsus is converted
44	Herod Agrippa I dies (Acts 12:20-23)
c. 47-48	Paul's first missionary journey (Acts 13–14)
c. 49	The Council of Jerusalem (Acts 15)
c. 49-52	Paul's second missionary journey (Acts 16:1–18:22)
c. 52-56	Paul's third missionary journey (Acts 18:23–21:17)
c. 57	Paul arrested in Jerusalem (Acts 21:27–23:30)
c. 57-59	Paul imprisoned in Caesarea (Acts 23:31–26:32)
c. 60-61	Paul at liberty under house arrest in Rome (Acts 28:14–31)
c.62-64	Paul at liberty again
64	The fire of Rome. Nero persecutes Christians
c. 65	Paul martyred in Rome
70	Jerusalem destroyed by Titus
81-96	Widespread persecution of Christians during reign of Emperor Domitian

NOTES

1. Eusebius, *Ecclesiastical History* III.39.16.

2. For a brief but thorough and fair discussion of the problems raised by the Fourth Gospel, see the introductory essay in *The New Bible Commentary Revised*, 3rd ed. (IVP, 1970). A fuller, critical but conservative treatment may be found in Stephen S. Smalley, *John, Evangelist and Interpreter* (Paternoster, 1980) and D. A. Carson, *The Gospel according to John* (IVP/Eerdmans, 1991).

3. John mentions three Passovers in his narrative (2:13; 6:4; 11:55).

4. The story of Nicodemus is recorded in John 3:1 ff and of the woman of Samaria in John 4:4 ff.

5. The story of the first missionary journey is told in Acts 13:4–14:28.

6. The Greek word translated sexual immorality in Acts 15:20, 29 may refer to fornication in particular, or to immorality in general, or (it has been argued) to Jewish regulations regarding marriage within the prohibited degrees.

7. The story of the second missionary journey is told in Acts 15:36–18:22.

8. The story of the third missionary journey is told in Acts 18:23–21:16.

9. See 1 Pet. 5:13 where "Babylon" is almost certainly a symbol for Rome.

10. Gnosticism is the name given to a number of heretical movements which were a threat to the early church. The product of attempts to reconcile Greek philosophy and Christian faith, Gnosticism taught, for example, that God could never have created the material world or become a human being, that the flesh is an evil, trapping the divine spark in human beings, and that salvation depends on knowledge and ritual. Early church writings show a continuing conflict with incipient Gnostic teachings.

5. The Message of the Bible

❖ *What are the two basic truths we need to know about God?*

❖ *What is the nature of God's covenant?*

❖ *Describe the three stages in the outworking of God's covenant.*

It is a fundamental Christian conviction that God has spoken, and spoken in a concrete historical and geographical setting. We have taken several chapters to survey the geography and the history; it is time now to listen to the message. Some of this has already been included in the story of the Bible, as the teaching of the prophets has been fitted into the life of Israel, and the teaching of Christ and his apostles into the New Testament story. We saw also in the first chapter that the message of the Bible concerns salvation through Christ. But this needs to be elaborated.

Since the Bible is a whole library of books, composed by many authors over more than a thousand years, it seems to some quite incredible that we can claim for it a single theme, let alone condense it into a single chapter. Besides, they say, do not the Old and New Testaments contradict each other? Does not the Old Testament portray Yahweh as a fearful God of wrath and judgment, who is entirely incompatible with the God and Father of our Lord Jesus Christ? How can we reconcile the thunders of Sinai with the meekness and gentleness of Christ?

I hope that the true answer to these questions will become plain as in this chapter I try to demonstrate further the astonishing unity of the Bible. Meanwhile, it will be enough to express the Bible's own claim that it contains neither a ragbag of miscellaneous contradictions, nor a gradual evolution of human ideas about God, as human beings grew up and discarded their childish notions, but a progressive revelation of truth by God.

Progression there undoubtedly is. For example, the great stress of the Old Testament is on the unity of God, in contrast to the degraded polytheism of the heathen nations. Although there are foreshadowings of it in the Old Testament, the doctrine of the Trinity is clearly stated only in the New Testament. Again, there is progression from the recorded teaching of Jesus to the fuller understanding of his person and work which we find in the Epistles and the prologue to the Fourth Gospel. But this is exactly what Jesus himself led us to expect by what he said to the apostles in the Upper Room:

> I have much more to say to you, more than you can now bear. But when he, the Spirit of truth, comes; he will guide you into all truth. He will not speak on his own; he will speak only what he hears, and he will tell you what is yet to come. He will bring glory to me by taking from what is mine and making it known to you. All that belongs to the Father is mine. That is why I said the Spirit will take from what is mine and make it known to you. (John 16:12-15)

Progression is not the same as contradiction, however. An artist begins by making a sketch, and then applies oils to the canvas bit by bit until the whole picture (apparent to his mind from the start, though not to the beholder's) finally emerges. Again, parents teach their children step by step, "rule on rule, rule on rule; a little here, a little there" (Isa. 28:10). But if they

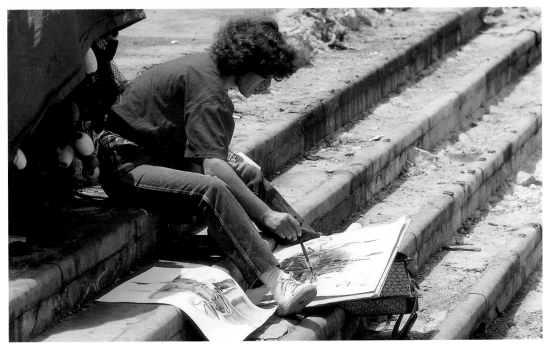

An artist begins by making a sketch, and then applies oils to the canvas bit by bit until the whole picture finally emerges.

are wise, they do not teach anything in the early stages which needs later to be contradicted. Their later teaching supplements what has gone before and builds on it; it does not come into collision with it. So God has gradually filled out his revelation, constantly expanding it but never repudiating it, until at last it was complete in Christ the Word made flesh (than whom a higher revelation is inconceivable) and in the witness of the apostles to Christ.

The Letter to the Hebrews opens with a very valuable statement of this truth:

> In the past God spoke to our forefathers through the prophets at many times and in various ways, but in these last days he has spoken to us by his Son. (Heb. 1:1-2)

Here the author concedes that there are several differences between the Old and New Testament revelations. The revelation was given at different times ("in the past" and "in these last days"), to different people ("to our forefathers" and "to us") and especially in different modes ("through the prophets at many times and in various ways" and "by his Son"). But though the occasion, the recipients and the manner of revelation were different, its author was the same. It is *God* who has spoken to us in and through his Son.

In the light of this we should not hesitate to claim God himself as the ultimate Author of both Testaments or to designate the whole of Scripture "the Word of God." I shall have more to say in the next chapter about this.

What, then, has God spoken? The Bible is essentially a revelation of God. It is, in fact, a divine self-disclosure. In the Bible we hear God speaking about God. To say this is not inconsistent with the thesis developed in the first chapter that the Bible is concerned with salvation and bears witness to Christ. For what God says about himself is, above all else, that he has conceived and fulfilled a plan to save fallen men through Christ.

The living and consistent God

But before we come to his saving activity, there are two basic truths about him to consider, which Scripture emphasizes throughout. The first is that he is a living and sovereign God; the second that he is consistent, always the same, "the Father of the heavenly lights, who does not change like shifting shadows" (Jas. 1:17).

Again and again the one, living and true God is contrasted with the dead idols of heathendom. Prophets and psalmists hold heathen idols up to ridicule. Isaiah describes the scene in one of the temples when Babylon was captured. He pictures the chief Babylonian deities being snatched ignominiously from their pedestals, carried out on men's shoulders and loaded on to carts outside. Fancy gods being carried by men and becoming "burdens on weary beasts"! And when the laughter subsides, the voice of God is heard. He is no idol needing to be carried about by men, for it is he who carries his people:

Listen to me, O house of Jacob,
    all you who remain of the house of Israel,
you whom I have upheld since you were
    conceived,
and have carried since your birth.
Even to your old age and gray hairs
    I am he, I am he who will sustain you.
I have made you and I will carry you.
(Isa. 46:3-4)

Not only the idols' inability to save aroused the prophets' scorn, but their total lifelessness:

Their idols are silver and gold,
    made by the hands of men.
They have mouths, but cannot speak,
    eyes, but they cannot see;
they have ears, but cannot hear,
    noses, but they cannot smell;
they have hands, but cannot feel,
    feet, but they cannot walk;
    nor can they utter a sound with their
    throats. (Ps. 115:4-7)

In contrast to them, "our God is in heaven; he does whatever pleases him" (Ps. 115:3). He is the living God, who sees and hears and speaks and acts.

This living God is sovereign, a great king over all the earth. He is king of nature, and king of the nations also.

As king of nature he sustains the universe he has made and all its creatures. Even the ferocious elements are under his control. "The sea is his, for he made it" (Ps. 95:5), and the "stormy winds" fulfill his command (Ps. 148:8). Psalm 29 gives a dramatic description of a thunderstorm, in which "the voice of the LORD" breaks the cedars of Lebanon. The lightning flashes. The wilderness is shaken. The forests are stripped bare. The rain causes floods. As havoc spreads, one would expect apprehension and alarm to spread with it. But the Psalmist remains quietly confident that God is in control:

The LORD sits enthroned over the flood;
    the LORD is enthroned as King forever.
(Ps. 29:10)

Psalm 104 is an early study in ecology. In it the psalmist marvels (Ps. 104:17-18) at the way storks make their homes in fir trees, while "the high mountains belong to the wild goats" and "the crags are a refuge for the coneys" (that is, the rock badger, or hyrax). The psalm goes onto describe how God feeds all animals:

These all look to you
    to give them their food at the proper time.
When you give it to them,
    they gather it up;
when you open your hand,
    they are satisfied with good things.
(Ps. 104:27-28)

Entirely in keeping with this Old Testament insistence that God is the Lord of nature is the teaching of Jesus in the Sermon on the Mount, that God rules the animate and inanimate worlds. On the one hand, he feeds the birds of the air and clothes the lilies of the field; on the other, "he causes his sun to rise on the evil and the good, and sends rain on the righteous and the unrighteous" (Matt: 5:45; 6:26-30).

The King of nature is also King of nations.

Galilee from the Mount of Beatitudes. In the Sermon on the Mount Jesus teaches that God rules the animate and inanimate worlds.

As Daniel said to King Nebuchadnezzar, "The Most High is sovereign over the kingdoms of men and gives them to anyone he wishes" (Dan. 4:32). We saw in an earlier chapter how the little countries of Israel and Judah often seemed no more than pawns on an international chessboard. The great power blocs of the day were the empires of Egypt and Mesopotamia. As they confronted each other on the battlefield, and the tide of war ebbed and flowed, it was Israel and Judah and the small neighboring states which got caught in between. Yet Israel continually uttered the splendid shout of faith:

The LORD reigns, let the nations tremble!
(Ps.99:1)

No power on earth, whether alone or in coalition with others, could triumph over God's people without God's permission. Do the nations scheme and plot, and set themselves against the Lord and against his anointed?

The One enthroned in heaven laughs;
the Lord scoffs at them. (Ps. 2:4)

The apostles of Jesus in New Testament days had the same conviction. When Peter and John were forbidden to speak or teach at all in the name of Jesus, they called their friends to prayer. They lifted their voices together to God as the "sovereign Lord," the creator of the universe. Then they recited the first two verses of Psalm 2 (from which I have just quoted) and applied them to Herod and Pontius Pilate, the Gentiles and the rulers of Israel. These had conspired together in Jerusalem against Jesus. To do what? "What your power and will had decided beforehand should happen" (Acts 4:18, 23-28).

More than that. The prophets taught that the mighty soldier-emperors of the day, some of whom were cruel and ruthless men, were still instruments in the hand of the Lord. Shalmaneser of Assyria was the rod of his anger, the staff of his fury, with which to punish Samaria (Isa. 10:5-6), Nebuchadnezzar of

Babylon his "servant" through whom he would destroy Jerusalem (Jer. 25:9; 27:6) and Cyrus of Persia his "anointed" to free his people from their captivity (Isa. 45:1-4; cf. 44:28).

If the God of the Bible is the living and the sovereign God, he is also always self-consistent. His sovereign power is never arbitrarily used. On the contrary, his activity is always consistent with his nature. One of the most important statements about God in Scripture is that "he cannot disown himself" (2 Tim. 2:13). Does it come as a surprise that it is said God "cannot" do something? Can he not do *anything*? Is he not omnipotent? Yes, he can do anything he pleases to do, anything which is consistent with his nature to do. But his omnipotence does not mean that he can do absolutely anything whatsoever; for he limits it by his own self-consistency.

God's love and wrath, together with his works of salvation and of judgment, are sometimes set over against each other by critics as supposedly incompatible. We have already mentioned how some people imagine the God of the Old Testament to be a God of anger and the God of the New Testament to be a God of mercy. But this is a false antithesis. The Old Testament also reveals him as a God of mercy, while the New Testament also reveals him as a God of judgment. Indeed the whole Bible, Old and New Testaments alike, presents him as a God of love and wrath simultaneously. The biblical authors are not embarrassed by this, as many moderns seem to be. Thus, the apostle John can tell his readers how "God so loved the world that he gave his one and only Son"; and at the end of the same chapter declare that on him who does not obey the Son the wrath of God remains (John 3:16, 36). Similarly, the apostle Paul can describe his readers as "like the rest . . . by nature objects of wrath" and in the very next verse write that God is "rich in mercy" and has loved us with a great love (Eph. 2:3-4).

The only explanation the Bible gives of the loving and wrathful activity of God, of his deeds of salvation and of judgment, is simply that he is like that. That is the kind of God he

is, and this is why he acts that way. "God is love," and therefore he loves the world and has given his Son for us (1 John 4:8-9). But also "our God is a consuming fire" (Heb. 12:29; cf. Deut. 4:24). His nature of perfect holiness can never compromise with evil but, as it were, "devours" it. Always he sets himself implacably against it.

One of the ways in which Scripture dares to express this truth of God's self-consistency is to say that he must and will "satisfy himself."[1] That is to say, he is always perfectly himself and acts in a way that is true to himself. In every situation he expresses *himself* as he is, in mercy and in judgment. But it was supremely in the cross that he demonstrated in equal measure his justice and his love (Rom. 3:25, 26; 5:8).

Having now drawn attention to the biblical revelation of God as both living and sovereign on the one hand, and self-consistent on the other, there can be no doubt that the principal way in which the living God has expressed himself is in "grace." No one can understand the message of Scripture who does not know the meaning of grace. The God of the Bible is "the God of all grace" (1 Pet. 5:10). Grace is love, but love of a special sort. It is love which stoops and sacrifices and serves, love which is kind to the unkind, and generous to the ungrateful and undeserving. Grace is God's free and unmerited favor, loving the unlovable, seeking the fugitive, rescuing the hopeless, and lifting the beggar from the dunghill to make him sit among princes (Ps. 113:7-8).

It is grace which led God to establish his covenant with a particular people. God's grace is covenant grace. True, it is also shown to everybody without distinction. This is called his "common grace," by which he gives to all men indiscriminately such blessings as reason and conscience, love and beauty, life and food, marriage and children, work and leisure, ordered government and many other gifts besides. Yet God's entering into a special covenant with a special people may be described as his characteristic act of grace. For in it he took the initiative to pick a people for himself and to pledge himself to be their God. He did not choose

Mount Sinai at dawn. The covenant of grace was confirmed and renewed at Sinai.

Israel because they were greater or better than other peoples. The reason for his choice lay in him, not in them. As Moses explained it,

> The LORD . . . set his affection on you . . . because the LORD loved you. (Deut. 7:7-8)

"Covenant" is a legal term, and signifies any binding undertaking. When used in Scripture to describe what God has done, however, it is not to be thought of as an agreement between two equal parties, a kind of mutual contract. It is more like a "testament" or will in which the testator has sole and entire discretion in the disposal of his own estate: Indeed, the English words "covenant" and "testament" can be used interchangeably, which is why the two halves of the Bible are known as the Old and New "Testaments." The Greek word *diatheke* can mean either, and twice in the Epistles there is a play on the two meanings of the word, in order to make it plain that God's covenant is like a "last will and testament" in that he has freely made certain promises (Gal. 3:15-18; Heb. 9:15-18). His covenant promises are not uncon-

ditional, since his people are required to obey his commands and this is their part of the covenant, but God himself lays down the commands as well as the promises. So even at Sinai God's covenant remains a covenant of grace.

It is important to grasp, then, that the covenant of God is the same throughout, from Abraham to Christ, so that those who are Christ's by faith are thereby Abraham's children and heirs of the promises God made him (Gal. 3:29). The law which was given at Sinai did not annul the covenant of grace. On the contrary, the covenant of grace was confirmed and renewed at Sinai. What the law did was to emphasis and expand the requirement of obedience. It is only when the law is considered in isolation from the covenant of grace that it is contrasted with the gospel. Then the law is seen to condemn the sinner for his disobedience, while the gospel offers him life by grace.

We are now in a position to think about what may be described as three stages in the outworking of God's covenant, expressed in the three words "redemption," "adoption" and "glorification."

Redemption

Redemption was originally not a theological but a commercial word. Often in the Old Testament (as today) we read about the redemption of land, which had been alienated from the owner's possession, or mortgaged. There were people also who needed to be redeemed, such as slaves and prisoners. In each case something or somebody was bought, in fact bought back, from some state of alienation or bondage. To redeem was to purchase somebody's freedom, to recover by payment of a price something which had been lost.

This is the word which came to be applied to God's first act of grace towards his people. When they had somehow got lost, separated from him and from their homeland in exile or captivity, he delivered them from their bondage and restored them to their land. This pattern repeated itself three times in Israel's history. First, he called Abraham from Ur of the Chaldees (not, strictly speaking, a redemption because Abraham had not yet been in Canaan), then he delivered Israel from their Egyptian bondage, and finally the exiles from their Babylonian captivity. In each he called, he acted, he delivered and he brought them to the land of promise.

This is the Old Testament background to Jesus Christ's great work of redemption. Now humankind's alienation and bondage are spiritual. It is our sin – our rebellion against both our Creator's authority and our neighbor's welfare – which has enslaved us and separated us from God. Our sin has brought us under judgment; we deserve nothing for our revolt but death.

Into this situation of helplessness and despair came Jesus Christ. He took upon him our nature when he was born and our guilt when he died. In the stark, unvarnished language of the New Testament he first "became flesh," and then "was made sin," and even "became a curse" for us (John 1:14; 2 Cor. 5:21; Gal. 3:13). For the simple truth is that he took our place. He identified himself so completely with us in our predicament that he bore our sin and died our death. Our life was forfeit because of sin. He died instead of us, experiencing in our place the desolation of God-forsaken darkness.

The New Testament authors several times draw an analogy between the Passover, which initiated Israel's redemption from Egypt, and the death of Christ which has secured our redemption from sin. The life of every first-born in Egypt was forfeit, but God made provision for the life of a lamb to be acceptable instead, if its blood was first shed and then sprinkled on the lintel and side posts of the front door. When God saw the blood, he passed over the house to protect it from his own judgment.

The New Testament fulfillment is dramatic. John showed in his Gospel that by one reckoning Jesus was shedding his blood on the cross at the precise time when the Passover lambs were being killed (John 13:1; 18:28). Paul wrote that "Christ, our Passover lamb, has been sacrificed" (1 Cor. 5:7), while Peter referred to "the precious blood of Christ, a lamb without blemish or defect," which was shed to redeem us and must (symbolically, of course) be "sprinkled" upon us (1 Pet. 1:2, 18-19).

When Christ the Lamb of God had offered himself as our Passover sacrifice, had shed his blood and died, God raised him from the dead to vindicate him, and to demonstrate that his sacrifice for sin had not been offered in vain. Now he is described as "seated at God's right hand," resting from his finished work of redemption and crowned with glory and honor. He has won an "eternal redemption" (Heb. 9:12) for us. And throughout eternity the multitudes of heaven will sing, "Worthy is the Lamb, who was slain" (Rev. 5: 12. See also 5:9, 10)

Adoption

Redemption is a largely negative concept. It concentrates on the plight from which we have been delivered and on the price which had to be paid. True, to be redeemed from sin by

Passover dish, with a lamb's shank. Paul wrote that "Christ, our Passover lamb, has been sacrificed."

Christ's blood is to be redeemed "for God" (Rev. 5:9). But this positive aspect of our salvation is emphasized rather in the notion of our adoption to be his children. Paul brings the two together as virtually inseparable when he writes:

When the time had fully come, God sent his Son, born of a woman, born under law, to redeem those under law, that we might receive the full rights of sons; . . . So you are no longer a slave, but a son, and since you are a son, God has made you also an heir. (Gal. 4:4-7)

Redeemed from slavery and adopted into sonship – that is the glorious double privilege of those who put their trust in Christ. Our relationship to God as his children is an essential part of his covenant promise.

Already this fact of "belonging to God" was plain in Old Testament days. The covenant formula, used each time the covenant was renewed, was "I will be your God and you shall be my people." Moreover, this adoption of Israel to be the people of God immediately followed their redemption. Again and again God had to remind them of this, saying "I am the LORD your God, who brought you out of Egypt, out of the land of slavery" (Exod. 20:2). He had redeemed them. They were his. He spelled it out very clearly to them during the period between their redemption from Egypt and the renewal of the covenant at Sinai:

You yourselves have seen what I did to Egypt, and how I carried you on eagles' wings and brought you to myself. Now if you obey me fully and keep my covenant, then out of all nations you will be my treasured possession. Although the whole earth is mine, you will be for me a kingdom of priests and a holy nation. (Exod. 19:4-6)

Often this covenant, by which God's redeemed people became his own possession, his special treasure, was likened to a marriage covenant. Yahweh was the husband of his people. He had delighted in his bride's early love and devotion in the wilderness (Jer. 2:2; 31:32). But in Canaan she went after her "lovers," the baals of the local shrines. She became an adulteress, even a prostitute. She broke the covenant.

The marriage metaphor is continued and expanded in the New Testament. The apostle Paul described how "Christ loved the church and gave himself up for her," but he added elsewhere how anxious he was, even to the extent of feeling divine "jealousy," lest this bride should be led astray from "sincere and pure devotion to Christ" (Eph. 5:25; 2 Cor. 11:2-3).

The relation between God and his people in New Testament days is expressed more often in terms of the father and his family; however, than of the husband and his wife. It is a development of the Old Testament conviction that Israel was God's "firstborn son" (for example, Exod. 4:22). Jesus regularly taught his disciples to regard God as their heavenly Father and themselves as his beloved children, to pray to him as their Father, to trust his fatherly care to supply their material needs and to become concerned for their Father's name, kingdom and will.

One of the greatest privileges of being God's children is to have the Holy Spirit dwelling within us. The personal and abiding presence of the Holy Spirit in our hearts is a distinctive blessing, distinctive both of the Christian era itself (Jer. 31:33) and of the individual Christian. It is because we are sons or daughters that "God sent the Spirit of his Son into our hearts" (Gal. 4:6). Paul enlarges on this:

Those who are led by the Spirit of God are sons of God. For you did not receive a spirit that makes you a slave again to fear, but you received the Spirit of sonship. And by him we cry, "Abba, Father." The Spirit himself testifies with our spirit that we are God's children. (Rom. 8:14-16)

So the life of God's children may be described as "life in the Spirit." It is a life lived under the direction and by the power of the Holy Spirit. He bears witness with our spirit that we are indeed God's children. As the "Spirit of wisdom and revelation" in our knowledge of Christ (Eph. 1:17), he also opens the eyes of our hearts to know him better. And he is the *Holy* Spirit, seeking to lead us into *holiness,* to make us like Christ (2 Cor. 3:18). He subdues the power of our flesh (or fallen nature) and causes to ripen in our character his fruit of "love, joy, peace, patience, kindness, goodness, faithfulness, gentleness and self-control" (Gal. 5:16-23).

The children of God together form his family, the church, enjoying a direct continuity with God's people in Old Testament days. This fellowship of brothers and sisters in Christ transcends all barriers. It is hard for us to imagine how great was "the dividing wall of hostility" between Jew and Gentile. But Christ broke it down, and Paul devoted much of his Ephesian letter to the theme that Jews and Gentiles share in Christ on equal terms, being fellow citizens of God's kingdom and fellow members of God's family (Eph. 2:11-19; 3:6).

Other great contemporary rifts in society existed between men and women, and those who were slaves and those who were free. In the Roman empire slaves had no rights before the law; all the privileges belonged to the free. But when Paul led to Christ a runaway slave called Onesimus, he sent him back to his master Philemon, begging him to welcome him "no longer as a slave, but better than a slave, as a dear brother" (Philem. 16).

Also in ancient society women were almost universally despised. Jesus, however, treated them with honour, and Paul affirmed that men and women are equally in Christ God's children. The social effects of the gospel were explosive.

To sum up this unity, this equality, of all the members of God's family, Paul wrote:

There is neither Jew nor Greek, slave nor free, male nor female, for you are all one in Christ Jesus. (Gal. 3:28)

The people of God are "holy" people, that is, distinct or separate people, set apart from the rest of humankind to belong to God. Therefore they are called to be what they are, to manifest in their character and conduct the holiness of their status or position. They are "called to be holy," that is, called to be different from the secular world, and not to be conformed to its outlook or standards. "You must not do as they do," God had said to Israel in the wilderness, referring both to the Egyptians and to the Canaanites (Lev. 18:1-5). Similarly, "do not be like them," Jesus said during the Sermon on the Mount, referring both to the Gentiles and to the Pharisees.

Instead, the Christian is to follow Christ. And his absolute ethical standards are set forth without compromise in both the Gospels and the Epistles, just as God's standards were set before Israel in the Law and the Prophets.

It must not be thought, however, that Christ's call to his people to be "holy" or "different" provides any excuse for withdrawal from the world into a pietistic isolation. On the contrary, the very same people whom Christ has "chosen out of the world" he sends back "into the world" as his representatives, to give themselves to other people in humble service and witness (John 15:19; 17:15-19).

Further, as they remain in the world for Christ, seeking to serve the world's needs but refusing to become assimilated to the world's standards, they will experience the world's opposition. The world will hate them for their very difference, Christ warned, and persecute them too (John 15:18-25; 17:14). So they will suffer. Indeed, to suffer unjustly and to forbear revenge is another part of the calling of Christians. For Christ left us an example of this, that we should follow in his footsteps (1 Pet. 2:18-23).

But suffering leads to glory. It was so for Christ. It is so for the followers of Christ. Peter commands us to rejoice both in our share of Christ's sufferings and in our anticipated share in the glory which is to be revealed (1 Pet. 4:13; 5:1, 10). The apostle Paul said the same thing:

A Roman slave badge. Paul claimed that Christ broke all barriers between slaves and the free.

Now if we are children, then we are heirs
– heirs of God and co–heirs with Christ,
if indeed we share in his sufferings in
order that we may also share in his glory.
(Rom. 8:17)

These are some of the implications of our "adoption" into God's family. As children of our Father God, we are the dwelling place of his Spirit, united as brothers and sisters to all other Christian people, the ambassadors of Christ in the world, serving and suffering for his cause, and Christ's fellow heirs as well.

For to be a son is to be an heir. Suffering is the pledge of glory. This leads us straight to the third stage in God's unfolding plan of salvation, namely "glorification."

Glorification

The New Testament is full of the Christian hope. It reminds us that, although in the past we have been redeemed from sin by Christ and are now enjoying the privileges which adoption into God's family has brought us, there is still far more to come. To this consummation we are eagerly looking forward. For our Christian "hope" has no uncertainty about it. It is a joyful and confident expectation, based upon the promises of God. And it sustains us as we travel like pilgrims to our eternal home.

What is the object of our hope? To what are we looking forward? Paul called it "the hope of glory" (Rom. 5:2). But what does this mean?

First, the return of Christ. It is not fashionable to believe in this today, or at least, not in any literal sense. But Jesus clearly and repeatedly said that he was going to come back, and that his return would be "in power and great glory." The apostles enlarged on this assurance. His coming will be personal and visible, although it will also have a transcendent quality which puts it beyond our present understanding:

> For as lightning that comes from the east
> is visible even in the west, so will be the
> coming of the Son of Man. (Matt. 24:27)

Secondly, the resurrection. Resurrection means neither resuscitation nor survival. "Resuscitation" denotes the restoration of the body to this life, without change. "Survival" denotes the continuance of the soul, without the body. "Resurrection," however, denotes the simultaneous raising and changing of the body into a new vehicle of our personality, possessing new powers such as those exhibited by the risen Christ.

Those whom Jesus raised from death during his earthly ministry were resuscitated. They came back from death, resumed their former way of life, and then later died a second time. Resurrection, however, means the beginning of a new, different and immortal life. So our resurrected bodies, though retaining some kind of continuity with our present bodies, will also be changed. They will be as different, Paul says, as the plant is from the seed out of which it grows. They will be set free both from decay and from "the flesh," the fallen nature which in some sense belongs to them. They will also have new powers. In fact our resurrection body will be a "body of glory." Like Christ's (see Phil. 3:21; 1 Cor. 15:35-37).

Thirdly, the judgment. When Christ comes,

both salvation and judgment will be brought to completion. For both are processes begun in this life, as Jesus made plain (John 5:19-29). We shall be judged according to our works (Matt. 16:27; John 5:28-29; Rom. 2:6; Rev. 20:11-15). We cannot be justified (brought into acceptance with God) by our works; justification is only by God's grace through faith in Christ and his finished work. But we shall be judged by our works, because the judgment will be a public occasion, and our "works" – what we have said and done – will be the only public evidence that can be brought forward to prove the presence (or absence) of any saving faith. Those whose works reveal that they have disobeyed the gospel and rejected Christ will be lost. Whatever its precise nature may be, hell is a terrible reality. Christ called it "outer darkness" and "destruction." He told us to fear God "who can destroy both soul and body in hell" (Matt. 10:28).

Fourthly, the new universe. It is variously described. There will be "a new heaven and a new earth" (2 Pet. 3:13; Rev. 21:1), for God will make "everything new" (Rev. 21:5). Jesus called it "the rebirth" (Matt. 19:28, literal translation), Paul, the uniting of all things under Christ as head (Eph. 1:10), and Peter, the "restoration of all things" (Acts 3:21, literal translation).

Popular Christian devotion has perhaps concentrated too much on the negative joys of heaven, that is, on the promises of the Revelation that there will be no more hunger or thirst, no more scorching heat or sunstroke, no more tears or pain, no more night, no more curse, no more death. Thank God for these absences. But thank God even more for their cause, namely the presence – the central, dominating presence – of the throne of God.

When John was granted his vision of heavenly reality, and was permitted to peer through "an open door," the first thing on which his eye rested was "a throne" (Rev. 4:1-2), the symbol of God's sovereignty. Everything else in his vision was related to this throne. The Father sat on it, and the Lamb shared it, together with "the seven spirits of God" representing the Holy Spirit. Round it in concentric circles were twenty-four elders symbolizing the church and four living creatures symbolizing the creation, and beyond them myriads of angels. Flashes of lightning and peals of thunder issued from the throne, and before the throne stood the great gathering of the redeemed, drawn from every nation and language, wearing white robes of righteousness, waving palm branches of victory, and ascribing their salvation to their God who sits on the throne and to the Lamb (Rev. 4–7).

The Bible begins with the creation of the universe and ends with the re-creation of the universe. It goes on at its beginning to describe the fall of man in a garden and paradise lost; it concludes in a garden, with paradise regained. Here are the tree of life for food and for healing, and the water of life for refreshment. And the river of the water of life is seen to be "flowing from the throne of God and of the Lamb" (Rev. 22:1). For at last God's kingdom has been consummated. All creation is subject to him. And the blessings of our inheritance will be due to his perfect rule. So the great multitude sings:

Hallelujah! For our Lord God Almighty reigns. (Rev. 19:6)

And somehow, we are told, his redeemed, adopted, glorified people will share his reign:

They will reign for ever and ever. (Rev. 22:5)

NOTE

1. For verses in which God says he will "spend," "satisfy" (RSV) or "give full vent to his anger" and thus judge his people for their inveterate rebellion, see, for example, Ezek. 5:13 ff.; 6:12; 7:8; 16:42, 43; 24:13, 14 and Lam. 4:11. In Psalm 89:33ff., however, it is his steadfast love according to his covenant promise and oath which direct him. "I will not . . . betray my faithfulness," he says (v. 33). Compare the declaration in Isa. 53:11 that the Lord's suffering servant, seeing the fruit of his soul's travail, will "be satisfied."

6. The Authority of the Bible

❧ *How are biblical revelation, inspiration and authority different, and what are the three disclaimers we must add to these words?*

❧ *How did Jesus put his seal on both the Old Testament and the New Testament?*

❧ *How do we know that the apostles had the authority to speak for God?*

I tried in the preceding chapter to summarize the message of the Bible, and in the previous three to outline the geographical and historical settings in which this message was given and received. But is the biblical message really the divine revelation it claims to be? Can we trust the Bible? Has it any continuing authority?

Drop the word "authority" into any conversation today, and it sets off in people a whole range of different vibrations. None of us has escaped the crisis of recent decades. The widespread, conscious revolt against all established authority – government, university, church, family, tradition, Bible – broke out in 1968 when students and workers took to the barricades in Paris and the "Free Speech" movement erupted on the Berkeley campus of the University of California. Since then some genuine gains can be registered, in that contemporary society is more open and participatory than before. But there have been serious losses too, especially in the rejection of values and standards. Existentialists insist that nothing has meaning any longer, and that therefore no intellectual or moral authority of any kind is left. And now, as the third millennium has dawned, post-modernism is hostile to all truth-claims.

The Christian witness, who seeks to infiltrate the defenses of relativism, will not begin with the authority of the Bible, but rather with the authority of Christ. For Jesus of Nazareth remains an attractive figure to them, in spite of the fact that he somehow managed to combine with his radical challenges to tradition a strangely conservative attitude to God and to Scripture. Moreover, his humble submissiveness had a self-authenticating quality, and still has when embodied in his followers. His authority does not simply impose itself from above; it commends itself from below. It is unexpectedly liberating.

My concern in this chapter is not with rebels and relativists, however, for they are not likely to be found among the readers of this book. I am concerned rather with those who profess and call themselves Christians, and who accept that the words "authority" and "submission," although in constant need of redefinition, cannot possibly be dropped from the Christian vocabulary. For have we not confessed that "Jesus Christ is Lord"? And does not our confession of his lordship inevitably involve a submission to his authority? Further, should not our submission to his authority bring with it a submission to the Bible's authority? Could it be that his exhortation "he who has an ear, let him hear what the Spirit says to the churches" (Rev. 2–3) is an invitation to us to listen to *Scripture* through which Christ by his Spirit still speaks to the church? These are the questions I want to raise. They are crucial questions, which must be answered and cannot be dodged.

For one thing, the Bible claims (as we have seen) to be a book of salvation, to "make us wise for salvation." Therefore we must know whether the way of salvation it unfolds is true or false. The eternal destiny of human beings depends upon it.

For another thing, the contemporary church

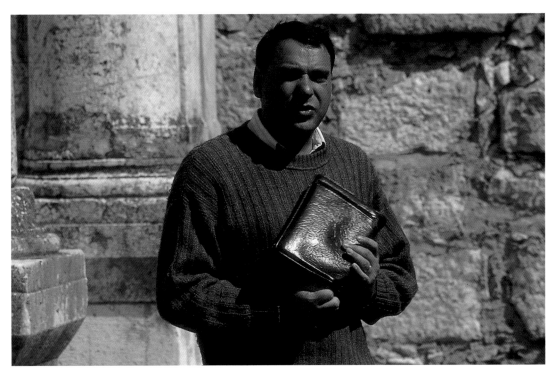

The Bible claims to be a book of salvation, to "make us wise for salvation."

is confused. The non-Christian world is constantly being treated to the bewildering spectacle of Christians in disagreement and discord. Why is this? The primary cause of confusion in the church is the lack of an agreed authority. The church will never recover either its morale or its mission unless it first rediscovers the source of its authority.

In addition, it is fashionable nowadays to deny to every religion whatever exclusive elements it may claim. Other religions also have their holy books; what is so special about the Christian Scriptures, the Bible?

Three definitions

Aware, then, of the importance of our subject and of the disfavor with which many will regard our attempt to defend the uniqueness of the Bible, we shall begin with some definitions. The three great words commonly used by Christians in this connection are "revelation," "inspiration" and "authority." They are related but distinct.

The fundamental word is "revelation." Derived from a Latin noun meaning "unveiling," it indicates that God has taken the initiative to make himself known. The reasonableness of this concept should be plain. For whoever or whatever God may be, he is altogether beyond our knowledge. "Can you fathom the mysteries of God? Can you probe the limits of the Almighty?" (Job 11:7) Indeed not. His infinite greatness is veiled from our eyes. We cannot discover him by ourselves. If we are ever to know him, he must make himself known.

The second word, "inspiration," indicates the chief mode God has chosen by which to reveal himself. He has revealed himself partly in nature and supremely in Christ, but also by "speaking" to particular people. And it is this process of verbal communication which is called "inspiration." We do not use it in the general sense that we may say a poet or musician is "inspired." On the contrary, it has a special and precise connotation, namely that "all Scripture is God-breathed" (2 Tim. 3:16) – a phrase translating a single Greek expression, less precisely translated in some versions as "inspired by God." The meaning, then, is not that God breathed into the writers, nor that he somehow breathed into the writings to give them their special character, but that what was written by the human authors was breathed out by God. He spoke through them. They were his spokesmen.

Further, we do not hesitate to say that this inspiration was "verbal inspiration," in that it extended to the very words used by the human authors. This is what they claimed. The apostle Paul, for example, could declare that in communicating to others what God had revealed to him, he used "not words taught us by human wisdom but . . . taught by the Spirit" (1 Cor. 2:13). Nor is this in the least surprising, since it is not possible to convey a precise message in any other way than in precise words.

"Authority," the third word, is the power or weight which Scripture possesses because of what it is, namely a divine revelation given by divine inspiration. If it is a word from God, it has authority over us. For behind every word that anybody utters stands the person who speaks it. It is the speaker himself (his character, knowledge and position) who determines how people regard his words. So God's Word carries God's authority. It is because of who he is that we should believe what he has said.

This is the lesson Simon Peter learned when Jesus told him on the lake of Galilee to put out into deep water and let down his nets for a catch. All his fisherman's expertise, gathered from years of experience, rebelled against the suggestion. He even protested, "Master, we've worked hard all night and haven't caught anything." Yet wisely he added, "But because you say so, I will let down the nets" (Luke 5:4-5).

Our claim, then, is that God has revealed himself by speaking; that this divine ("God-breathed") speech has been written down and preserved in Scripture; and that Scripture is, in fact, God's Word written, which therefore is true and reliable and has divine authority over us.

Three disclaimers

It seems necessary now to add to these definitions certain disclaimers which may anticipate objections and disarm possible criticism.

First, the process of inspiration was not a mechanical one. God did not treat the human authors of Scripture as dictating machines or tape recorders, but as living and responsible persons. Sometimes he spoke to them in dreams and visions, sometimes by an audible voice, sometimes by angels. At other times we are not told how the word of God came to them. They may well not have been conscious of it at all. Thus in the case of Luke the evangelist divine inspiration was certainly not incompatible with human research, for he tells us in the preface to his Gospel about the painstaking enquiries he had pursued. Whatever means of communication God employed in speaking to human beings, it never obliterated their own personality. On the contrary, as they wrote, their literary style and vocabulary were their own. So too – more important still – was their theme. It is not an accident that Amos was the prophet of God's justice, Hosea of his love and Isaiah of his kingly sovereignty, nor that Paul was the apostle of grace and faith, James of works, John of love and Peter of hope. The internal evidence, gathered from reading the biblical text, is that God made full use of the personality, temperament, background and experience of the biblical authors, in order to convey through each an appropriate and distinctive message.

So, then, Scripture is equally the word of God and the word of human beings. This is, indeed, how it describes itself. If it is true that "the mouth of the LORD has spoken" (for example, Isa. 1:20), it is also true that God spoke "through his holy prophets" (for example, Acts 3:21). Similarly, "God spoke . . . through the prophets" (Heb. 1:1), and "men spoke from God" (2 Pet. 1:21). Again, the law could be described by one author in a single passage both as "the Law of Moses" and as "the Law of the Lord" (Luke 2:22-23).

The dual authorship of Scripture is an important truth to be carefully guarded. On

Simon Peter learned to believe God's Word when Jesus told him on the lake of Galilee to put out into deep water and let down his nets for a catch.

the one hand, *God* spoke, revealing the truth and preserving the human authors from error, yet without violating their personality. On the other hand, *men* spoke, using their own faculties freely, yet without distorting the divine message. Their words were truly their own words. Yet they were (and still are) also God's words, so that what Scripture says, God says.

My second disclaimer is that, although Scripture as God's Word is true, this does not mean – to quote a common claim – that "every word of the Bible is literally true." Such a statement would need to be qualified in several ways. Although I am here trespassing slightly upon what I shall write in the next chapter about biblical interpretation, I think I need to say something about it here.

To begin with, every word of the Bible is true only in its context. Isolated from its context, it may be quite untrue. The best example of what I mean is the Book of Job, the bulk of which consists of a dialogue between the grief-stricken Job and his three "comforters," together with a fourth who appears later. This part occupies chapters 1–37. Then God reveals

himself to Job in chapters 38–42. Some of what Job and his comforters say about suffering in the first thirty-seven chapters is mistaken. It is recorded in order to be contradicted, not in order to be believed. We are told so at the end of the book when Job says to God, "I spoke of things I did not understand," and God says to Job's comforters "you have not spoken of me what is right" (Job 42:3, 7). It would be quite impossible, therefore, to take any verse from the Book of Job and say "this is the word of God," for it may not be. The book as a whole is God's Word, but the first thirty-seven chapters can be understood only in the light of the last five.

The key principle, already mentioned in chapter 2 and to be further elaborated in the next chapter, was well expressed in the Lausanne Covenant (1974), namely that Scripture is "without error in all that it affirms." This phrase indicates that not everything contained in the Bible is affirmed by the Bible (as we have seen in the Book of Job). It then adds that whatever is affirmed by Scripture is true and without error, because its affirmations are God's. This vital principle has not always been apparent in the so-called "inerrancy debate" in the United States. We should be able to agree that whatever Scripture affirms is true, whether in the field of religion or ethics, history or science, its own nature or origins. But this leaves the major question of interpretation: precisely what is the Bible affirming in these areas?

Then again much of Scripture is deliberately presented in a highly figurative manner. Thus, there are many "anthropomorphic" descriptions of God, representing him in human form, and referring to his eyes and ears, his "outstretched arm," "mighty hand" and fingers, his mouth, his breath and his nostrils. We do not interpret these *literally* for the simple reason that "God is spirit" (John 4:24) and therefore has no body. So when we read that "the eyes of the LORD range throughout the earth to strengthen those whose hearts are fully committed to him" (2 Chron. 16:9), we do not try to visualize a pair of divine eyes literally running about over the earth's surface, but understand, rather, that God sees everyone everywhere and is always ready to save and to strengthen those who trust in him. In the same way, when we read of people hiding under his "wings," we do not picture him as a bird with feathers, but learn that he protects those who take refuge in him.

Similarly, when the psalmist writes that the sun comes forth "like a bridegroom . . . from his pavilion, like a champion rejoicing to run his course," and when he goes on to refer to the sun's "rising" and "circuit" from one end of the heavens to the other (Ps. 19:1-6), he does not commit us to a pre-Copernican view of the solar system. For he is evidently describing the sun's resplendent magnificence both in poetic imagery and from the point of view of an earthbound observer. Even sophisticated technocrats of the third millennium can wax eloquent about the sun, and can talk of its "rising" and "setting." They do not need to apologize for doing so. People recognize that they are using the language of poetry, and of ordinary observations, not of science.

The third disclaimer I would make concerns what the inspired text of Scripture is, which alone can be regarded as God's Word written. This is the original Hebrew or Greek text as it came from the authors' hands. We claim no special inspiration or authority for any particular translation *as a translation* – whether ancient Latin or modern English, nor indeed for any particular interpretation.

It is true that no actual autograph has survived. Their loss is presumably due to a deliberate providence of God, which may have been to prevent us giving superstitious reverence to pieces of paper. Nevertheless, we know something of the scrupulous care with which scribes copied the sacred Hebrew text (as evidenced in the Dead Sea scrolls), and the same would have been true of the New Testament documents. Further, we possess a great many more early copies of the original text than of any other ancient literature. By comparing these with each other, with the early "versions" (that is, translations) and with biblical quotations in the writings of the church fathers, scholars (called "textual critics") have been able to establish the authentic text (especially of the New Testament) beyond any reasonable doubt. The uncertainties which remain are almost entirely trivial; no doctrine of any importance hangs upon them.

So far I have tried to clear the ground by indicating both what we do and what we do not claim for the Bible. It is time to ask on what grounds we base our assurance that it is God's Word written, originating with God and authoritative for us. Many different answers have been given. I will touch on the first three briefly and concentrate on the fourth and decisive argument.

Arguments for the authority of Scripture

The first point to make is that the historic Christian churches have consistently maintained and defended the divine origin of Scripture. Only in comparatively recent times

One of the Dead Sea scrolls is the centerpiece of the Shrine of the Book museum, Jerusalem.

have some churches changed their official doctrine on this matter. Whether we consult the formularies of Protestant churches (for example, Anglican, Presbyterian and Lutheran) or of the Roman Catholic and Orthodox Churches, the witness is virtually unanimous. Now this is not a conclusive argument and may not appeal at all to some. Nevertheless, the consensus of the centuries is very impressive and is not to be lightly set aside or despised.

Secondly, we turn from what the historic churches have consistently taught to what the biblical writers themselves claimed. This is even more impressive. For example, Moses said he had received the law from God. The prophets introduced their oracles with formulae like "Thus says the LORD" or "The word of the LORD came to me, saying." And the apostles could write such statements as this one from Paul:

When you received the word of God, which you heard from us, you accepted it not as the word of men, but as it actually is, the word of God, which is at work in you who believe. (1 Thess. 2:13)

The biblical authors also make similar claims for each other. We find in Scripture an elaborate pattern of cross-authorization. For example, the prophets endorsed the law, and the psalmists extolled its truth, beauty and sweetness (for example, Pss. 19; 119). Above all, the New Testament confirms the Old, the apostolic authors drawing from it a rich variety of quotations as divine warrant for what they were writing. There is even the famous passage in which the apostle Peter refers to the letters of "our dear brother Paul," comments on the "wisdom" given to him, and equates his epistles with Scripture (2 Pet. 3:15-16).

The third line of evidence for the inspiration and authority of Scripture is supplied not by the writers but by the readers of Scripture. For there are certain characteristics of the Bible which cannot fail to strike the observant reader. There is, for instance, the books' remarkable unity and coherence, on which I have tried to enlarge in earlier chapters. In view of the diversity of human authorship and topic, the best explanation of this unity seems to be the overshadowing activity of a single divine author behind the human authors. There is also, as one aspect of this overall unity, the striking phenomenon of fulfilled prophecy. Then there are the nobility and dignity of the great themes of Scripture and the extraordinary relevance of its message thousands of years later, to which its continuing popularity bears witness.

Further, there is the power which the Bible has had (God's power through it, we believe) in human lives, disturbing the complacent and comforting the sorrowful, humbling the proud, reforming the sinful, encouraging the faint-hearted, bringing hope to the bereaved and giving direction to those who have lost their way. Added to all this is what the Reformers called "the inward witness of the Holy Spirit." It is the deep assurance that Scripture is truth from God, an assurance arising not from external confirmation such as archaeological discoveries (helpful as these are), but internally from the Holy Spirit himself It is the experience of the "burning heart," given first to the disciples on the Emmaus Road, but still granted to Christian disciples of the modern world:

> Were not our hearts burning within us
> while he talked with us on the road and
> opened the Scriptures to us? (Luke 24:32)

However, the first and foremost reason why Christians believe in the divine inspiration and authority of Scripture is not because of what the churches teach, the writers claimed or the readers sense, but because of what Jesus Christ himself said. Since he endorsed the authority of Scripture, we are bound to conclude that his authority and Scripture's authority either stand or fall together.

Some may at once retort that to rely on Christ's witness to Scripture is to employ a circular argument, which might be expressed like this: "How do I know that Scripture is inspired? Because of Christ, who says so. How do I know that Christ says so? Because of Scripture, which

is inspired." This, our critics point out, is to beg the question, for it is to assume the very truth we are wanting to prove. But they have misstated our argument. When we make our first approach to the Bible, we bring with us no assumptions about its divine inspiration. We accept it merely as a collection of historical documents, containing in particular the witness of first-century Christians to Christ. As we read their testimony, we come to believe in Christ, still without formulating any particular doctrine of Scripture. But then the Christ we have come to believe in sends us back to Scripture. He gives us a new understanding of it because he endorses its authority for us.

But how did Christ endorse Scripture? Scripture consists, of course, of two separate sections, the Old and the New Testaments. And the way in which Jesus Christ set his seal on each is different.

Christ's view of the Old Testament

Take the Old Testament first. There can be no doubt, as any careful reader of the Gospels will agree, that Jesus gave his reverent assent to the authority of Old Testament Scripture, for he submitted to its authority himself. I will give three examples to demonstrate this.

First, Jesus submitted to the Old Testament in his personal conduct. Thus, he countered each of the temptations of the devil by an apt biblical quotation. It is sometimes said that he quoted Scripture "at the devil." This is not so. It would be more accurate to say that he quoted Scripture at himself in the presence of the devil. For when the devil offered him the kingdoms of the world if he would fall down and worship him, Jesus replied:

> Away from me, Satan! For it is written:
> "Worship the Lord your God, and serve
> him only." (Matt. 4:10)

Jesus was not applying this text to Satan, but to himself. He knew from Scripture that

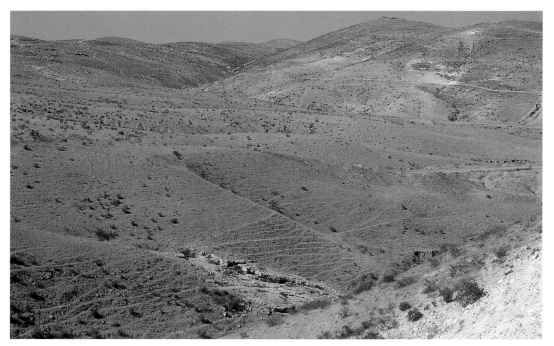

The barren Judean Wilderness, where Jesus was tempted by Satan.

worship was due to God alone. Therefore he would obey. As man he would worship God, not Satan. The simple word *gegraptai* ("it stands written") was enough for him. There was no need to question, discuss, argue or negotiate. The matter had already been settled by Scripture. This voluntary, personal submission of God's Son to the authority of God's Word is extremely significant.

Secondly, Jesus submitted to the Old Testament in the fulfillment of his mission. He seems to have come to an understanding of his messianic role from a study of Old Testament Scripture. He knew himself to be both Isaiah's suffering servant and Daniel's Son of Man. So he accepted that he could enter into his glory only by the road of suffering and death. This explains the sense of necessity, of compulsion, which constrained him:

> The Son of Man *must* suffer many things and be rejected . . . and he *must* be killed and after three days rise again. (Mark 8:31)

Why *"must"*? Because the Scripture said so.

Voluntarily and deliberately he put himself under its authority. He was determined to fulfill what stood written in his mission as in his conduct. So when Peter tried to prevent Christ's arrest in the Garden of Gethsemane, he told him to sheathe his sword. He had no need of human defense. Could he not appeal to his Father for legions of defending angels? Then why did he not do so? Here is the reason he gave:

> How then would the Scriptures be fulfilled that say it *must* happen in this way? (Matt. 26:54)

He was of the same opinion after the Resurrection, and confirmed it both to the two Emmaus disciples and to the wider group of his followers:

> Did not the Christ have to suffer these things and then enter his glory? . . . This is what I told you while I was still with you: Everything *must* be fulfilled that is written about me in the Law of Moses, the Prophets and the Psalms. (Luke 24:26, 44)

Thirdly, Jesus submitted to the Old Testament in his controversies. He found himself engaged in continuous debate with the religious leaders of his day, and whenever there was a difference of opinion between them, he regarded Scripture as the final court of appeal. "What is written in the Law?" he would ask. "How do you read it?" (Luke 10:26). Again, "Haven't you read this scripture?" (Mark 12:10). One of his chief criticisms of his contemporaries concerned their disrespect for Scripture. The Pharisees added to it and the Sadducees subtracted from it. So to the Pharisees he said:

> You have a fine way of setting aside the commands of God in order to observe your own traditions! . . . Thus you nullify the word of God by your tradition that you have handed down. (Mark 7:9, 13)

And to the Sadducees who denied the supernatural:

> Are you not in error because you do not know the Scriptures or the power of God? (Mark 12:24)

It is beyond question, then, that Jesus Christ was himself personally submissive to Scripture. In his own ethical standards, in his understanding of his mission and in debate with the Jewish leaders, what the Scripture said was decisive for him. "Scripture cannot be broken," he affirmed. And again,

> I tell you the truth, until heaven and earth disappear, not the smallest letter, not the least stroke of a pen, will by any means disappear from the Law until everything is accomplished. (Matt. 5:18)

There is no example of Christ contradicting the divine origin of Old Testament Scripture. Some people have supposed that he did so in the six antitheses of the Sermon on the Mount, in which he said, "You have heard that it was said . . . but I say to you. . . ." However, it is not Moses with whom he was at odds, but the scribal perversions of Moses; not Scripture (what was "written"), but oral tradition (what was "said"). All the available evidence confirms that Jesus Christ assented in his mind and submitted in his life to the authority of Old Testament Scripture. Is it not inconceivable that his followers should have a lower view of it than he?

Christ's provision for the New Testament

Christ's way of endorsing the New Testament was, of course, different from his way of endorsing the Old, for none of the books of the New Testament had yet been written. If, then, the writing of the New Testament belonged entirely to the future, how could he endorse it at all?

The answer to this question lies in his appointment of the apostles. Jesus seems to have foreseen the need for Scriptures of the New Testament corresponding to the Scriptures of the Old. In the Old Testament God was active in redeeming and judging Israel, and himself raised up prophets to give a true record and interpretation of what he was doing. Now God was active, through Christ, in redeeming and judging the world. Was this supreme and final revelation of God in Christ to be lost to future generations? No, there must be authoritative scribes and interpreters of this revelation as well. So Jesus made provision for this very thing. He carefully (after a whole night of prayer) chose and appointed, and then went on to train and authorize, the twelve apostles to be his witnesses, as God had chosen the prophets in Old Testament days:

> One of those days Jesus went out to a mountainside to pray, and spent the night praying to God. When morning came, he called his disciples to him and chose twelve of them, whom he also designated apostles. (Luke 6:12-13)

All the followers of Jesus were "disciples";

Cleopatra's Gate, Tarsus. Paul of Tarsus was one of the restricted circle of "apostles of Christ."

only the twelve were named "apostles." A study of the New Testament use of the title shows that, although there were "apostles of the churches" roughly equivalent to modern missionaries (for example, 2 Cor. 8:23; Acts 13:1-3; 14:14; Phil. 2:25), "the apostles of Christ" were a small and restricted circle consisting of the Twelve, Matthias (who replaced Judas), Paul, James the Lord's brother, and perhaps one or two others. Although the whole church is apostolic in the sense that Christ sends it into the world on his mission, and although every Christian should be involved in this mission, yet "apostle" is not a general word for a Christian in the New Testament. Even Paul's loyal and trusted colleagues like Timothy were not apostles. He deliberately drew a distinction between himself and them. Thus, he began his letter to the Colossians: "Paul, an apostle of Christ Jesus by the will of God, and Timothy our brother." Timothy was a brother. Indeed, all Christians are brothers and sisters. But he was not an apostle of Christ like Paul.

Modern research suggests that the Greek word *apostolos* is the equivalent of the Aramaic *shaliach,* and that the *shaliach* in rabbinic Judaism was a person with a clearly defined role. He was an emissary of the Sanhedrin, sent out to the Jews of the dispersion to teach in the Council's name. It was said of him, "the one sent by a person is as this person himself." In other words, he was a plenipotentiary, speaking with the authority of the person or body that had commissioned him. Thus Saul of Tarsus went to the synagogues at Damascus, armed "with the authority and commission of the chief priests" (Acts 26:12; cf. 9:1-2; 22:5).

It is against this background that Jesus chose twelve men and deliberately gave them this title. The apostles were to be his personal representatives, endowed with his authority to speak in his name. When he sent them out, he said to them, "He who receives you receives me" (Matt. 10:40; John 13:20).

The apostles of Jesus appear to have had a fourfold uniqueness.

First, they had a personal call and authorization by Jesus. This was clear in the case of the Twelve, and Paul claimed something comparable. He vehemently asserted and defended his apostolic authority, insisting that he had received his commission to be an apostle "not from men nor by man, but by Jesus Christ and God the Father" (Gal. 1:1). It is further significant that in one of the accounts of Paul's conversion in the Acts, the very words which Jesus used to commission him are recorded (although Luke has translated them into Greek), namely *ego apostello se*, "I send you" or "I make you an apostle" (Acts 26:17; cf. 22:21).

Secondly, they had an eyewitness experience of Christ. The Twelve were appointed, Mark says, to be "with him, and that he might send them out to preach." The verb *"send* out" is again *apostellein*, and their essential qualification for the work of apostleship was to be "with him." Similarly, shortly before he died, Jesus said to them:

> You also must testify, for you have been
> with me from the beginning. (John 15:27)

So he gave them unrivaled opportunities to hear his words and see his works, so that they might later bear witness to what they had seen and heard (cf. 1 John 1:1-3). Especially was it important for them to be witnesses of his resurrection. It was for this that Matthias was chosen, "to take over this apostolic ministry, which Judas left to go where he belongs" (Acts 1:21-26).

It is true, of course, that Paul was not one of the original twelve apostles, that he did not have the eyewitness experience of Jesus which they had, and that probably he never even saw Jesus in the flesh. Some have conjectured that the three years he spent in Arabia, during which he says he received his gospel "by revelation from Jesus Christ" (Gal. 1:11-12, 17-18), were deliberately intended to compensate him for the three years of Christ's public ministry which he had missed. Be that as it may, he fulfilled this second apostolic qualification by being a witness of the resurrection. "Am I not an apostle?" he cried. "Have I not seen Jesus our Lord?" (1 Cor. 9:1). His reference is of course to his encounter with Christ on the Damascus Road. Although it took place after the ascension, and was therefore abnormal, nevertheless he claims that it was an actual, objective resurrection appearance, and he adds that it was the last. At the end of his catalogue of the resurrection appearances he writes:

> Last of all he appeared to me also, as to
> one abnormally born. (1 Cor. 15:8-9)

Thirdly, they had an extraordinary inspiration of the Holy Spirit. We saw in the previous chapter that the indwelling and illumination of the Holy Spirit are the privilege of all God's children. This privilege was not restricted to the apostles. Nevertheless, the ministry of the Spirit which Christ promised the apostles was something quite unique, as should be clear from these words:

> All this I have spoken while still with
> you. But the Counselor, the Holy Spirit,
> whom the Father will send in my name,
> will teach you all things and will remind
> you of everything I have said to you. . . .
>   I have much more to say to you, more
> than you can now bear. When he, the
> Spirit of truth, comes, he will guide you
> into all truth. (John 14:25-26; 16:12-13)

These wonderful promises have sometimes been applied to all Christian people, and doubtless they do have a secondary reference to us all. But their primary reference is evidently to the apostles who were gathered round Jesus in the Upper Room, of whom he could say, "All this I have spoken to *you* while still with *you* and "I have much more to say to *you*, more than *you* can now bear."

What he promised them was twofold. First, that the Holy Spirit would remind them of the teaching he had given them, and secondly that he would supplement it, leading them into all the truth which they could not at the moment receive. The major fulfillment of these promises was in the writing of the Gospels and the epistles of the New Testament.

Fourthly, they had the power to work miracles. The Book of Acts is rightly called "The Acts of the Apostles" (cf. Acts 1:1-2; 2:43; 5:12), and Paul designates the "signs and wonders and miracles" which he had performed "the things that mark an apostle" (2 Cor. 2:12). This does not mean that every single miracle was performed by an apostle (for Stephen and Philip were not apostles), but rather that the major purpose of the miraculous power given to the apostles was to authenticate their apostolic commission and message:

> How shall we escape if we ignore such a great salvation? This salvation, which was first announced by the Lord, was confirmed to us by those who heard him [that is, the apostolic eyewitnesses]. God also testified to it by signs, wonders and various miracles, and gifts of the Holy Spirit distributed according to his will. (Heb. 2:3-4)

In these four ways the apostles seem to have been unique.

The apostles' authority confirmed

Our impression of the uniqueness of the apostles is confirmed in two ways. First the themselves knew it, and so exhibit in the New Testament their self-conscious apostolic authority. This is certainly so of Paul and John. Paul not only defends his authority as an apostle (as we have seen); he asserts it. Listen to the dogmatic instructions he gave the Thessalonian church:

> We have confidence in the Lord that you are doing and will continue to do the things we command. . . . In the name of the Lord Jesus Christ, we command you, brothers. . . . For even when we were with you, we gave you this rule. . . . Such people we command and urge in the Lord Jesus Christ. . . . If anyone does not obey

our instruction in this letter, take special note of him. (2 Thess. 3:4, 6, 10, 12, 14)

Who is this "we"? It is the plural of apostolic authority. And who is it who presumes to issue these authoritative commands and to demand obedience? Again, it is an apostle of Christ, who speaks in the name of Christ. He claims that Christ was speaking in and through him (2 Cor. 13:3). As a result, when he first visited Galatia, although he was disfigured by illness, the Galatians did not scorn or despise him, but actually received him "as . . . an angel of God, as . . . Christ Jesus" (Gal. 4:14). Paul does not rebuke them for paying him an exaggerated deference. On the contrary, they were right to receive him thus, for he was an apostle, an ambassador, an authorized representative of Jesus Christ.

John also used the plural of apostolic authority (for example, 3 John 9) and constantly recalled his readers to the original teaching he had given them. In view of the prevalence of false teachers he dared even to write:

> We are from God, and whoever knows God listens to us; but whoever is not from God does not listen to us. This is how we recognize the Spirit of truth and the spirit of falsehood. (1 John 4:6)

In other words, a safe test by which John's readers could discern between truth and error was whether what was taught was in accord with his teaching. False teachers would show their error by not listening to John, while the true Christian would authenticate himself by his submission to the apostle's authority.

The second way in which the unique authority of the apostles is substantiated is that the early church recognized it. For example, in the post-apostolic period, round about AD 110, soon after John the last apostle had died, Bishop Ignatius of Antioch sent letters to several churches of Asia Minor and Europe. In his Epistle to the Romans (ch. 4), he wrote:

I do not, as Peter and Paul, issue commandments unto you. They were apostles; I am but a condemned man.

He was a bishop. But he recognized that even a bishop's authority was not comparable to an apostle's.

When in the fourth century the church came finally to settle which books should be included in the New Testament canon and which excluded, the test they applied was whether a book came from the apostles. That is, was it written by an apostle? If not, did it nevertheless emanate from the circle of the apostles and carry the endorsement of their authority? It is important to add this, for not every New Testament book was written by an apostle. But it seems to have been recognized that if a non-apostolic document nevertheless carried a kind of apostolic imprimatur, it should be recognized as "apostolic." For example, Luke was known to have been a regular companion and colleague of Paul, and Mark was described by the early church fathers Papias and Irenaeus as "the interpreter of Peter," who faithfully recorded Peter's memories of Christ and the substance of his preaching.[1] Thus, the church was in no sense conferring authority on the canonical books; it was simply recognizing the authority they already possessed.

It is time now to summarize the argument which has been developed. Christ endorsed the authority of the Old Testament. He also made provision for the New Testament by authorizing his apostles to teach in his name. Therefore, if we desire to bow to Christ's authority, we must bow to Scripture's. It is because of Jesus Christ that Christians submit to both Old and New Testaments.

What are the alternatives to this conclusion? There are only two.

The first is to say that Christ was mistaken in his view of Scripture. In this case the argument would run somewhat as follows: "The incarnation imprisoned Jesus in the limited mentality of a first-century Jew. Of course he accepted the authority of Scripture, for this is what the Jews of his day believed. But that is

Modern Thessaloniki. Paul emphasized his apostolic authority to the church at Thessalonica.

no reason why we should. Their view and his are outmoded." This is the so-called theory of "kenosis," from the Greek word which declares that he "emptied himself" (Phil. 2:7 RSV) or "made himself nothing" (NIV) when he became man. He certainly emptied himself of his glory when he took the form of a servant. But he did not empty himself of his deity in becoming human. And although as a human being he seems to have been ignorant of certain matters (he said he did not know the day of his return, Mark 13:32), the remarkable fact is that he was not ignorant of his ignorance. He knew the limits of his knowledge. Consequently in his instruction he never strayed beyond these limits. On the contrary, he insisted that he taught only what the Father gave him to teach (for example, John 7:14-17; 12:49; 17:8). Therefore we claim that he was inerrant, that all, his teaching was true, including his endorsement of the authority of Scripture.

The second alternative which has been proposed may be expressed like this: "Jesus knew perfectly well that Scripture was not entirely the Word of God and reliable. Yet because his contemporaries all believed that it was, he accommodated himself to their position. There is no need for us to do so." But this suggestion is quite intolerable. It is derogatory to Christ, and incompatible with his claim to be the truth and to teach the truth. Besides, he never hesitated to disagree with his contemporaries on other matters, so why should he have done so on this? Further, this reconstruction would attribute to Jesus the very thing he detested most – religious pretense, or hypocrisy.

So we reject both the "kenosis" and the "accommodation" theories. Over against them we must insist that Jesus knew what he was talking about, and that he meant it. He taught knowledgeably, deliberately and with entire sincerity. He declared the divine origin of all Scripture for the straightforward reason that he believed it. And what he believed and taught is true.

Some conclusions

In conclusion, let me emphasize both the rightness and the reasonableness of submitting to the authority of Scripture.

First, to accept the authority of the Bible is a Christian thing to do. It is neither a religious eccentricity, nor a case of discreditable obscurantism, but the good sense of Christian faith and humility. It is essentially "Christian" because it is what Christ himself requires of us. The traditional view of Scripture (that it is God's Word written) may be called the "Christian" view precisely because it is Christ's view.

Secondly, what shall we do with the problems? To accept the divine origin of the Bible is not to pretend that there are not problems. To be candid, there are many problems – literary, historical, theological and moral. So what shall we do with them? Is it compatible with intellectual integrity to accept the unique authority of Scripture when so many residual problems remain? Yes indeed it is.

We need to learn to do with the problems surrounding Scripture exactly what we do with the problems surrounding any other Christian doctrine. Every Christian doctrine has its problems. No doctrine is entirely free of them. Take as an example the doctrine of the love of God. Every Christian of every conceivable hue believes that God is love. It is a fundamental Christian doctrine. To disbelieve this would be to disqualify oneself as a Christian. But the problems surrounding the doctrine are massive. What, then, do we do when someone brings us a problem touching God's love, a problem of evil or of undeserved suffering, for instance? In the first place, we shall wrestle with the problem and may be granted some fresh light on it. But we are not likely to solve it altogether. So then what? Must we abandon our belief in the love of God until we have solved all the problems? No. We shall maintain our belief in the love of God, in spite of the problems, for one reason and for one reason only, namely that Jesus Christ taught it and exhibited it. That is why we believe that God is love. And the problems do not overthrow our belief

So with Scripture. Someone brings us a problem, or we stumble across one ourselves, maybe an apparent discrepancy or a question of literary criticism. What shall we do? To begin with, it is essential that we wrestle honestly with biblical problems. It is not Christian to bury our heads in the sand, pretending that no problems exist. Nor is it Christian to manipulate Scripture in order to achieve a forced, artificial harmonization. No, we work at the problems with intellectual integrity. During this process (as I can testify from my own experience) some problems, which at first seemed intractable, are satisfactorily solved. To others, however, we can see no immediate solution. So then what? Must we abandon our belief in the Word of God until we have solved all the problems? No. We shall maintain our belief in God's Word, just as we maintain our belief in God's love, in spite of the problems, ultimately for one reason and one reason only, namely that Jesus Christ taught it and exhibited it. It is no more obscurantist to cling to the one belief than the other. Indeed, it is not obscurantist at all. To follow Christ is always sober, humble, Christian realism.

Thirdly, the ultimate issue in the question of authority concerns the Lordship of Christ. "You call me 'Teacher' and 'Lord,'" he said, "and rightly so, for that is what I am" (John 13:13). If Jesus Christ is truly our teacher and our Lord, we are under both his instruction and his authority. We must therefore bring our mind into subjection to him as our teacher and our will into subjection to him as our Lord. We have no liberty to disagree with him or to disobey him. So we bow to the authority of Scripture because we bow to the authority of Christ.

NOTE

1. See Eusebius' *Ecclesiastical History* III.xxxix, 15 and Irenaeus' *Adversus Haereses* III.l.i.

7. The Interpretation of the Bible

❖ What are the three teachers God has given to instruct his people, and what do we learn from them?[1]

❖ What are the three principles of interpretation?

❖ What are some examples of why we should see the Bible as a whole?

I once heard Dr. Alan Cole of Sydney, Australia, remark that, surprising as it may seem, God sometimes blesses "a poor exegesis of a bad translation of a doubtful reading of an obscure verse of a minor prophet!"

This is true. He does. But it gives us no possible excuse for slovenliness in biblical interpretation. On the contrary, if the Bible is indeed God's Word written, we should spare no pains and grudge no effort to discover what he has said (and says) in Scripture.

How then shall the student of the Bible grasp its message with accuracy? Where are we to look for help? Perhaps we should begin our answer by warning the reader against any pretension to infallibility. God's Word is infallible, for what he has said is true. But no Christian individual, group or church has ever been or will ever be an infallible interpreter of God's Word. Human interpretations belong to the sphere of tradition, and an appeal may always be made against tradition to the Scripture itself

How shall the student of the Bible grasp its message with accuracy?

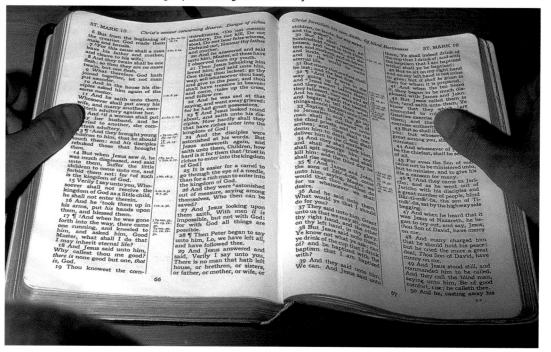

which tradition claims to interpret.

Nevertheless, God has made provision for us to grow in our understanding of the truth and to be protected from the worst forms of misinterpretation. He has given us three teachers to instruct us, and three principles to guide us.

The enlightenment of the Holy Spirit

Our foremost teacher is the Holy Spirit. "Hermeneutics" is the technical name given to the science of interpreting Scripture, and it should be obvious that a truly biblical hermeneutic will be consistent with the nature of the Bible itself. If, then, the biblical authors spoke from God, not on their own impulse but as they were moved by the Holy Spirit (2 Pet. 1:21), it is the Holy Spirit who can interpret what he caused them to speak. The best interpreter of every book is its author, since he alone knows what he intended to say. So God's book can be interpreted by God's Spirit alone.

The work of the Holy Spirit in communicating God's truth is now seen to have two stages. The first and objective stage is "revelation," the disclosure of the truth in Scripture. The second and subjective stage may be called "illumination," the enlightenment of our minds to comprehend the truth disclosed in Scripture. Each process is indispensable. Without revelation we have no truth to perceive; without illumination no faculty with which to perceive it.

An illustration comes from the days of Isaiah when, in judgment upon his rebellious people, God ceased to speak to them. His truth became like a sealed book, and his people like illiterate children. There were thus two barriers to their receiving his word:

> If you give the scroll to someone who can read, and say to him, "Read this, please," he will answer, "I can't; it is sealed." Or if you give the scroll to someone who cannot read, and say, "Read this, please," he will answer, "I don't know how to read." (Isa. 29:11-12)

Once we grant the necessity of the Holy Spirit's illumination before we can understand God's Word, we are ready to consider the kind of people the Holy Spirit enlightens.

First, the Holy Spirit enlightens the regenerate, or born-again, person. An experience of rebirth is essential before we are able to grasp heavenly truth. "No one can see the kingdom of God unless he is born again," Jesus said (John 3:3). This fact the apostle Paul echoed:

> The man without the Spirit [the "natural" or "unregenerate" man] does not accept the things that come from the Spirit of God, for they are foolishness to him and he cannot understand them, because they are spiritually discerned. (1 Cor.2:14)

Many have borne witness to this out of their own experience. For example, William Grimshaw, one of the leading English evangelicals in the eighteenth century, said to a friend after his conversion that "if God had drawn up his Bible to heaven, and sent him down another, it would not have been newer to him."[1]

I can myself testify to something very similar. My mother brought me up to read a passage of the Bible every day. For her sake and out of habit I continued the practice until my late teens. But it was a largely meaningless routine; for I did not understand what I was reading. After my conversion, however, the Bible immediately began to become a living book to me. I am not of course claiming that I suddenly understood it all. Nor do I pretend that I no longer found some of it dull and difficult. But it assumed a new relevance for me, as the Holy Spirit illumined and applied its message to my life.

Secondly, the Holy Spirit enlightens the humble. There is no greater hindrance to understanding than pride, and no more essential condition than humility. Jesus put the matter beyond dispute:

> I praise you, Father, Lord of heaven and earth, because you have hidden these

In Jesus' time, Scripture was written on scrolls.

things from the wise and learned, and revealed them to little children. Yes, Father, for this was your good pleasure. (Matt. 11:25-26)

The "wise and learned" from whom God hides himself are the intellectually proud, and "little children" the humble and sincere. It is not the ignorance or even the simplicity of a child which Jesus commended, but its open, receptive and unprejudiced approach. It is to such only that God reveals himself. As Charles Simeon wrote:

In the beginning of my enquiries I said to myself, I am a fool; of that I am quite certain. One thing I know assuredly, that in religion of myself I know nothing. I do not therefore sit down to the perusal of Scripture in order to impose a sense on the inspired writers; but to receive one, as they give it me. I pretend not to teach them, I wish like a child to be taught by them.[2]

There is only one way to express such an

attitude of humble expectancy before God, and that is by prayer. We need both to pray before we read Scripture and to read it in a prayerful frame of mind, and many Christians have found it helpful to use some of the Bible's own prayers for illumination. For example, the psalmist's petition:

Open my eyes that I may see wonderful things in your law. (Ps. 119:18)

Or one of Paul's great prayers, in all of which he asks in some way for an increase of knowledge or understanding. For example:

That the God of our Lord Jesus Christ, the glorious Father, may give you the Spirit of wisdom and revelation, so that you may know him better. I pray also that the eyes of your heart may be enlightened in order that you may know the hope to which he has called you, the riches of his glorious inheritance in the saints, and his incomparably great power for us who believe. (Eph. 1:17-19)

Such a humbling of ourselves before God, acknowledging our darkness and appealing for his enlightenment, will not go unrewarded. Not long after his conversion at Pembroke College, Oxford, George Whitefield wrote in his journal:

> I began to read the Holy Scriptures upon my knees, laying aside all other books, and praying over, if possible, every line and word. This proved meat indeed and drink indeed to my soul. I daily received fresh life, light and power from above.[3]

Thirdly, the Holy Spirit enlightens the obedient. This is much emphasized. Since God's purpose through Scripture is not merely to "instruct" in general terms but specifically "to make you wise for salvation" (2 Tim. 3:15), he is concerned about the response which readers give to his Word. And the degree of our responsiveness, of our willingness to hear and obey, will to a large extent determine the degree of understanding we receive. Thus Jesus promised that those who have a will to do God's will would know whether his teaching was true, and that he would show himself personally to those who proved their love for him by their obedience (John 7:17; 11:21). Conversely, it is those who violate their conscience by disobedience who shipwreck their faith (1 Tim. 1:19). Nobody who does not practice what he already knows can expect to advance in his knowledge.

Fourthly, the Holy Spirit enlightens the communicative. The understanding he gives us is not intended for our private enjoyment alone; it is given us to be shared with others. We hold it on trust. A lamp is not brought into a room to be put under a bed, Jesus said, but on a stand. In the same way he intended his teaching to be made known, not to be kept secret. The apostles were to take heed what and how they heard. They were to listen to their Master's teaching, in order to communicate it. Otherwise, they would not receive any more:

> With the measure you use, it will be measured to you – and even more. (Mark 4:21-25)

The Christian's disciplined study

If the Holy Spirit is our first and foremost teacher, there is a sense in which we ourselves, in our very dependence on the Spirit, must also teach ourselves. That is to say, in the process of divine education we are not wholly passive, but are expected to use our own reason responsibly. For in our reading of Scripture divine illumination is no substitute for human endeavor. Nor is humility in seeking light from God inconsistent with the most disciplined industry in study.

Scripture itself lays great stress on the conscientious Christian use of the mind, not of course in order to stand in judgment on God's Word, but rather in order to submit to it, to grapple with it, to understand it and to relate it to the contemporary scene. Indeed, there are frequent complaints in Scripture that we keep forgetting our basic rationality as human beings made in God's image and behave instead "like the horse or the mule, which have no understanding" (Ps. 32:9).

For Jesus rebukes his apostles for their lack of understanding and their failure to use their common sense (for example, Mark 8:17-21). He reproached the multitudes similarly:

> Why don't you judge for yourselves what is right? (Luke 12:57)

This command to "judge for yourselves" is particularly prominent in Paul's first letter to Corinth. Here was a church which laid claim to great wisdom, but failed to exhibit it. Again and again Paul asks incredulously, "Do you not know . . . ?" (1 Cor. 3:16; 5:6; 6:2-3, 9, 15-16, 19) and introduces his apostolic instruction with formulae like "I want you to know, brothers" or "I do not want you to be ignorant" (for example, 1 Cor. 10:1; 12:1). He is

Remains of the basilica, ancient Corinth. The Corinthian church laid claim to great wisdom, but failed to exhibit it.

clear that, whereas the natural or unregenerate person is unable to understand God's truth, the spiritual or regenerate person "makes judgments about all things." That is, what the natural person cannot discern, the spiritual person can and does, because he or she is inhabited and ruled by the Holy Spirit and so has "the mind of Christ" (1 Cor. 2:14-16).

This conviction leads Paul, in this same Corinthian letter, to appeal to his readers' reason. He writes:

> I speak to sensible people; judge for yourselves what I say.
> (1 Cor. 10:15; cf. 11:13)

In other New Testament letters similar exhortations occur. Christians are to "test the spirits" (that is, human teachers claiming divine inspiration) and indeed to test everything they hear (1 John 4:1). Again, when faced with difficult ethical decisions, they are to give their minds to the problem, so that each may be "fully convinced in his own mind" (Rom. 14:5). It is a mark of Christian maturity to have our faculties trained "by constant use . . . to distinguish good from evil" (Heb. 5:14).

We must, then, take seriously this biblical injunction to use our rational and critical powers. We are not to oppose prayer and thought as alternative means of increasing our understanding of Scripture, but to combine them. Daniel in the Old Testament and Paul in the New are good examples of this balance:

> Do not be afraid, Daniel. Since the first day that you set your mind to gain understanding and to humble yourself before your God, your words were heard. . . . (Dan. 10:12)

> Reflect on what I am saying, for the Lord will give you insight into all this.
> (2 Tim. 2:7)

It is not enough to humble ourselves before God and look to him for understanding; we must also set our minds to understand Scripture and think over what is written in it. As Charles Simeon put it:

For the attainment of divine knowledge, we are directed to combine a dependence on God's Spirit with our own researches. Let us, then, not presume to separate what God has thus united.[4]

Sometimes our growth in understanding is inhibited by a proud and prayerless self-confidence, but at other times by sheer laziness and indiscipline. Those who would increase in the knowledge of God must abase themselves before the Spirit of truth and commit themselves to a lifetime of study.

The teaching of the church

Our third teacher is the church. So far our portrayal of how God teaches his people from his Word has been entirely individualistic. And it has been true. For it is God's loving purpose to enlighten, save, reform and nourish his people by his Word as each hears it or reads it for himself. Our sixteenth-century reformers were quite right to want to translate the Bible into plain English and put it into the hands of plain people. For they were appalled at the widespread ignorance of Scripture. Hence William Tyndale's famous jibe to a clergyman critic:

If God spare my life, ere many years pass I will cause a boy that driveth the plough shall know more of the Scriptures than thou dost.[5]

We must also agree with the reformers' insistence on what they termed "the right of private judgment," the birthright of every child of God to hear his Father's voice speaking to him directly through Scripture. This they asserted over against the claim of the Church of Rome that she had been given a unique "magisterium" or teaching authority, because of which she alone could supply the true interpretation of Scripture.

Nevertheless, in rejecting every attempt to interpose the church or any other authoritative teaching body between God and his people, we must not deny that the church has a place in God's plan to give his people a right understanding of his Word. The individual Christian's humble, prayerful, diligent and obedient study of Scripture is not the only way the Holy Spirit makes clear what he has revealed. It would hardly be humble to ignore what the Spirit may have shown to others. The Holy Spirit is indeed our teacher, but he teaches us indirectly through others as well as directly to our own minds. It was not to one man that he revealed the truths now enshrined in Scripture, but to a multiplicity of prophets and apostles; his work of illumination is given to many also. It is not as individuals merely, but "with all the saints" that we are given "power . . . to grasp how wide and long and high and deep is the love of Christ . . . that surpasses knowledge" (Eph. 3:18-19).

A recognition of this truth will give us more respect than we customarily have for "tradition," that is, for the understanding of biblical truth which has been handed down from the past to the present. Although the Holy Spirit's work of biblical inspiration was unique, his teaching ministry did not cease when the last apostle died. It changed from revelation to illumination. Gradually and progressively over the centuries of church history, the Spirit of truth enabled the church to grasp, clarify and formulate the great doctrines of Scripture. We owe much to the so-called Catholic Creeds ("catholic" because they were accepted by the whole church) and Reformation confessions, together with the biblical commentaries and theological treatises of individual scholars.

If we should not despise the heritage of the past, neither should we despise the teachers of the contemporary church. The pastoral ministry is a teaching ministry, and "pastors and teachers" are gifts which the ascended Christ still bestows upon his church (Eph. 4:11-12). We should also be willing to listen to each other and learn from each other. The Holy Spirit can illumine our minds through group as well as individual Bible study. The apostle Paul clearly envisaged this kind of mutual instruction in the local church when he wrote:

Let the word of Christ dwell in you
richly, as you teach and admonish one
another with all wisdom. (Col. 3:16)

Luke gives a striking example of the role of
the teacher in Acts 8:26-39. An Ethiopian minister of state, while traveling home from
Jerusalem by chariot, was reading the prophecy of Isaiah. Philip the evangelist asked him:
"Do you understand what you are reading?"
To which he replied: "How can I, unless someone explains it to me?" So Philip went up to sit
beside him and to explain the Scripture to him.
Calvin comments:

That is also why the reading of Scripture
bears fruit with such a few people today,
because scarcely one in a hundred is to be
found who gladly submits himself to
teaching. . . .
   Now if any of us is diffident about
himself, but shows that he is teachable,
angels will come down from heaven to
teach us, rather than that the Lord allow
us to labour in vain. However, following
the example of the (Ethiopian) eunuch, we
must make use of all the aids which the
Lord sets before us for the understanding
of Scripture. Fanatics seek inspiration
from heaven, and at the same time despise
the minister of God, by whose hand they
ought to have been ruled. Others, relying
on their own penetrating insight, do not
deign to hear anybody or to read any
commentaries. But God does not wish the
aids, which he appoints for us, to be
despised, and does not allow contempt of
them to go unpunished. And we must
keep in mind here, that not only is
Scripture given to us, but interpreters and
teachers are also added to help us. That is
why the Lord chose Philip for the eunuch,
rather than an angel.[6]

Of course no human teacher is infallible,
either of the past or of the present, and Christ
forbade us to give any human teacher a slavish
following (Matt. 23:8-10). Ultimately, God

himself is our Teacher and, speaking ideally,
we may all be described as "taught by God"
(Isa. 54:13; John 6:45; 1 Thess. 4:9). Indeed,
in principle, because of the apostolic word and
the anointing Spirit given to us all, we "do not
need anyone to teach us." The right of private
judgment must not be taken away from us.
Sometimes it is even necessary for us, out of
loyalty to the plain meaning of Scripture, to
disagree with teachers in the church and say
(I hope humbly):

I have more insight than all my teachers,
for I meditate on your statutes.
(Ps. 119:99)

Nevertheless, I must repeat that God has
appointed teachers in his church. It is our
Christian duty to listen to them with respect,
humility and eagerness, and to feed upon
God's Word from their lips when they faithfully expound it, at the same time ourselves
"examining the Scriptures every day" to see if
what they say is true (Acts 17:11).
   Our three teachers, then, whom I have mentioned are the Holy Spirit, ourselves and the
church. It is by receiving the illumination of
the Spirit, by using our own reason and by listening to the teaching of others in the church
that we grow in our understanding of
Scripture. I am anxious not to be misunderstood. I am emphatically not saying that
Scripture, reason and tradition are a threefold
authority of equal importance by which we
come to know God's truth. No. Scripture
alone is God's Word written, and the Holy
Spirit its ultimate interpreter. The place of the
individual's reason and of the church's tradition lies in the elucidation and application of
Scripture. But both are subordinate to God
himself as he speaks to us through his Word.
   We turn now from the three teachers who
instruct us to the three principles which are to
guide us in our interpretation of Scripture.
   It is often said by our critics, especially by
those who know what a high view of Scripture
we take, that "you can make the Bible mean
anything you like." They are probably think-

ing of non-Christian and semi-Christian cults which support their particular opinions by an arbitrary selection and interpretation of proof texts. But the New Testament itself condemns those who "distort the word of God" and twist it to suit their own purposes (2 Cor. 4:2; 2 Pet. 3:16). To those who accuse us of this, I always reply: "You are quite right. You *can* make the Bible mean anything you like – if you are unscrupulous enough. But if you are scrupulously honest in your approach to the Bible and in your use of sound principles of interpretation, far from you being able to manipulate Scripture, you will find Scripture controlling and directing you." What, then, are these sound principles of interpretation?

The natural sense

First, we must look for the *natural* sense of the biblical text. I will call this the principle of simplicity.

One of our basic Christian convictions is that "God is light; in him there is no darkness at all" (1 John 1:5). That is to say, it is as much the nature of God to reveal himself as it is the nature of light to shine. Now God has revealed himself chiefly by speaking. We may be quite sure, therefore, that he has spoken in order to be understood, and that he has intended Scripture (the record of the divine speech) to be plain to its readers. For the whole purpose of revelation is clarity not confusion, a readily intelligible message, not a set of dark and mysterious riddles.

This principle of simplicity strikes at the root of much popular interpretation. For example, the destructive criticism of radical Christians would limit the truth to a tiny minority of scholars who claim the competence to sift the wheat from the chaff in Scripture, while the fanciful reconstructions of some evangelical Christians would turn Scripture into a complicated jigsaw puzzle to which they alone possess the key. Over against these distortions we must assert that God's whole purpose in speaking and in causing his speech to be preserved is that he wanted to communicate to ordinary people and save them.

It is true that in some matters Scripture is not as plain as in others. This is apparent from the fact that, although devout and careful students of the Bible, deeply concerned to submit to its authority, enjoy a very wide measure of agreement on the great fundamentals of historic Christianity, they still disagree on some points. One thinks, for example, of such questions as these: whether baptism should be administered only to adult believers or to the children of Christian parents as well, and whether candidates should be immersed in the water or have it poured over them; whether our doctrine of the church should be "independent" (each local church being autonomous) or "connectional" (local churches being in some way federated); whether the ministry of the church should be episcopal or presbyterian, or indeed whether the local assembly should rather have a nonprofessional pastoral oversight; whether miracles (for example, the instantaneous healing of organic diseases without medical means) should be expected in the contemporary church regularly, occasionally or never; and whether the "millennium" (the reign of Christ for a thousand years) is intended to be understood literally as a future earthly event or symbolically as a present spiritual reality.

When equally biblical Christians disagree on such matters, what should we do? We should be humble enough to reexamine them ourselves in the light of sound principles of interpretation. And we should be mature enough to discuss them with one another without rancor. If then we still disagree, we must regard such disputed points as being secondary in importance, and respect one another with mutual Christian love and tolerance. We should also rejoice that in all the central doctrines of the faith we remain agreed, for in these the Scripture is plain, clearly expressed and virtually self-interpreting.

God chose human language as the vehicle of his self-revelation. As a result, although Scripture is unlike all other books in being the Word of God, it is also like all other books in being the words of human beings. Since it is

Biblical Christians disagree over such issues such as baptism, church government and the "millennium."

unique because divine, we must study it like no other book, praying to the Holy Spirit for illumination. Since it is also ordinary because human, we must study it like every other book, paying attention to the common rules of vocabulary, grammar and syntax. For if (as we saw in the previous chapter) God did no violence to the agents of his revelation (human persons), he did no violence to its instrument, either (human language).

It follows that no serious Bible reader can escape the discipline of linguistic study. Best of all (especially for the church's accredited teachers) would be a knowledge of the original languages, Hebrew and Greek. But most will read in English, and for them an accurate modern version is essential. Although popular paraphrases are useful additional helps, there is no substitute for a careful, scholarly translation like the Revised Version or the Revised Standard Version (both revisions of the Authorized/King James Version) or the New International Version (O.T. 1973, N.T. 1978), whose text has been quoted throughout this book. These are probably the best translations

available in English. The Good News Bible also deserves a special mention, since it combines reliability with unusually simple and straightforward language. An analytical concordance (like Young's or Strong's) is another extremely valuable tool, for it not only groups the biblical words according to the English (AV) text but then subdivides them into the original Hebrew and Greek words and gives their meaning. Excellent concordances are now available for both the New International Version and the Good News Bible, although neither divides the words according to the original Greek or Hebrew.

In reading the words and sentences of the biblical text, we must look first of all for their obvious and natural meaning. In Sir Charles Odgers' standard book on the interpretation of legal deeds and documents his third rule is that "words are to be taken in their literal meaning." Unless the subject matter shows otherwise, he writes, "the plain, ordinary meaning of the words used is to be adopted in construing a document."[7]

Unfortunately, the fanciful allegorization of

Scripture has often brought serious Bible reading into disrepute. It was already indulged in by Jewish commentators before Christ, of whom Philo of Alexandria was the notorious example. It is not surprising that some Christian commentators in the post-apostolic period tried their hand at the same game. The so-called *Epistle of Barnabas*, for instance, an apocryphal work of (probably) the early second century AD, contains some outrageous allegorizations. In one passage the author quotes the Mosaic regulation that the Jews might eat every animal that divides the hoof and chews the cud, and explains it thus:

> Cleave unto those that fear the Lord, . . . with those who know that meditation is a work of gladness and who chew the cud of the word of the Lord. But why that which divides the hoof? Because the righteous man both walks in this world and at the same time looks for the holy world to come.[8]

Now certainly to "chew the cud" of God's Word is a very suggestive expression for Bible meditation, and also the Christian is a citizen of two worlds. But equally certainly this is not what Moses had in mind when he wrote about cud-chewing, cloven-hoofed animals!

The allegorical school of interpretation was further promoted by Origen of Alexandria in the fourth century AD and by medieval churchmen. It is greatly to the credit of the sixteenth-century reformers that they rescued Scripture from this kind of arbitrary treatment and insisted that what is simple and straightforward is always to be preferred to subtleties. John Calvin put it admirably:

> Let us know, then, that the true meaning of Scripture is the natural and obvious meaning; and let us embrace and abide by it resolutely. Let us not only neglect as doubtful, but boldly set aside as deadly corruptions, those pretended expositions which lead us away from the natural meaning.[9]

To look for the *natural* meaning of Scripture is not necessarily the same as looking for the *literal* meaning. For sometimes the natural meaning is figurative rather than literal. Jesus himself had to reproach some of his hearers for their excessive literalism. Nicodemus misunderstood his reference to a second birth so completely that he asked incredulously whether we can reenter our mother's womb and be born. The Samaritan woman seems to have supposed that the living, thirst-quenching water which he offered her was down Jacob's well. And when later Jesus claimed he could satisfy people's hunger by giving himself to them as living bread, they asked, "How can this man give us his flesh to eat?" (John 3:3-4; 4:10-15; 6:51-52). These examples should be enough to warn us against a dead and rigid literalism. It should have been obvious that Jesus was using figures of speech.

His favorite form of instruction was the parable, though occasionally he used the allegory. The difference between them is that in an allegory the similitude is drawn at many points, whereas the parable is an everyday story told to illustrate one main lesson, the wealth of detail being added not to teach subsidiary lessons but for dramatic effect. Examples of the allegory are the good shepherd in John 10, the vine and the branches in John 15 and the sower in Mark 4. An example of the parable is the Good Samaritan (Luke 10:29-37). Jesus told it in answer to the question "Who is my neighbor?" and taught from it that true neighbor-love transcends the barriers of race and religion. It is not legitimate to press the details – for example, to suggest that the inn represents the church and the two denarii given to the innkeeper the two sacraments. This would be to turn an obvious parable into an allegory and to provoke questions about what is represented by the brigands, the oil, the wine and the donkey.

Scripture is very rich in metaphorical language, and in every metaphor it is essential to ask at what point the analogy is being drawn. We must avoid arguing from analogy, that is, elaborating the correspondence beyond the limits which Scripture sets. Thus, God is our

Father and we are his children. As our Father, he has begotten us, he loves us and cares for us. As his children, we depend on him and must love and obey him. But we have no liberty to argue, for example, that since God is our heavenly Father, we must also have a heavenly mother, on the ground that no child can have a father without a mother. Nor can we argue that because we are called "children," we can avoid the responsibility of adult thought and action. For the same Scripture which commends to us the humility of a little child also condemns in us a child's immaturity.

If some Scripture is literal and some figurative, how are we to tell which is which? The fundamental answer is that we are to look for the *natural* sense. Common sense will usually guide us. In particular, it is wise to ask ourselves what the intention of the author or speaker is. Let me give two examples.

First, it is often said that the Old Testament authors conceived the universe as a "three-decker" construction with earth as man's dwelling place, heaven above him like a great canopy punctured with holes through which the stars peeped, and *sheol* (the abode of the dead) beneath him; that they believed this in a literal and spatial way; and that when it rained, for instance, God had literally "opened the windows of heaven." I do not of course deny that this is the kind of language they used, but I do seriously doubt whether they believed it literally or intended their readers to understand it literally. Take Psalm 75. In verse 3 God is represented as saying that "when the earth quakes," it is he who holds its pillars firm. Did the psalmist think that the earth was literally balanced on stilts? I think not. In the next verse God commands the wicked "do not lift up your horns" (a symbol of prosperity and success) and in verse 10 it is written that "I will cut off the horns of all the wicked," while in verse 8 we are told that in the Lord's hand there "is a cup full of foaming wine" (a symbol of his wrath). It is quite gratuitous to insist that the author thought the earth was set on literal pillars, unless we are prepared equally to insist that he thought the wicked have literal horns (which will one day be cut off) and that God literally holds a cup of foaming wine which he will one day pour out upon all the wicked of the earth.

My other example is taken from the special form of biblical literature called "apocalyptic," which claims to set forth hidden truths of both present reality and future history, usually in a series of weird and wonderful images. The Book of Revelation is a Christian apocalypse. In it God's redeemed people, gathered round his throne, are said to be wearing white robes which they have "washed . . . and made . . . white in the blood of the Lamb" (Rev. 7:14). Now to take this literally would be rather repulsive. It would also be impossible, since robes laundered in lamb's blood would not come out white. No. The author clearly intends the expression as a symbol to be interpreted, not as an image to be visualized. We are to understand that the righteousness of God's people (their "white robes") is due entirely to the death of Christ ("the blood of the Lamb") in which they have put their trust ("washed their robes"). Thus, in this case, too, the "natural" sense is the figurative, not the literal.

The original sense

Secondly, we must look for the *original* sense of Scripture. This is the principle of history.

We have seen in earlier chapters that God chose to reveal himself in precise historical contexts. Although his self-revelation is addressed to every person of every age and every country, each part of it was addressed in the first instance to a particular people of a particular age in a particular country. Therefore the permanent and universal message of Scripture can be understood only in the light of the circumstances in which it was originally given. It would obviously be very misleading to read back into Scripture the notions of a later age. As Charles Simeon wrote about the ideals of his preaching ministry:

My endeavour is *to bring out of Scripture*

what is there, and not to thrust in what I think might be there. I have a great jealousy on this head; never to speak more or less than I believe to be the mind of the Spirit in the passage I am expounding.[10]

So, as we read the Bible, we need to keep asking ourselves: What did the author intend to convey by this? What is he actually asserting? What will his original hearers have understood him to have meant? This inquiry is commonly known as the "grammatico-historical" method of interpretation. J. Gresham Machen described it well:

Scientific historical method in the interpretation of the Bible requires that the biblical writers should be allowed to speak for themselves. A generation or so ago that feature of scientific method was exalted to the dignity of a principle, and was honored by a long name. It was called "grammatico-historical exegesis." The fundamental notion of it was that the modern student should distinguish sharply between what he would have said or what he would have liked to have the biblical writer say, and what the writer actually did say.[11]

As we attempt to transport ourselves back into the author's mind and times, and to listen to his words as if we were among his first readers, we shall need particularly to consider the situation, the style and the language in which he wrote.

First, the situation. The proper function of literary and historical criticism is to reconstruct the *mise-en-scène* of the biblical book in question. Who wrote it and to whom? Under what circumstances? For what reason? Floods of light are thrown on the text of the Old Testament prophets, for example, if we can fit them into the story of Israel. The same is true of the New Testament epistles and the story of the early church as Luke tells it in the Acts, and especially the missionary journeys of Paul.

For example, Paul's Letter to the Philippians becomes a much more human document if on the one hand we can picture the author under house arrest in Rome (or possibly Ephesus) and on the other Lydia, the jailer and the slave girl (whose conversions are described in Acts 16) as among its first readers.

A careful consideration of the historical background to the letters of Paul and James would have protected Luther from finding them contradictory and from rejecting James' letter as made of "straw." It is true that Paul declared a sinner "justified by faith apart from observing the law" and gave Abraham as an example (Rom. 3:28; 4:1-3), whereas James declared a sinner "justified by what he does and not by faith alone" and also quoted Abraham as an example (Jas. 2:21-24). But their positions are not mutually irreconcilable. Paul was tilting at legalists who believed in salvation by works, James at religionists who believed in salvation by orthodoxy. Both believed that salvation was by faith and that a saving faith would manifest itself in good works. It was natural in their particular circumstances, however, that Paul should stress the faith which issues in works, and James the works which spring from faith.

Secondly, the style. It is important to take note of the literary *genre* of each biblical book. Is it prose or poetry, historical narrative or wisdom literature? Is it law, prophecy, psalm or apocalyptic? Is it a drama, or a letter, or that distinctively Christian form called a "Gospel," a collection of the words and deeds of Jesus which bear witness to him? How we interpret what we read, not least whether we take it literally or figuratively, will depend largely on its form and style.

Thirdly, the language. All human language is a living, changing thing. The meaning of words alters from century to century and culture to culture. We cannot read the word "love" in Scripture and immediately suppose we know what it means. Four different Greek words are used in the New Testament, all translated "love" in English. But each has a distinctive meaning, and only one expresses what

A grain ship similar to the vessel in which Paul was shipwrecked. Acts is a more human document if we picture the journeys of Paul.

Christians mean by love, which is poles apart from the erotica of today's glossy magazines.

For many centuries scholars were not able to recognize the kind of Greek in which the New Testament was written. It was neither classical Greek nor modern Greek. Some thought it was made up specially for the purpose. They even called it "the language of the Holy Ghost." But towards the close of the last century, in the dry sands of Egypt, archaeologists began to discover large quantities of ancient papyrus rolls. They were mostly secular and non-literary documents. Many had come from the wastepaper baskets of public record offices, whose contents had been dumped on the local rubbish heap. And their Greek (the *koine* or common language of every day) was found to be largely the same as that of the New Testament. So now the meaning of New Testament Greek words has to be sought

against a background not only of classical Greek and of Hebrew thought but also of the secular language of the day. I will give one example only.

In his two letters to the Thessalonians Paul several times refers to those he describes as *ataktos*. In classical Greek the word was commonly used of soldiers who broke rank, of an army in disarray. So the Authorized Version translates the word "disorderly," and it was assumed that there was an undisciplined group of some kind in the Thessalonian church. But two or three apprenticeship contracts were discovered among the papyri which contain an undertaking that should the boy play truant from work or exceed his annual holiday, the lost time would be made good. And the word for playing truant is *ataktos*, or rather its cognate verb. So the New International Version renders it not "disorderly" but "idle." It seems probable that some Thessalonian Christians, believing that the Lord's return was imminent, were playing truant from work. It is these idle Christians whom Paul commands to mind their own affairs, work with their own hands and earn their own living, adding that if a person will not work, he shall not eat (1 Thess. 4:11; 5:14; 2 Thess. 3:6-12).

In addition to situation, style and language there is the vital question of culture. Since God's revelation was given in particular historical and geographical situations, this means that it had a particular cultural setting as well. The social customs which form the background of some biblical instruction are entirely foreign to those of our day. Are we then to reject the teaching because it is culturally dated? Or are we to go to the other extreme and try to invest both teaching and setting with the same permanent validity? Neither of these seems to be the right way to escape the dilemma. The third and better way is to accept the biblical instruction itself as permanently binding, but to translate it into contemporary cultural terms. Thus, Jesus commanded his disciples to wash one another's feet as a mark of the mutual love which humbles itself to serve (John 13:12-17), and the apostles Paul and Peter commanded their readers, when they came together, to greet one another with a holy kiss or a kiss of love (Rom. 16:16; 2 Cor. 13:12; 1 Thess. 5:26; 1 Pet. 5:14). We have no liberty to repudiate these commandments. But nor should we give them a slavishly literal obedience. For nowadays (at least in the West) we do not walk through dusty streets in sandals, and therefore do not need to have our feet washed. Nor is it customary to go round kissing everybody in public. Nevertheless, we can and must obey Christ's injunction through other outward forms of humble service, and obey the apostles' command by a "handshake all round," as J. B. Phillips aptly paraphrases the kiss of peace.

A more difficult example of the tension between the permanently valid and the culturally dated concerns the status, behavior and dress of women. Are we to retain all the detailed biblical requirements, or – in deference to many voices in the feminist movement – jettison the lot? Again there seems to be a wiser middle course. Consider the question of the veiling of women, to which Paul devotes half a chapter in First Corinthians (11). He insists that it is dishonorable, even disgraceful, for a woman to pray or prophesy in public with her head unveiled. He appeals to reason, nature, ecclesiastical custom and his own apostolic authority in support of his teaching. What are we to make of this? Perhaps the commonest and most superficial reaction is to suppose that the apostle's requirement is met if women wear hats in church. But eastern veils and western hats are entirely different, theologically as well as culturally! One of the crucial statements of Paul's argument occurs in verse 10 where, in referring to a woman's duty "to have a veil on her head" (RSV), he actually writes that she ought to wear "authority" (RSV margin and New International Version) on her head. This is the point. In those days the veil a woman wore was a symbol of her husband's authority over her. Not only does a woman's hat not have this significance today, but some modern modes appear to symbolize the exact reverse – liberation, not submission. What is permanently valid in Paul's teaching is the "headship" of the husband, for he grounds it on unchanging theological truths concerning creation. What is culturally dated is the veil. We must find other social customs which express a woman's submission to her husband.

In addition, we must be very careful how we interpret the husband's "authority." The word is by no means a synonym for authoritarianism. Nor can it be taken to express any "superiority" of the male or "inferiority" of the female. For – centuries in advance of his time – Paul emphatically declared that in Christ "there is neither . . . male nor female" (Gal. 3:28). He also drew a profound analogy between the relationship of husband and wife in marriage and the relationship between the Father and the Son in the Godhead (1 Cor. 11:3). This suggests that the husband's "headship" over his wife is not incompatible with their equality, any more than is the Father's

Remains of the Roman theater, Thessalonica. Some Thessalonian Christians, believing that the Lord's return was imminent, appear to have played truant from work.

"headship" over Christ. Perhaps the husband's authority should be understood in terms rather of responsibility than of autocracy, the responsibility of a loving care (Eph. 5:21-33).

It is essential to recognize that the purpose of "cultural transposition" (the practice of transposing the teaching of Scripture from one culture into another) is not to avoid obedience but rather to ensure it, by making it contemporary.

If so far I have concentrated on "exegesis," that is, on how to elucidate the original meaning of each biblical text, it is only because this is an indispensable preliminary to asking the next question: what has the text to say today, in our own generation and culture, or (better) what is God saying to us through it? The great merit of the so-called "new hermeneutic" is that it lays its emphasis here. Mind you, it sometimes goes too far. Its more extreme proponents teach that a text's *only* meaning is what it means to *me*. This is absurd. A text cannot with any possible legitimacy mean to me something substantially different from what it meant to its original author and readers. To claim that it can is to sink into the quicksands of subjectivity. Besides, every flower cut from its roots is bound to wither and die. Nevertheless, there is the opposite danger of scrutinizing a text "over there" as if it had nothing to say to us today. This is to lapse into irresponsible objectivity. The third and right way is to combine the historical and the contemporary, and to relate the past to the present. To be concerned only with the ancient text and ignore its modern application is antiquarianism; to search for a living message without first wrestling with the original meaning is existentialism. Meaning and message must be held together. Moreover, in going beyond meaning to message, we must be ready for the text to penetrate our defenses, challenge our assumptions, disturb our complacency and judge our compromises. Otherwise, if we come to Scripture with our mind already made up, all we are likely to hear is the reassuring echoes of our own cultural prejudice.

The general sense

Thirdly, we must look for the *general* sense of Scripture. This is the principle of harmony.

From a human standpoint the Bible is a symposium with a wide assortment of contributors. From the divine standpoint, however, the whole Bible emanates from one mind. It is the Word of God expressing the mind of God, and so possesses an organic unity. For this reason we must approach Scripture with the confidence both that God has spoken and that, in speaking, he has not contradicted himself

Sir Charles Odgers, in the book mentioned earlier, gives as his seventh rule for interpreting legal documents "the deed is to be construed as a whole." He goes on:

> The deed must be read and interpreted as a whole in order to extract the meaning of any particular expression. . . . Every part of the deed ought to be compared with the other and one entire sense ought to be made thereof. . . . Every part of it may be brought into action in order to collect from the whole one uniform and consistent sense, if that may be done. . . . The words of each clause should be so interpreted as to bring them into harmony with the other provisions of the deed if that interpretation does no violence to the meaning of which they are naturally susceptible.[12]

As with legal documents, so with the biblical text, we should seek to resolve apparent discrepancies and interpret Scripture as one harmonious whole. This will lead us to interpret Scripture by Scripture, especially what is obscure by what is plain, and never so to "expound one place of Scripture that it be repugnant to another."[13]

This was John Knox's argument with Mary Queen of Scots. In a private debate with her in Edinburgh in 1561 he asserted that the Church of Rome (which she said she would defend as the true Church of God) had declined from the purity of religion taught by the apostles. The Queen herself, he added, possessed little right knowledge, since she had heard no teachers but those allowed by the Pope and his Cardinals. At this the Queen said:

> Ye interpret the Scriptures in one manner, and they in another; whom shall I believe, and who shall judge?

John Knox replied:

> Believe God, that plainly speaketh in his Word: and further than the Word teacheth you, ye shall neither believe the one nor the other. The word of God is plain in itself; and if there appear any obscurity in one place, the Holy Ghost, which is never contrarious to himself, explains the same more clearly in other places.[14]

We may say, therefore, that every text of Scripture has a double context, historical and scriptural. Its context in history is the situation in which it was written. Its context in Scripture is the place where it is found. So each text must be understood against both its historical and its scriptural background. These are our second and third principles of interpretation respectively, the principles of history and harmony.

Further, the scriptural context of every text is both immediate (the paragraph, chapter and book in which it is embedded) and distant (the total biblical revelation).

The immediate context is the more obvious. To wrench a text from its context is an inexcusable blunder, and many horrific tales are told of preachers who have done it. In his instruction on the local church's responsibility to discipline an impenitent offender, Jesus said: "If he refuses to hear the church, let him be to you as a Gentile" – that is, let him be excommunicated (Matt. 18:17, AV). Now during the Tractarian movement, which sought to restore the Church of England's "Catholic" authority, its followers preached so often on the three words of this verse "hear the church" that they provoked Archbishop Whately to retort with a sermon on the equally truncated text "if he refuses to hear the church, let him"!

Perhaps this kind of trickery, which exploits a combination of words without any respect for their true contextual meaning, is so outrageous as to be comparatively rare. Yet I was myself greatly disturbed that the World Council of Churches (which ought to have known better) should take as the text for their Fourth Assembly at Uppsala in 1967 God's great words in Revelation 21:5 (RSV), "Behold, I make all things new." For this sentence applies to what God is going to do in the end when he makes a new heaven and a new earth. But the WCC, without any conceivable justification, applied it to the revolutionary political and social movements of the 1960s.

It is in some ways even more important that we should learn to see the Bible as a whole, and to read each text in the light of all. Let me give some examples of what I mean.

I promised in chapter 3 that I would say something more about the early chapters of Genesis. Perhaps these chapters are specially susceptible to misunderstanding whenever they are isolated from the rest of Scripture. My own position is to accept the historicity of Adam and Eve, but to remain agnostic about some details of the story like the precise nature of the tree of life and of the serpent. This is not to be arbitrary or inconsistent, however, for I have biblical reasons for both. That Adam and Eve were literal people seems clear from Romans 5:12-21, where Paul draws a deliberate contrast between the disobedience of Adam through which sin and death entered the world and the obedience of Christ who secured salvation and life. The analogy would be meaningless if Adam's act of disobedience were not an event as historical as Christ's act of obedience. But as for the serpent and the tree of life, they both reappear in the Book of Revelation, where they are clearly symbolical, the serpent representing Satan and the tree eternal life. So I have a *biblical* (New Testament) reason for believing that Adam and Eve were historical, and an equally *biblical* reason for sup-

posing that the serpent and the trees in the story may in some sense be meant to be figurative.

Some readers, uneasy about the notion that Genesis 3 may contain a figurative element, will declare my suggestion ill-advised on at least two counts. First, to question the literal nature of the serpent and the trees in Genesis on the ground of their symbolic appearance in Revelation is to confuse two quite distinct literary genres, they say, Genesis being narrative and Revelation apocalyptic. Secondly, it opens the door too wide: shall we not now be able to argue that all Old Testament references to snakes and trees are figurative, and even references to Jerusalem too since it reappears in the Revelation as a symbol? But no, my argument cannot be so easily dismissed. The Jerusalem of the Old Testament is obviously a literal city, and the many other Old Testament allusions to snakes and trees are also obviously literal. None of us has any difficulty with them. In Genesis 2 and 3, however, the text itself raises question in every reader's mind. The serpent is certainly no ordinary snake, since it not only talked but actually presumed to deceive Adam and Eve by contradicting God's Word and denigrating his goodness. As for the trees, although all other Old Testament trees are readily recognizable (oak, cedar, sycamore, balsam, olive, etc.), which of us has ever had in our woods or orchards a "tree of life" or a "tree of the knowledge of good and evil"? So what were they? Zoology cannot identify the snake, nor dendrology the trees. It is when these puzzled questions rise in our minds – about this specific snake and those specific trees – that the further reference to them in the Revelation comes helpfully to our aid.

Let me give another example of the need to let Scripture interpret Scripture. When I was a Cambridge undergraduate, I can remember being rather perplexed by the verse which says that the ten commandments were written on stone tablets by the finger of God (Exod. 31:18; Deut. 9:10). Was I required to believe this literally? Did a divine finger really appear and somehow inscribe Hebrew letters on stone? Certainly it is not impossible, for "the fingers of a human hand appeared and wrote on the plaster of the wall, near the lampstand in the royal palace" in the case of King Belshazzar, announcing his imminent doom (Dan. 5:5, 24-28). But today I am not so sure that we were ever meant to take literally the statement about the finger of God writing the law. For now I have read the Bible more thoroughly, and I have come across other references to God's fingers, all of which are symbolical. Thus, David referred to the heavens as the work of God's fingers (Ps. 8:3). Again, after the plague of gnats on man and beast the Egyptian magicians said to Pharaoh, "This is the finger of God," and after Jesus had begun to cast out demons he claimed to do it "by the finger of God" (Exod. 8:19; Luke 11:20). If, then, the reference to God's finger in the writing of the law is comparable to these other references, it seems that "the finger of God" is a biblical figure of speech for God's immediate intervention whether in creation (the heavens), in revelation (the law), in judgment (the plagues) or in salvation (the exorcism of demons). Such an interpretation would be in keeping with the principle of harmony.

Another example of the importance of considering each part of Scripture's teaching on any subject in the light of the whole is the second coming of Christ. It would be easy (and dangerous) to be selective in the texts from which we build up our doctrine. Thus, some passages indicate that Christ's return will be personal and visible, indeed that he will come "in the same way" as he went (Acts 1:11). But before we press this into meaning that the Return will be a kind of Ascension in reverse, like a film played backwards, and that Christ will set his feet on the precise spot on the Mount of Olives from which he was taken up, we need to consider something Jesus said to counter those who wanted to localize his return:

> For the Son of Man in his day will be like the lightning, which flashes and lights up the sky from one end to the other. (Luke 17:24; cf. Matt. 24:27)

The truly biblical Christian, anxious to be faithful to all Scripture, will want to do equal justice to both these strands of teaching. The coming of the Lord will indeed be personal, historical and visible; but it will also be "in power and great glory:' as universal as the lightning, a transcendent event of which the whole human population of both hemispheres will be simultaneously aware.

In my last examples of the need to see Scripture as a whole, I want to say something about both the Mosaic law and the fulfillment of prophecy. This will throw light on the relation between the Old and the New Testament, and so on the question of progressive revelation. The principle of harmony does not deny that there has been progression in God's revelation of himself and of his purposes, but emphasizes rather that the progression has not been from error to truth, but from truth to more truth.

Take the law of Moses. It is recognized in both Old and New Testaments that Moses' law was God's law. Moses was but the intermediary through whom God gave his law to his people. But does the divine origin of the law mean that it is all still permanently binding on Christian people? No. For Moses' law was a complex code, consisting of moral instructions, ceremonial regulations and civil statutes. The New Testament clearly teaches that the *ceremonial* rules are now obsolete, the temple, priesthood and sacrifices having been fulfilled in Christ and the food laws having been abolished by him.[15] The *civil* laws of Moses still have importance as indications of divine righteousness and justice, but no church or nation is under obligation to enact and enforce them in detail today. There are several reasons for this. For one thing, the civil code of Moses was framed for a people who belonged to God by redemption; they were both a nation and a church simultaneously, whereas today no church is a nation and no nation a church. For another, it was adapted to an emergent nation, who were first a nomadic and then an agricultural community. The *moral* laws of Moses, however, have not been abrogated. On the contrary, they are still in force.

The Israeli parliament, or Knesset. Some biblical Christians believe the modern State of Israel is at least a partial fulfillment of Old Testament promises.

Christ died that the righteous requirement of the law might be fulfilled in us, and the Holy Spirit writes God's law in our hearts (Rom. 8:3-4; Jer. 31:33; cf. 2 Cor. 3:6-8). Article VII of the Church of England's *Thirty-nine Articles* sums up these distinctions well:

> Although the laws given from God by Moses, as touching ceremonies and rites, do not bind Christian men, nor the civil precepts thereof ought of necessity to be received in any commonwealth; yet notwithstanding, no Christian man whatsoever is free from the obedience of the commandments which are called moral.

We turn now from law to prophecy. The great conviction of the New Testament authors is that with Jesus Christ the "last days" foretold throughout the Old Testament had come, and that in him and in his people the great promises of God found their fulfillment. Paul could even claim before King Agrippa:

> I stand here and testify to small and great alike. I am saying nothing beyond what the prophets and Moses said would happen. (Acts 26:22)

There is some disagreement among biblical Christians, however, as to whether we are to expect the Old Testament promises about Israel's future to be literally fulfilled, and whether the modern State of Israel in its occupation of the Holy Land is at least a partial fulfillment of them. Certainly God has a great future for the Jews, which is figuratively set forth by Paul as the grafting back into their own olive tree of the natural branches which had been broken off (Rom. 11:13-27). But there is no mention in the New Testament of any literal return of the Jews to the promised land. The overwhelming emphasis of the New Testament is that the Christian church is now "the Israel of God," "the circumcision," "a chosen people, a royal priesthood, a holy nation, a people belonging to God" (Gal. 6:16; Phil. 3:3; 1 Pet. 2:9), and that God's great promises to Abraham of both a posterity and a land are fulfilled spiritually in Christ and his church:

The Jews lament the destruction of the Temple at Jerusalem's Western Wall; but today the Christian church is "a holy temple in the Lord."

Understand, then, that those who believe are children of Abraham . . . those who have faith are blessed along with Abraham, the man of faith. . . .

Christ redeemed us from the curse of the law by becoming a curse for us . . . in order that the blessing given to Abraham might come to the Gentiles through Christ Jesus, so that by faith we might receive the promise of the Spirit. . . .

If you belong to Christ, then you are Abraham's seed, and heirs according to the promise.[16]

To be more precise, the fulfillment of Old Testament prophecy is usually in three stages. First came an immediate or literal fulfillment. The second stage, in which we are living, is the gospel or spiritual fulfillment. One day will come the third stage, which will be the final or heavenly fulfillment. Thus, the promise to Abraham of an innumerable posterity was historically fulfilled in the children of Israel (cf. Num. 23:10; 1 Kings 4:20), is being fulfilled today in Christ's people, and will be consum-

mated in heaven in the "great multitude that no one could count" round God's throne (Rev. 7:9). Again, the Old Testament prophets predicted the rebuilding of the temple, and there was an immediate and literal rebuilding under Zerubbabel. Today, however, it is the Christian church which is "a holy temple in the Lord, . . . a dwelling in which God lives by his Spirit,"[17] and so is the individual Christian's body also (1 Cor. 6:19-20). In the new or heavenly Jerusalem, however, there will be no separate temple, because the Lord God Almighty and the Lamb are its temple dwelling in the midst of his people forevermore (Rev. 21:3, 22).

In conclusion, let me emphasize that the three principles of biblical interpretation which we have been considering are not arbitrary. They are derived from the character of the Bible itself as God's Word written, and from the character of God as revealed in it.

We look for the *natural* meaning because we believe that God addressed his word to those who first heard it, and that it can be received by subsequent generations only insofar as they understand it historically. Our understanding may be fuller than that of the first hearers (for example, of the prophecies of Christ); it cannot be substantially different.

We look for the *general* meaning because we believe that God is self-consistent, and that his revelation is self-consistent also.

So our three principles (of simplicity, history and harmony) arise partly from the nature of God and partly from the nature of Scripture as a plain, historical, consistent communication from God to human beings. They lay upon us a solemn responsibility to make our treatment of Scripture coincide with our view of it.

NOTES

1. Bishop J. C. Ryle, *Five Christian Leaders of the Eighteenth Century,* first published 1868 (Banner of Truth edition, 1960), p. 28.
2. J. J. Gurney's memoir of an afternoon spent in Cambridge with Simeon in 1831, recorded in *Memoirs of the Life of the Rev. Charles Simeon,* ed. William Carus (Hatchard, 1847), p. 674.
3. *George Whitefield's Journals,* first published between 1738 and 1741 (Banner of Truth edition, 1960), p. 60.
4. Sermon 975 in *Horae Homileticae* (1819).
5. Recorded in Foxe's *Book of Martyrs,* vol. IV.
6. Commentary on Acts 8:31 in the Oliver and Boyd edition, p. 247.
7. *The Construction of Deeds and Statutes,* first published by Sweet and Maxwell in 1939 (fourth edition, 1956), p. 27.
8. *The Apostolic Fathers* ed. J. B. Lightfoot (Macmillan, 1891), p. 279.
9. Comment on Galatians 4:22, William Pringle's translation (Calvin Translation Society, 1854), p. 136.
10. The italics are Simeon's. The quotation comes from a letter to his publisher Mr. Holdsworth (undated, although apparently 1832) in *Memoirs of the Life of the Rev. Charles Simeon,* 2nd edition, ed. William Carus (Hachard, 1847), p. 703.
11. J. Gresham Machen *What Is Faith?* first published 1925 (Hodder edition, n.d, p. 24).
12. *The Construction of Deeds and Statues,* p. 39.
13. Article XX *Of the Authority of the Church* from the Church of England's Thirty-nine Articles.
14. The debate is recorded near the beginning of Book 4 of John Knox, *The History of the Reformation of the Church of Scotland,* unfinished edition 1587, first complete edition 1644, p. 314.
15. Consider the use of the words "shadow" and "copy" in Heb. 8:5; 9:24; 10:1 and Mark's editorial comment in 7:19.
16. Gal. 3:7, 9, 13, 14, 29; cf. Rom. 4:13, 16. In verse 13 God's promise to Abraham and his descendants is "that he would be heir of the world," cf. 1 Cor.3:21-23.
17. Eph. 2:21-22; cf. 1 Cor. 3:16. Consider also how James saw the Gentiles' inclusion in the church a fulfillment of God's promise through Amos to rebuild the ruins of David's dwelling. Acts 15:13-18; Amos 9:11-12.

8. The Use of the Bible

❖ *What are the marks of a "doer of the Word"?*

❖ *In what different ways can we hear and learn God's Word?*

❖ *Why does the Bible have an essential place
in the lives of Christians?*

Basic to our Christian faith is the conviction that our God, far from being dead and dumb, is living and vocal. He has spoken a precise message in precise historical and geographical contexts, and has caused it to be written and preserved in the Bible. Moreover, as we have considered, there are sound reasons for accepting the Bible's authority and sound principles to guide us in its interpretation.

So what? Why have we spent so much time on these matters? For one reason only, that God still speaks through what he has spoken. What he said centuries ago has a vital relevance to contemporary men and women. The Bible is not an antique piece whose proper home is a museum. On the contrary, it is a "lamp" to our feet and a "light" to our path (Ps. 119:105; cf. 2 Pet. 1:19). God's words can be our "counselors" in all the perplexities of modern life. They give wisdom and under-standing to the simple (Pss. 119:24, 34; 19:7).

But whether we derive any benefit from Scripture depends on how we use it, on what response we make to its message. One of God's recurring complaints in the biblical record itself is that his people continually turned a deaf ear to his Word. His messengers had to keep pleading with Israel:

Today, if you hear his voice, do not
harden your hearts. (Ps. 95:7-8)

There are in the end only two possible atti-tudes to God's Word, to receive it or to reject it. Those who are receptive to it are portrayed with vivid figures of speech. They are said to

"tremble" at it, just because it is the word of the great God himself (Isa. 66:2, 5; Ezra 9:4). They prize it like gold and relish it like honey (Pss. 19:10; 119:103, 127). They rejoice over it "like one who finds great spoil." They thirst for it with the ardor of a suckled child (Ps. 119:162; 1 Pet. 2:2). On the other hand, those who reject it are said to have closed their ears and refused to listen; they are "stiff-necked" and follow "the stubbornness of [their] evil heart" (for example, Jer. 17:23; 18:12; 19:15). Of such there is no more notorious example than King Jehoiakim, who, as the scroll of God's words through Jeremiah was read to him, first used a penknife to cut it into pieces and then threw the pieces into the fire until the whole scroll had been burned (Jer. 36:21-23).

Jesus similarly warned his contemporaries about their response to his teaching. In the parable of the sower the different soils into which the seed fell were intended to exemplify the varying reception which people give God's Word. Jesus solemnly insisted that we shall be judged on the last day by the word he has spo-ken (John 12:47-48). All of us are building our life on some foundation. Those who build on rock, whose house will survive the storms of adversity and of judgment, are those who lis-ten to Christ's teaching and put it into practice (Matt. 7:24-27).

To begin with, to listen involves time. Do we really believe that *God* has spoken, that *God's* words are recorded in Scripture, and that as we read it we may hear *God's* voice addressing us? Then we shall not grudge the time to listen. Instead, we shall want to register our protest

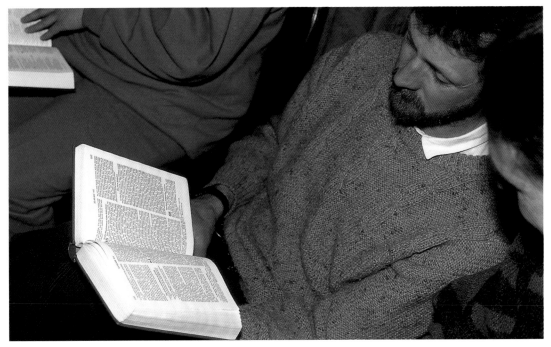

We can hear God's Word by personal and family Bible reading and through group Bible studies.

against the rat-race of modern life and strive to recover the lost art of meditation. It is not a casual, superficial acquaintance with Scripture that the modern church needs, but rather to heed our Master's exhortation: "Let these words sink into your ears" (Luke 9:44 RSV).

There is no particular secret about how to do it. It just takes time, purposefully redeemed from our busy lives, in which to turn Scripture over and over in our minds until it sinks into our hearts and so regulates everything we think and do. It is those who thus "meditate day and night" in God's Word whom he pronounces "blessed" (Pss. 1:1-2; 119:97; Josh. 1:8).

If there is no single secret, there are no hard and fast rules either. For example, the practice of the daily "Quiet Time" of Bible reading and prayer, preferably first thing in the morning and last thing at night, is not an inviolable tradition. It has certainly stood the test of time and brought untold profit to many generations of Christians. I am myself old-fashioned enough to retain confidence in it as an extremely valuable discipline. But it is still only a tradition; it has not been laid down in Scripture. So we have no liberty to add it to the

Decalogue as a kind of eleventh commandment. Nor was such a practice possible before the invention of printing and the availability of cheap Bibles for all. To insist on it as indispensable to Christian living would be to disqualify the millions of Christians who lived in the first fifteen centuries, and many more millions in our day who cannot read.

The great value of some Scripture meditation and prayer (however brief) at the beginning of each day is that it prepares us to bear the day's responsibilities and face the day's temptations. It seems unwise, to say the least, to go into the conflict unarmed. Nevertheless, the mother who has to cook the breakfast, and then get husband off to work and children off to school, may have to postpone her time with God until later in the morning, while the breadwinner who leaves home very early may prefer to requisition a little time from his (or her) lunch break.

However busy one's daily timetable may be, with the increased leisure of modern times, most people should be able to devote a longer time to Bible reading and prayer over the weekend. Sunday afternoon has obvious possibilities, or even Sunday evening since there is nothing in Scripture requiring Christians to attend church twice every Sunday! Further, if daily family prayers are impossible from Monday to Friday because work and school demand staggered mealtimes, a weekly time when the family honors God together in their home, whatever form it takes, should be possible during the weekend.

It is not only by personal or family Bible reading that we can hear God's Word, however. It is also through group Bible studies, whether organized by the local church or a Christian organization or by ourselves in our own home, and (above all) through the public exposition of Scripture in church. I long that modern Christians should take this more seriously. It is easy to blame the pulpit, but very often the pew gets the kind of pulpit ministry it wants. God said to Jeremiah:

A horrible and shocking thing has
happened in the land: the prophets
prophesy lies, the priests rule by their
own authority, *and my people love it this
way.* (Jer. 5:30-31)

Congregations have far more responsibility than they commonly recognize for the kind of ministry they receive. They should encourage their pastor to expound Scripture. They should come to church in a receptive and expectant mood, preferably bringing their Bible with them, hungry to hear what the Lord God may have to say to them through the lessons and the sermon. It may also be wise to take some steps to retain the message in the memory, perhaps by writing the text on a card and then meditating on it during the rest of the week. And if the church we attend is not blessed with a ministry of biblical exposition, audiocassettes bring the ministry of other Bible teachers within reach of many people, for personal or group listening.

Precisely how the individual Christian or the Christian family seeks to receive the message of the Bible is not the most important question. What is vital is that in some way at some time, and that regularly, we learn to listen to

God's Word and to feed upon it in our hearts.

This listening to God's voice in and through his Word is only the beginning, however. It is not enough to "know these things," Jesus said; we shall be blessed only if we "do them" (John 13:17). For according to the New Testament the truth is something to be "done," not merely "known" (for example, 1 John 1:6, literally). Perhaps no apostle put this more clearly than James, the Lord's brother, who wrote:

Do not merely listen to the word, and so
deceive yourselves. Do what it says.
(Jas. 1:22)

To "do" the truth is to practice what it teaches, to translate its message into action. This sounds simple, but it has far-reaching implications simply because the truth we have to "do" is so rich. Let me give five facets of the lifestyle of a "doer of the word."

Worship

First, worship. Worship is impossible without a knowledge of the truth. I grant that Paul found an altar in Athens which was inscribed "to an unknown God." But it is ludicrous to try to worship a deity we do not know, for if we do not know him we do not know what kind of worship he desires. Conversely, as soon as we have begun to know the living and true God, we must worship him. And the more we come to know him, the more we shall realize that he is worthy of our devotion. For to worship is to praise God's name, to glory in who and what he is in the splendor of his being and his works:

Let them praise the name of the LORD,
    for his name alone is exalted;
    his splendor is above the earth and the
        heavens. (Ps. 148:13)

Since worship is always a response to the truth of God we perceive, it is supremely the Word of God (his self-revelation) which evokes the worship of God. Therefore the Bible has an indispensable place in both public and private worship. In all public worship there should be a reading (or readings) of Scripture, and an exhortation or instruction based on it (cf. Neh. 8:8; 1 Tim. 4:13). Far from being an intrusion into the service, both are essential to worship. So those who have the privilege of reading lessons in church should take pains to understand the passage, and those who are called to preach should be conscientious in studying both God's Word and the contemporary world in order to relate the one to the other. Only when God speaks through his Word, making himself known in the greatness of his glory and grace, does the congregation truly bow down and worship.

The same principle applies to private devotion. Apart from a prayer for illumination, we should worship and pray *after* our Bible reading. For it is from Scripture that we shall learn whom to worship and how to pray according to God's will (1 John 5:14; John 15:7).

Repentance and faith

The second mark of a "doer of the word" is repentance. For God's Word tells us what *we* are as well as what he is, discloses to us our sin, and calls us to confess and forsake it. Several of the graphic similes of Scripture enforce this truth. The Word of God is like a mirror, showing us what we are like (Jas. 1:23-25), like a sword to prick our guilty conscience (Eph. 6:17; Heb. 4:12; Acts 2:37), and like both a hammer and a fire to break and purify us (Jer. 23:29). Whenever we read the Scripture we hear God saying to us:

This is what the Lord Almighty, the God of Israel, says: Reform your ways and your actions. . . . Take your evil deeds out of my sight! Stop doing wrong, learn to do right! (Jer. 7:3; Isa. 1:16-17)

The third characteristic of the "doer of the word" is faith. Faith is an integral part of the Christian life, for "without faith it is impossible to please God" (Heb. 11:6). Christians are frequently described in the New Testament as

"believers" who "through faith and patience inherit what has been promised" (Heb. 6:12). But faith is very commonly misunderstood. It is not screwing ourselves up to believe something which we strongly suspect is not true; it is resting confidently on him who is true. Faith cannot exist in a vacuum or in isolation; it is always a trustful response to a trustworthy person. We must never set faith and knowledge over against one another as if they were mutually exclusive. For faith is based on knowledge: "Those who know your name will trust in you" (Ps. 9:10).

We trust God because we know him to be trustworthy. How? Because he has revealed himself to be such. As we read in Scripture about the character and mighty deeds of God, about his faithfulness to his covenant in the history of Israel, about "his very great and precious promises" (2 Pet. 1:4), about Jesus Christ in whom all God's promises find their "yes" (2 Cor. 1:20), and about the men of faith who were "fully persuaded that God had power to do what he had promised" (Rom. 4:21), our faith is quickened, nourished and matured.

So then it is no use moaning that we seem to suffer from a chronic unbelief, or envying others ("I wish I had your faith"), as if our lack of faith were like our temperament, a congenital condition which cannot be changed. For God himself has given us the means to increase our faith:

Faith comes from hearing the message, and the message is heard through the word of Christ. (Rom. 10:17)

We have to take time and trouble to hear in order to believe. Christians who want to grow in faith must spend time meditating on God's Word. They will soon discover what is meant by "the encouragement of the Scriptures" (Rom. 15:4).

Obedience

Obedience is the fourth way by which we become "doers" of the word and not only "hearers." Yet obedience involves submission to authority, and this is out of fashion today. However, if Jesus Christ himself lived in humble obedience to God's Word, obeying its commands as well as believing its promises, there can be no doubt that we must also. For the servant is not greater than his master.

Jesus went further than that. He indicated that, just as ancient Israel was to prove her love for God by obeying him, so Christian disciples must prove their love for Christ by their obedience:

> If you love me, you will obey what I command. . . . Whoever has my commands and obeys them, he is the one who loves me. . . . If anyone loves me, he will obey my teaching; . . . He who does not love me will not obey my teaching. (John 14:15, 21, 23-24)

It seems to me that we should be more grateful to God than we customarily are that he has revealed his will so clearly on so many subjects in his Word. For the very first step towards holiness of life is a knowledge of what is pleasing and displeasing to God (cf. 1 Thess. 4:1). So the Christian's dearest ambition is "to live according to Scripture" (see 2 Cor. 4:6), for there is not other way to be sure of living according to his will.

This goes for social as well as personal righteousness. For the will of God in the Word of God for the people of God relates to the whole of our lives. It tells us to love God, to control ourselves and to love and serve our neighbor. And the requirement of neighbor-love has many and wide ramifications. For my neighbor is a human being, and human beings have a body as well as a soul, and live by God's ordering in a community. So I cannot claim to love my neighbor if I ignore either their physical or their social well-being.

We have already seen with what detailed applications the Hebrew prophets proclaimed the righteousness of God. The home, the marketplace, the lawcourt, the farm – these were the places where righteousness was to be prac-

ticed. And where it was lacking, there the judgment of God would fall. The prophets were fearless in thundering their woes upon the unrighteous, upon the trader who cheated his customers by using false weights and measures, upon the greedy landowner who joined houses to house and field to field until there was no more room, upon the magistrate who perverted justice by taking bribes from the guilty rich and condemning the innocent poor, upon the husband who profaned the divine institutions of marriage and home by his sexual unfaithfulness, upon the moneylender who charged extortionate rates of interest, even upon the king who oppressed the people instead of serving them. And by contrast the Book of Proverbs, full of practical wisdom, extols the virtues of honesty, industry, generosity, humility, chastity and justice.

The apostles too, in the ethical sections of their letters, lay great stress on social righteousness. They portray what should be the mutual relations between husband and wife, parents and children, employers and employees. Paul exposes the gravity of tolerating in the Christian community such sins as factions due to a personality cult, litigation and immorality. The liar is to learn to speak the truth, and the thief to earn his own living so that he can give to those in need. All bitterness, anger, slander and malice are to be put away. Christians are to be kind, tenderhearted, forbearing, tolerant, and even (as Jesus taught) to love and serve their enemies. James inveighs against class distinctions in the Christian fellowship, against our unruly tongues, and against jealousy and selfish ambition. In the last chapter of his letter he sounds just like an Old Testament prophet as he condemns the rich for their luxurious living and their fraudulent treatment of their own farm laborers.

It is true that there are many complex ethical questions of the contemporary world on which Scripture does not directly pronounce. But the principles are there on which we must form a responsible Christian judgment. Whether the issue is war or violent revolution, pollution, pornography or poverty, or political

Bethlehem Market. The Old Testament prophets were fearless in thundering their woes upon the trader who cheated his customers by using false weights and measures.

and economic theory, we cannot escape the labor – and sometimes the pain – of seeking to formulate a biblically conditioned Christian opinion.

Witness

The fifth mark of a Christian who "does" God's Word is witness. For truth cannot be concealed or monopolized. If our eyes have been opened to receive it, we know ourselves under compulsion to pass it on. We are "those entrusted with the secret things of God" (1 Cor. 4:1), trustees of his secrets. Not only must we bear witness to the Christ we have come to know, but we cannot bear witness without this knowledge.

The words "witness" and "testimony" have been much devalued, and are sometimes employed to describe what is little more than an essay in religious autobiography. But Christian witness is witness to Christ. And the Christ to whom we have a responsibility to witness is not merely the Christ of our personal experience, but the historic Christ, the Christ of the apostolic testimony. There is no other Christ. So if Scripture leads to witness, witness also depends on Scripture.

The Bible, then, has an essential place in the life of a Christian. For the revelation of God leads to worship, the warnings of God to repentance, the promises of God to faith, the commands of God to obedience and the truth of God to witness. It is no exaggeration to say that without Scripture a Christian life is impossible. True, there are still many in the world who are illiterate, and cannot read the Bible. Others can read, but do not or not much, either because of their cultural background or because of the electronic revolution or because of some innate reluctance. Is a Christian life to be denied to them? No, of course not. If (for whatever reason) they do not read Scripture and meditate on it by themselves, I am bound to say I think they will be spiritually impoverished. But they can certainly receive God's Word in other ways as I have indicated earlier – through sermons, through tapes, through the Internet, through group study, through the mass media and through person-to-person communication.

Nevertheless, God's Word is indispensable to us, by whatever means we receive it. Jesus himself put this beyond question when he quoted from Deuteronomy:

Man does not live on bread alone, but on every word that comes from the mouth of God. (Matt. 4:4)

God's Word is as essential to us spiritually as food is to us physically. Both life and health are – quite literally – impossible without it. It is by his Word that God implants spiritual life within us (Jas. 1:21; 1 Pet. 1:23-25). It is by the same Word that he instructs, reforms, nourishes, encourages and strengthens us. It is truly by his Word alone that the man or woman of God grows into maturity and becomes "equipped for every good work" (2 Tim. 3:17).

INDEX